Ecopoetry

Ecopoetry

A Critical Introduction

Edited by
J. Scott Bryson

Foreword by
John Elder

The University of Utah Press
Salt Lake City

Acknowledgments:

Scott Bryson. Some of the editor's introductory material orginally appeared in altered form in "Seeing the West Side of Any Mountain: Thoreau and the New Ecological Poetry," from *Thoreau's Sense of Place: Essays in American Environmental Writing*, edited by Richard J. Schneider (University of Iowa Press, 1999).

W. S. Merwin. "The Saint of the Uplands," "For a Coming Extinction," and "Finding a Teacher," from *The Second Four Book of Poems* (Copper Canyon Press, 1993), copyright 1993 by W. S. Merwin.

06 05 04 03 02
5 4 3 2 1

Library of Congrss Cataloging-in-Publication Data

Ecopoetry : a critical introduction / edited by J. Scott Bryson.
p. cm.
1. American poetry—History and criticism. 2. Nature in literature. 2. English poetry—History and criticism. 4. Environmental protection in literature. 5. Environmental policy in literature. 6. Nature conservation in literature. 7. Wilderness areas in literature. 8. Landscape in literature. 9. Ecology in literature. I. Bryson, J. Scott, 1968–
PS310.N3 E26 2002
811.009'36—dc21

2001005653

For my parents

Contents

Foreword
John Elder ix

Introduction
J. Scott Bryson 1

Forerunners of Ecopoetry

Regarding Silence: Cross-Cultural Roots of Ecopoetic Meditation
David Gilcrest 17

Emerson, Divinity, and Rhetoric in Transcendentalist Nature Writing and Twentieth-Century Ecopoetry
Roger Thompson 29

Landscape and the Self in W. B. Yeats and Robinson Jeffers
Deborah Fleming 39

William Carlos Williams, Ecocriticism, and Contemporary American Nature Poetry
Mark Long 58

Contemporary Ecopoets

Gary Snyder and the Post-Pastoral
Terry Gifford 77

Earth's Echo: Answering Nature in Ammons's Poetry
Gyorgyi Voros 88

"Between the Earth and Silence": Place and Space in the Poetry of W. S. Merwin
J. Scott Bryson 101

Panentheistic Epistemology: The Style of Wendell Berry's *A Timbered Choir*
Leonard M. Scigaj 117

The Pragmatic Mysticism of Mary Oliver
Laird Christensen 135

"Everything Blooming Bows Down in the Rain": Nature and the Work of Mourning in the Contemporary Elegy
Jeffrey Thomson 153

Genocide and Extinction in Linda Hogan's Ecopoetry
Emily Hegarty 162

Expanding the Boundaries

"The Redshifting Web": Arthur Sze's Ecopoetics
Zhou Xiaojing 179

In Her Element: Daphne Marlatt, the Lesbian Body, and the Environment
Beverly Curran 195

Postcolonial Romanticisms: Derek Walcott and the Melancholic Narrative of Landscape
Roy Osamu Kamada 207

A Woman Writing about Nature: Louise Glück and "the absence of intention"
Maggie Gordon 221

How to Love This World: The Transpersonal Wild in Margaret Atwood's Ecological Poetry
Richard Hunt 232

Primary Concerns: The Development of Current Environmental Identity Poetry
Bernard W. Quetchenbach 245

Contributors 263

Index 267

John Elder

Foreword

The attempt to combine words as reverberant as *ecology* and *poetry*, or to define one in terms of the other, can make people nervous. Ecologists worry about having their science taken to be an ethical or aesthetic system. Teachers and critics of literature may wonder whether a new technical frame of reference will interpose jargon between reader and text. But the present volume reveals how valuable such a compound approach can be, so long as one views it as a dialogue and an adventure rather than as an easy connection of any kind. Specifically, the success of this collection stems from the clear, concrete ways in which the authors explore two specific propositions. One is that poetry derives from the living earth as surely as our human bodies and minds do. The health and beauty of culture are ultimately inseparable from those of nature. The second is that poetry itself can manifest the intricate, adaptive, and evolving balance of an ecosystem. This can be true in the case of individual poems; in the sometimes surprising wholeness of a given poet's *oeuvre;* and in the ongoing process through which long-established writers and powerful new ones enrich each others' meanings—a process akin to the mutual honing of populations within a shared bioregion.

One of the reasons scientists rightly resist taking the term *ecological* as normative in any narrow sense is that ecosystems are, above all, shifting fields of adaptation. Populations respond continuously both to each other and to changes in the topography, hydrology, soils, and climate of their bioregions. Similarly, it is important to note that the present collection conveys a single vivid moment within a field of study that has rapidly evolved and that will continue to do so. One narrative of this evolution—among several implied by Scott Bryson's thoughtful table of contents—follows the emergence of ecological poetry from the work of Emerson and his circle. The transcendentalists scoured and resculpted the terrain of American literature, with Wordsworth as the sustained blizzard from which they gathered force. Yeats and Williams, as well as Stevens, Frost, Bishop, and Moore, reforested the twentieth century like the spruce and fir that follow in a glacier's wake. Jeffers, amid the stony shelves and outcroppings that he loved, announced an affinity between poetry and wilderness that many writers continue to affirm today. The second of this collection's three sections focuses on and celebrates a remarkable group of contemporary poets. Such figures as Snyder, Ammons, Wright, Merwin, Berry, and Oliver have, over the past several decades, directly inspired many of the new approaches to literary scholarship represented in this book.

That is one good way to tell the story. But biologists remind us to think of evolution as a web, not a single strand, as a proliferation with no center and no fixed goal. We may thus also find it helpful, as readers, to think of our own relationships with poetry as evolving ecosystems. I myself entered into the ecotone between literature and the natural world through discovering the work of Gary Snyder while I was a student in college. Although I had already read Emerson and Thoreau, the great modernists were still in store for me. In part because of Snyder's inspiration, the conversation between poetry and the earth has also included, for me, a long journey out of the Western tradition—toward the lineage of Basho. The 1990 publication of Mary Oliver's *House of Light* was an exciting new flinging-open of doors; it helped me both to understand the relationship between American and Japanese poetry more fully and to reground my reading in New England, where, like Oliver, my family and I live. In the first and last essays of this volume, as well as in the essays of the entire third section, I have glimpsed new possibilities for "expanding [my] boundaries." Specifically, I come away from this collection with an enhanced realization of the connection between cross-cultural and ecological interpretations of literature; with an awareness of the pertinence of Glück and Atwood, authors I have admired in other connections, to ecological poetry; with a fuller appreciation of Walcott and Sze's historical and ecological visions; and with a desire to read Daphne Marlatt, whose approach to the concepts of interdependence, surprise, and relocation feels enlivening and original.

I have ventured this personal sketch by way of transition to another level on which our critical conversation is itself an ecosystem. It is a dialogue that arises from and shifts with our own eccentric evolutions as readers; it exfoliates as our readings encounter one another. One of the greatest advantages of an ecological approach to poetry may in fact be that it releases us from the fractiousness of the prevailing scholarly culture. Sometimes academic discourse can feel like a conversation doomed to be carried out in rebukes and thus to have limited prospects for mutual understanding and growth. Perhaps respect for intellectual differences may be yet another value implicit in Aldo Leopold's great phrase "thinking like a mountain." Neither in the biological nor in the cultural realms does diversity mean, in any settled way, the Peaceable Kingdom. A. R. Ammons's "Corsons Inlet" records the gusty, insecure energy of life along the Jersey shore. But the poem also affirms that, amid the precarious beauty of such a world, "risk is full." Any discussion along the wavering shoreline of ecological poetry will likewise be marked by skirmishes and uncertainty; people have entered into the conversation from many different angles, and our different expectations will sometimes collide. We may be helped to celebrate such intersections and divergences by remembering the world of vectors that have sharpened the falcon's dive and that have tuned the tremulous rapture of a hare listening to the night. As readers, writers, and teachers, we too are encompassed by the process, described in "Corsons Inlet," of

> pulsations of order
> broken down, transferred through membranes
> to strengthen larger orders.

Most of the writers in this collection are, as many of its readers will be, teachers. The poets discussed here, and the terms of that discussion, may help us to conceive of education, too, in ecological terms. A pedagogy that focuses on a class as an ecosystem, and on each student's experience within it as another, is likely to end up challenging the assumptions about lecturing, grading, and the separation of scholarly disciplines that are such dominant features of most colleges and universities. Here, as in our conversation about ecological poetry, experimentation, constructive disagreement, and collaboration will all be required before we can find an approach to teaching that is appropriate to the insights and themes of the poets celebrated here. Perhaps a hallmark of literary criticism in this area will come to be direct discussion of the pedagogy implicit in a certain kind of reading. Perhaps, too, the landscapes of reader and writer alike will be more commonly acknowledged as elements within the ecosystem of a poem's meaning. Once one has begun to draw certain kinds of connections, as tenuous and shifting as they may be, there is a bracing awareness of living not simply in a niche but in the circling seasons of a watershed.

J. Scott Bryson

Introduction

The original vision for this book arose in the summer of 1997 as I prepared for my Ph.D. qualifying exams, one of which covered contemporary American nature poetry. As I read the work of the best-known contemporary nature poets, I was not surprised to discover that at a time when problems such as overpopulation, species extinction, pollution, global warming, and ozone depletion appear almost daily in national headlines, writers who are considered "nature poets" were less and less composing traditional romantic nature lyrics and were more and more taking up ecological and environmental issues. What did surprise me, however, was that as far as I could tell, this widespread and significant trend was garnering almost no critical notice. I was aware that the very young field of ecocriticism was exploding onto the critical scene, and as I read poetry that seemed to represent a departure from traditional nature poetry—at the time I wanted to call it "ecological poetry"—I assumed secondary sources existed that would introduce me to this field. Instead, my research demonstrated that within the new world of ecocriticism, scholars were largely ignoring the work of ecologically oriented poets and were focusing almost exclusively on nonfiction and some fiction, examining the works of Thoreau, Leopold, Dillard, Abbey, and other prose nature writers.

My research did turn up a handful of helpful secondary texts, the two most useful being John Elder's compelling and widely read *Imagining the Earth: Poetry and the Vision of Nature* and Terry Gifford's *Green Voices: Understanding Contemporary Nature Poetry.* Both are excellent works and provided the bulk of the theoretical grounding I was to receive in the field, yet as important as they were in providing some critical underpinnings for my scholarship, they stood alone as relevant examinations of the field[1] In addition, I encountered a handful of anthologies containing contemporary nature poetry, but for the most part these were simply collections of poems rather than treatments of the genre.[2] I also found that some fine work had been produced exploring the writing of individual nature poets but that very little attention had been paid to the genre as a whole.

Within the last few years, though, some interesting and evocative work that examines ecopoetry itself has begun to appear. In 1997 Gyorgyi Voros published *Notations of the Wild: Ecology in the Poetry of Wallace Stevens,* in which she employs contemporary environmental theory to argue for "an ecological poetic," applying it to the work of Stevens. Then in 1999 appeared Leonard Scigaj's *Sustainable Poetry: Four Ecopoets,* the first book to take ecopoetry as its primary subject. The following year two additional studies appeared: Jonathan Bate's *The Song of the Earth,* in which Bate examines a wealth of world literature in light of what he presents as an "ecopoetics"; and Bernard W. Quetchenbach's *Back from the Far Field: American Nature Poets in the Late Twentieth Century,* which examines contemporary nature poetry in general and focuses on three contemporary U.S. poets—Robert Bly, Gary Snyder, and Wendell Berry. These four excellent works offer sophisticated treatments of the field and lay the foundation for future studies of ecopoetry.[3]

Thus, the situation has quickly evolved from its state of only a few years ago, when young scholars trying to educate themselves in the field's critical milieu discovered that the academic community was largely ignoring one of the most vibrant and dynamic expressions of contemporary literature. More and more voices have appeared as of late to engage in an exchange of ideas regarding ecopoetry. This book seeks to further that conversation by gathering some of the most significant established and emerging critical voices currently working in the field.

One of the first questions to confront is, Exactly what is ecopoetry? This question has much to do with the history of nature poetry in general, which can be traced back to the roots of language. For centuries, what has loosely been termed "nature poetry" dominated English literature. From *Beowulf* to Blake, much of the literature produced by English-speaking writers contained heavy doses of natural subject matter and imagery. Yet as Robert Langbaum has pointed out, by the latter part of the nineteenth century and the early part of the twentieth, what was considered an overly romantic nature poetry—steeped in pathetic fallacy—had lost credibility, largely as a result of nineteenth-century science and the drastic changes in the way Westerners envisioned themselves and the world around them. Darwinian theory and modern geology, after all, would hardly allow readers to accept a poem that unselfconsciously anthropomorphized nonhuman nature or that celebrated nature's benevolence toward humans. By the early part of the twentieth century, therefore, anything resembling romantic nature poetry was rarely written, and if it was, it was even more rarely taken seriously.[4]

However, in response (and in opposition) to this older, romantic vision of nature, a new form of nature poetry began to emerge, produced primarily by such antiromantics as Frost, Jeffers, Stevens, Moore, Williams. With these and other modern poets in mind, Langbaum wrote (in 1959) that the best twentieth-century nature poetry "defines itself precisely by opposing, or seeming to oppose, the pathetic fallacy (one cannot perhaps get round it)." He went on to explain that "to feel in nature an unalterably alien, even an unfeeling, existence is to carry empathy several steps farther than did the nineteenth-century poets who felt in nature a life different from but compatible with ours."[5] Out of this conviction arise lines like that of Stevens, from "The Snow Man," about a listener beholding "Nothing that is not there and the nothing that is," and like that of Moore, from "A Grave," that contends "the sea has nothing to give" to the perceiving human "but a well excavated grave."

In the latter half of the twentieth century, proceeding out of these modern poetic voices, a whole new generation of poets began to take up the theme of nature in a manner that diverged even further from that of nineteenth-century nature poets like Wordsworth and Longfellow. As the American population grew more aware of ecological and environmental issues such as nuclear proliferation, species extinction, and other potential disasters, poets began to speak to such matters in ways they had rarely spoken before. This new-sounding poetic voice coincided with a growing spirit of protest that appeared in the mid-twentieth century, along with the new freedom regarding "poetic subject matter" that surfaced as a result of the emergence of the Beat poets. Indeed, some of these poets—most notably Gary Snyder—became and have remained leading voices in the environmental movement. As that movement grew and the poetry of writers like Jeffers and Snyder was more widely read (along with prose works by authors like Rachel Carson), other poets increasingly took up many of the environmental themes these authors espoused, thus setting up the offshoot of nature poetry we are calling ecopoetry.

A precise definition of *ecopoetry* has not yet been established. However, most of us recognize, intuitively if by no other means, that this newer brand of nature poetry differs in many ways from the traditional romantic nature poetry produced by writers like Wordsworth or Whitman. When we read Gary Snyder describe commercial land developers as rapists who say to the land, "Spread your legs,"[6] or when we come across Denise Levertov's description of the earth as "a beaten child or a captive animal" who lies "waiting the next blow,"[7] we know that we are encountering a poem essentially different from "Tintern Abbey" or Bradstreet's "Contemplations." Although in many ways ecopoems fall in line with such canonical nature lyrics as "Contemplations," "Intimations of Immortality," and "Ode to a Nightingale," they just as clearly take visible steps beyond that tradition.

Compare, for instance, Whitman's treatment of the razing of a forest, in "Song of the Redwood-Tree," with W. S. Merwin's treatment of the same general subject in his well-known poem "The Last One." Whitman's speaker tells of a redwood's "song" that contains these lines, addressed to the other trees:

Farewell my brethren,
Farewell O earth and sky, farewell ye neighboring waters,
My time has ended, my term has come.
. . . .
Nor yield we mournfully majestic brothers,
We who have grandly fill'd our time;
With Nature's calm content, with tacit huge delight,
We welcome what we have wrought for through the past,
And leave the field for them.
For them predicted long,
For a superber race, they too to grandly fill their time,
For them we abdicate, in them ourselves ye forest kings.[8]

Notice that the poem becomes a propagandistic justification for the clearing of centuries-old redwoods, who are portrayed as willingly yielding to humanity, abdicating their thrones so that members of a "superber race" can "grandly fill their time." Now compare Whitman's treatment with Merwin's in "The Last One," a poem that also renders the removal of a forest but speaks out of a much different vision of the world. The opening lines set the tone for the entire poem as they describe the humans who approach the forest:

Well they'd made up their minds to be everywhere because why not.
Everywhere was theirs because they thought so.
They with two leaves they whom the birds despise.
In the middle of stones they made up their minds. They started to cut.
Well they cut everything because why not.
Everything was theirs because they thought so.[9]

As the poem continues, we notice that, just as in Whitman's poem, human and nonhuman nature interact. But instead of offering a benign natural world that cares for the advancement of the human race, Merwin's parable attempts to render the consequences we can expect from cutting down "the last one," the final tree in the forest (emblematic of the numerous natural "resources" myopically wasted and destroyed). As the final tree falls and the loggers take it away, its shadow remains and the people around it are unable to escape its darkness.

What becomes clear in the examination of these two poems is that although both "Song of the Redwood-Tree" and "The Last One" can technically be labeled "nature poems," their approach to nature is drastically different. One endorses the cutting of trees by giving them a voice that not only absolves but even celebrates humankind for its actions; the other takes as its starting point a condemnation of humanity for the same deeds, then spends the majority of the poem rendering the disastrous consequences. Although I find the rhetoric of Merwin's narrative much more persuasive (at least for our historical situation) than that of Whitman, my argument here is not that one poem is a better or worse nature poem but that the visions offered in the poems are different, and extremely different at that. A poet working from an ecological perspective on the world would not be able to present the poem as Whitman has; an ecopoet, in order to continue to write poems of nature, must necessarily alter his or her poetics. Granted, I have chosen extreme examples to clarify this point. However, differences such as these appear time and again in ecopoetry, as writers attempt to address contemporary issues and concerns that earlier nature poets have either been unaware of or have not been forced to deal with. In the work of these contemporary poets we get a perspective on the human-nonhuman relationship that distinguishes them from their nature poetry ancestors and marks them as ecopoets.

Any definition of the term *ecopoetry* should probably remain fluid at this point because scholars are only beginning to offer a thorough examination of the field. A few initial definitions have emerged in recent years. Gifford assigns the term *green poetry* to "those recent nature poems which engage directly with environmental issues."[10] And Scigaj writes that we "might define ecopoetry as poetry that persistently stresses human cooperation with nature conceived as a dynamic, interrelated series of cyclic feedback systems."[11] Lawrence Buell sets down overarching characteristics for "environmentally oriented works" in general—the presence of the nonhuman as more than mere backdrop, the expansion of human interest beyond humanity, a sense of human accountability to the environment and of the environment as a process rather than a constant or given—and these characteristics presumably apply to poetry as well.[12]

The definition I offer here coincides with those of Gifford, Scigaj, and Buell: Ecopoetry is a subset of nature poetry that, while adhering to certain conventions of romanticism, also advances beyond that tradition and takes on distinctly contemporary problems and issues, thus resulting in a version of nature poetry generally marked by three primary characteristics. The first is an emphasis on maintaining an ecocentric perspective that recognizes the interdependent nature of the world;[13] such a perspective leads to a devotion to specific places and to the land itself, along with those creatures that share it with humankind. This interconnection is part of what Black Elk called "the sacred hoop" that pulls all things into relationship, and it can be found throughout ecopoetry. Levertov's "Web," for example, demonstrates this interconnection, ostensibly describing the literal web of a spider but pointing also to what Levertov calls the "great web," which is

> Intricate and untraceable,
> weaving and interweaving,
> . . . designed, beyond all spiderly contrivance,
> to link, not to entrap."[14]

The "great web" here is the one that moves through and connects all people and things, both human and nonhuman. Levertov's web represents what Mohawk poet Peter Blue Cloud calls "the allness of the creation,"[15] and it points toward the same lesson Joy Harjo offers in her famous poem "Remember," which concludes with its speaker imploring her audience to "Remember you are all people and all people are you. / Remember you are this universe and this universe is you."[16]

This awareness of the world as a community tends to produce the second attribute of ecopoetry: an imperative toward humility in relationships with both human and nonhuman nature. You won't hear ecopoets endorsing Emerson's statement, "Every rational creature has all nature for his dowry and estate. It is his, if he will."[17] Instead, ecopoets are more likely to echo Frost's reminder of how little control we actually have over the wildness of nature: "Something there is that doesn't love a wall."[18] So instead of what Albert Gelpi describes as romanticism's inherent "aggrandizement of the individual ego,"[19] we read a Jeffers ecopoem that depicts extravagant royal tombs, then concludes with the lines, "Imagine what delusions of grandeur, / What suspicion-agonized eyes, what jellies of arrogance and terror / This earth has absorbed."[20] And we hear Blue Cloud define stars as "fire vessels / the universe happening / regardless of man."[21]

Related to this humility is the third attribute of ecopoetry: an intense skepticism concerning hyperrationality, a skepticism that usually leads to an indictment of an overtechnologized modern world and a warning concerning the very real potential for ecological catastrophe. Harjo, for example, criticizes time and again the effects of what Edward Abbey dubs modern "syphilization," mourning in one poem for those in the cities who are "learning not to hear the ground as it spins around / beneath them."[22] Snyder is more direct in his reproach, condemning Japan, that "once-great Buddhist nation," for "quibbl[ing] for words on / what kinds of whales they can kill," and "dribbl[ing] methyl mercury / like gonorrhea / in the sea."[23]

These three overarching characteristics—ecocentrism, a humble appreciation of wildness, and a skepticism toward hyperrationality and its resultant overreliance on technology—represent a broad definition of the field examined here. This volume explores the ways contemporary ecopoets deal with these concerns and issues. Exactly what name to give the current manifestation of contemporary nature poetry varies from critic to critic. Most of the authors in this volume call it ecopoetry or ecological poetry; some call it environmental poetry, some simply nature poetry, and Gifford, in his essay, introduces the term *post-pastoral.* Regardless of the terminology, each of the essays, in one way or another, deals with the present version of nature poetry that takes into account environmental and ecological lessons we have learned (or are currently learning) regarding the interaction between human and nonhuman nature.

The book is divided into three major sections that intersect and bleed into one another.

Section One: Forerunners of Ecopoetry

The first section explores the background of the field and examines the intersection between ecopoets and those who have come before. In the opening article David Gilcrest examines what he calls the "cross-cultural roots of ecopoetic meditation." Using the work of Chinese poets Han-shan and Ssu-K'ung T'u, along with that of Plato, Augustine, and Basho, Gilcrest demonstrates that although contemporary ecopoets' uncomfortable relationship with language reveals certain postmodern sensibilities, the desire to transcend language and linguistic limitations is actually an ancient one. Roger Thompson's following essay narrows that historical focus slightly but still offers a wide-angle view of history, surveying the last two centuries of rhetoric and poetry about the nonhuman world. Thompson points out that for nineteenth-century transcendentalists like Emerson, poetry and rhetoric were "conflated as unique expressions of divine eloquence"; in contrast, the work of most contemporary nature poets has become a more "consciously rhetorical act, whose purpose is social change."

Next, Deborah Fleming compares the poetry of Yeats to that of Robinson Jeffers, the poet whom many consider the father of ecopoetry. Fleming points out that Yeats employed landscape in his poetry in an effort to create a fresh and original literary tradition in Ireland, whereas Jeffers "celebrated the earth primarily" in his work. Mark Long then argues that the work of William Carlos Williams can serve as something of a corrective for contemporary ecopoets who prize a poetics of presence but neglect to pay attention to the role language and imagination play in that poetics. As Long explains, a "passionate commitment to the environment" must be combined with "a genuine commitment to language and its domain of human culture" in order for a poem to articulate more than its own local point of view.

Section Two: Established Ecopoets

Section two analyzes well-known poets who write from an ecological perspective and would appear in virtually any anthology of contemporary nature poets. Some of these authors are more overtly environmental and politically involved than others, but the group coheres around the commitment to examining the relationship between human and nonhuman nature and to writing out of the ecopoetic principles outlined above. In this section's first essay Terry Gifford argues for a "post-pastoral" literature that "avoids the traps both of idealization of the pastoral and of the simple corrective of the anti-pastoral." Offering the best work of Snyder as his primary example, and working from numerous other well-known texts from British and U.S. poetry, Gifford defines and explores the questions raised by post-pastoral poetry.

Gyorgyi Voros then looks at A. R. Ammons's poetic attempts "to effect a sustainable ecological relation between human and nonhuman Other." After demonstrating that, for Ammons, mirroring and other ocular imagery ultimately fail to achieve this goal, Voros turns her attention to "acts of voicing" in Ammons's verse. Working from Jungian psychologist Patricia Berry's reading of the Echo and Narcissus myth, Voros maintains that for Ammons it is the human voice, "however impervious nature is to 'hearing' it," that offers us the best chance to connect human and nonhuman nature. My own essay follows and explores similar themes in W. S. Merwin's poetry, examining it through the theoretical lens of cultural geographer Yi-Fu Tuan. Like most ecopoets, Merwin attempts to harmonize in his poetry two principal concepts: a commitment to place, and a humble awareness of the linguistic and epistemological obstacles a writer faces when he or she attempts to render an experience with the natural world. However, as a result of Merwin's expressed inability to achieve such a harmony, his poems have throughout his career consistently turned toward silence.

Leonard M. Scigaj works with another of the best-known ecopoets, Wendell Berry. Scigaj likens the vision presented in Berry's *A Timbered Choir* to that offered by Christian mystics, explaining that Berry's vision reverses normal perception by allowing a biocentric viewpoint to produce lessons that nonhuman nature teaches the poet rather than perceiving the poet as interrogating nature, the poem's subject. Scigaj argues that the crucial movement that takes place in Berry's poetics is the recognition of the "panentheistic" quality of the world, a concept Scigaj borrows from theologian Matthew Fox. By viewing the world from a panentheistic perspective and comprehending, in Scigaj's words, "the biocentric holiness of creation," Berry perceives the holiness therein and thus necessarily chooses to be seen by it and to allow it to alter him. In another cross-disciplinary essay, Laird Christensen explores the melding of postmodern and ecological approaches in Mary Oliver's poetry, asserting that her ecopoetry serves as a postmodern curative to outdated notions of human independence. As Christensen explains, Oliver views herself as one of many subjects in a multisubjective world, thus "constructing a subject position based on ecological interdependence," which Christensen calls "a clearly postmodern project undertaken to correct the destructive illusion of human independence from ecosystems."

In his essay on the contemporary elegy Jeffrey Thomson asserts that the ecological vision offered by certain current nature poets offers the opportunity for a different type of elegy. Using the work of Oliver and Jane Kenyon, Thomson examines contemporary elegies and argues that they achieve their power by resisting the false dialectic of either elevating nature to a naively benevolent position or submitting to utter sorrow. Rather, elegies in the work of poets like Kenyon and Oliver provide a third alternative that allows the speaker to recognize herself or himself as a member of the natural world and its life cycle. Thus, meaning emerges out of grief. In this section's final entry, Emily Hegarty uses government statistics and independent research to establish the historical reality of Native American genocide, then elucidates Linda Hogan's response to this modern horror. Contextualizing the poet's work within the broader realms of ecopoetry in general and native poetry in particular, Hegarty contends that Hogan's writing aims "to counteract the effects of physical and cultural genocide" and "reproduce for future generations Native American culture and the viable environment with which it is entwined."

Section Three: Expanding the Boundaries of Ecopoetry

The six essays in the book's final section explore the environmentally conscious work of poets who are either not known primarily as ecopoets or who are now emerging as poets worthy of critical study. Looking at the list of ecopoets covered in this section, one notices the breadth and diversity of the poets currently writing ecopoetry. Whereas nature writing has often been labeled a "privileged white male" venture, this grouping illustrates the inaccuracy of that labeling by examining the diversity within the ecopoetic branch of nature writing.

In her article on the American Indian influence on Arthur Sze's ecopoetry, for example, Zhou Xiaojing looks specifically at the way Sze uses metaphysics and quantum physics to articulate a worldview based on an understanding of the chaotic nature of the world. By abandoning a linear view of time and emphasizing the inherent interrelationality of human and nonhuman nature, Sze explores alternative modes of understanding humanity and its place in the larger world. In the following essay Beverly Curran also explores the subversive tendency of certain types of ecopoetry. Analyzing the poetry of Canadian author Daphne Marlatt, Curran explores the connections between Marlatt's lesbian verse and the sense of place that pervades it, explaining that Marlatt's poetry highlights connections between lesbian and ecological consciousness in order to challenge "the dominant power structures that have rendered workers exploited, lesbians invisible, and the environment subject to destruction in the name of economic dominance." In doing so Marlatt's work breaks down borders dividing prose from poetry, words from worlds, subject from object, human from nature.

Roy Osamu Kamada then offers a postcolonial reading of the work of the Caribbean Nobel Prize–winning poet Derek Walcott. Kamada examines Walcott's juxtaposition of a romantic desire to find beauty and the sublime in natural landscapes with the historical awareness of the dispossession and trauma his country and people have undergone. In Kamada's words, Walcott "explores landscape even as he explores the problematics of a postcolonial subjectivity." Next, Maggie Gordon, acknowledging that Louise Glück would not consider herself a nature writer, argues for considering the ecofeminist tendencies that pervade Glück's poetry. Using the work of Charlene Spretnak, Gordon illuminates these tendencies that guide Glück's poetry—namely "the sense of the interdependence of human and nonhuman nature and the profound awareness of human bodily nature"—and shows that despite Glück's "absence of intention," her poetry highlights these ecological themes. Richard Hunt then makes a compelling argument for considering Margaret Atwood an ecopoet. Traveling from her earliest books to her most recent poetry, Hunt renders the ecological vision Atwood has been working from since her earliest period. Using the terminology of philosopher Warwick Fox,

Hunt argues that the ethical premise underlying Atwood's poetry is an adherence to a "transpersonal ecology" that leads to an identification among all entities.

The book concludes with Bernard Quetchenbach's essay, which effectively draws all three sections together. Quetchenbach looks at the work of what he calls "current" poets, whom he distinguishes from "contemporary" poets. Drawing from the verse of such diverse writers as Jimmy Santiago Baca, Adrienne Rich, Paula Gunn Allen, Li-young Lee, Primus St. John, Marilyn Chin, and Simon Ortiz, Quetchenbach explores the assumptions made by current poets concerning the relationship among writer, subject, and audience. He demonstrates that, in their retention of the personal quality of contemporary poets, and in their increased emphasis on writing identity- and subject-based poems, current poets allow for a broadening of appeal for ecopoetry in that these recent developments set the work of ecopoets "in a new, more expansive, and less-isolated context."

Finally, a few words concerning the book's compilation are in order. First, it would obviously be impossible for a single volume to include analyses of all of the ecopoets working today. Some important ecopoets have therefore necessarily been excluded, poets like Denise Levertov, Robert Bly, Leslie Marmon Silko, Galway Kinnell, Pattiann Rogers, Joy Harjo, Theodore Roethke, to name only a few. Decisions regarding inclusion in the volume were based on its overall goal. That is, no effort was made to offer some sort of exhaustive coverage of the field (as if that were possible); we offer, rather, an introduction, more of an invitation really, to this vibrant and diverse mode of literature. Therefore, what appears here is an amalgam of historical and emerging poets, combined with those ecopoets whose critical reputations demand that they be included in such a collection. One should not conclude, based on the fact that a majority of the poets whose work is studied in this volume live in the United States, that ecopoetry is a strictly American phenomenon. Although much of the current critical attention on ecopoetry is focused on U.S. writers, this collection demonstrates the intriguing work that can appear when we use an ecological perspective to gaze beyond U.S. borders.

Generally speaking, the scholars here avoid offering conclusions that might shut down discussion of the field. Ours is something of a midterm report. Contemporary ecopoets, like the mode itself, are still coming into their own, still developing and defining who they are, how they present themselves, and how they relate to their subject matter. The same goes for these analyses of the field. They are introductory forays into the genre, ones that we hope will spark conversation and argument, for the field of contemporary ecopoetry is large and has yet to be studied anywhere near adequately.

Notes

1. John Elder, *Imagining the Earth: Poetry and the Vision of Nature* (Athens: University of Georgia Press, 1996); Terry Gifford, *Green Voices: Understanding Contemporary Nature Poetry* (Manchester: Manchester University Press, 1995). Two other studies of note appeared in 1991: Guy Rotella's *Reading and Writing Nature: The Poetry of Robert Frost, Wallace Stevens, Marianne Moore, and Elizabeth Bishop* (Boston: Northeastern University Press); and Jonathan Bate's *Romantic Ecology: Wordsworth and the Environmental Tradition* (New York: Routledge). Each is a first-rate work providing a good introduction to some of the issues facing contemporary poets of nature, but neither actually focuses on working ecopoets.

2. See, for instance, Robert Bly's *News of the Universe: Poems of a Twofold Consciousness* (San Francisco: Sierra Club Books, 1980); Sara Dunn and Alan Scholefield's *Beneath the Wide Wide Heaven: Poetry of the Environment from Antiquity to the Present* (London: Virago, 1991); Christopher Merrill's *The Forgotten Language: Contemporary Poets and Nature* (Salt Lake City: Peregrine Smith, 1991); Robert Pack and Jay Parini's *Poems for a Small Planet: Contemporary American Nature Poetry* (Hanover: Middlebury College Press, 1993); and John Daniel's *Wild Song: Poems of the Natural World* (Athens: University of Georgia Press, 1998).

3. Gyorgyi Voros, *Notations of the Wild: Ecology in the Poetry of Wallace Stevens* (Iowa City: University of Iowa Press, 1997); Leonard M. Scigaj, *Sustainable Poetry: Four Ecopoets* (Lexington: University Press of Kentucky, 1999); Jonathan Bate, *Song of the Earth* (Cambridge: Harvard University Press, 2000); Bernard W. Quetchenbach, *Back from the Far Field: American Nature Poets in the Late Twentieth Century* (Charlottesville: University Press of Virginia, 2000). Along with these works three dissertations of note have also appeared: David Gilcrest's "Greening the Lyre: Environmental Poetics and Ethics" (University of Oregon, 1996), Laird Christensen's "Spirit Astir in the World: Sacred Poetry in the Age of Ecology" (University of Oregon, 1999), and my own "Place and Space in Contemporary Ecological Poetry: Berry, Harjo, and Oliver" (University of Kentucky, 1999). One other valuable venue offering consistent examples of work on ecopoetics has been the journal *ISLE: Interdisciplinary Studies of Literature and the Environment.*

4. Robert Langbaum, "The New Nature Poetry," in *The Modern Spirit: Essays on the Continuity of Nineteenth- and Twentieth-Century Literature* (New York: Oxford, 1970), 101–126. First published in *American Scholar* 28, no. 3 (summer 1959): 323–340.

5. Langbaum, 104 (page citations are to the reprint).

6. Gary Snyder, *Turtle Island* (Boston: Shambhala, 1993), 32.

7. Denise Levertov, *The Life around Us: Selected Poems on Nature* (New York: New Directions, 1997), 20.

8. Walt Whitman, *Leaves of Grass, and Selected Prose,* ed. Sculley Bradley (New York: Holt, Rinehart, and Winston, 1949), 174–175.

9. W. S. Merwin, *The Second Four Books of Poems: The Moving Target, The Lice, The Carrier of Ladders, Writings to an Unfinished Accompaniment* (Port Townsend, Wash.: Copper Canyon Press, 1993), 86–88.

10. Gifford, 3.

11. Scigaj, 37.

12. Lawrence Buell, *The Environmental Imagination: Thoreau, Nature Writing, and the Formation of American Culture* (Cambridge: Harvard University Press, 1995), 7–8.

13. I use the term *ecocentric* here to describe a worldview that, in contrast to an egocentric or anthropocentric perspective, views the earth as an intersubjective community and values its many diverse (human and nonhuman) members.

14. Levertov, 17.

15. This line appears in Blue Cloud's "voice play" entitled "For Rattlesnake: A Dialogue of Creatures," from *The Remembered Earth: An Anthology of Contemporary Native American Literature,* ed. Geary Hobson (Albuquerque: University of New Mexico Press, 1980), 23.

16. Joy Harjo, *She Had Some Horses* (New York: Thunder's Mouth Press, 1997), 40.

17. Ralph Waldo Emerson, *The Complete Works of Ralph Waldo Emerson,* 12 vols., ed. Edward W. Emerson (Boston: Houghton Mifflin, 1903–1904), 1:20.

18. Robert Frost, *North of Boston,* 2nd ed. (New York: Henry Holt, 1915), 11.

19. Albert Gelpi, *A Coherent Splendor: The American Poetic Renaissance, 1910–1950* (Cambridge: Cambridge University Press, 1987), 518.

20. Robinson Jeffers, "Iona: The Graves of Kings," in *Selected Poems* (New York: Vintage, 1965), 52.

21. Blue Cloud, "fire/rain," in Hobson, 20.

22. "For Alva Benson, and for Those Who Have Learned to Speak," in Harjo, 18.

23. "Mother Earth: Her Whales," in Snyder, 82.

Forerunners of Ecopoetry

David Gilcrest

Regarding Silence
Cross-Cultural Roots of Ecopoetic Meditation

In his poem "Ars Poetica" Charles Wright finds himself between two worlds—the green world of pepper tree and aloe vera, and this other world of words, language, poetry:

ARS POETICA

I like it back here

Under the green swatch of the pepper tree and the aloe vera.
I like it because the wind repeats itself,
                                        and the leaves do.

I like it because I'm better here than I am there,

Surrounded by fetishes and figures of speech:
Dog's tooth and whale's tooth, my father's shoe, the dead weight
Of winter, the inarticulation of joy . . .

The spirits are everywhere.

And once I have them called down from the sky, and spinning and
                    dancing in the palm of my hand,
What will it satisfy?
                    I'll still have

The voices rising out of the ground,
The fallen star my blood feeds,
                                        this business I waste my heart on.

And nothing stops that.[1]

Wright's situation is in fact an increasingly familiar one to contemporary writers and readers of environmental poetry. The distinction between *res* and *verba,* between the things of this earth and our words for them, has taken on epistemological and ultimately ethical import as we grope our way back to the more-than-human world.

"I like it back here / Under the green swatch," announces the poet. He likes it because he is "better" here than "there," better and perhaps better off in the natural here and now than over there where the seemingly unnatural artifacts of "fetishes and figures of speech" surround him, hold sway. The poet prefers the realm of "organic" metaphor, the natural repetition of wind and leaf rather than the "artificial" redoubling of linguistic metaphor, language turned back on itself in its figuration.

As a statement of his poetic art, Wright presents in "Ars Poetica" an ironic perspective on the ostensible merits of his craft. Here the poet is quite capable of calling down the "spirits," which are "everywhere," and which are identified syntactically with the "fetishes and figures of speech" that surround him; however, these "spirits," which the poet compels to descend from the sky to spin and dance in the palm of his hand, satisfy nothing. The heavenly words of the poet cannot answer the "voices rising out of the ground," the utterly inarticulate yet insistent tongue of the earth. The spirits of poetry cannot satisfy the body, the "fallen star my blood feeds," unfed by aerial turns of phrase. The spirits of poetry fail even to satisfy the ambitions of the art, "this business I waste my heart on," the occupation and preoccupation of poetry itself.

The final line is, of course, ambiguous. Nothing keeps the poet from calling down his words and nothing stops the earth and the body from making demands that cannot be met yet must be answered if the business of poetry is to continue. The poet's place, Wright suggests, is both between world and word and between desire and the impossibility of its satisfaction, especially through the offices of language.

The claim of a state of being removed from, and perhaps prior to, language aligns this poem with a poetics that has received some critical attention of late. Wright's gesture beyond the pale of language in "Ars Poetica," and other poems identifies him as an "ecopoet" in the sense Leonard Scigaj gives the term. According to Scigaj, the ecopoet works to direct our gaze "beyond the printed page toward firsthand experiences that approximate the poet's intense involvement in the authentic experience that lies behind his originary language."[2] Such a gesture is predicated on experience of the world unmediated by language. The ecopoets Scigaj addresses in *Sustainable Poetry*—Ammons, Berry, Merwin, and Snyder—affirm that "human language is much more limited than the ecological processes of nature" (11). Ecopoets "recognize the limits of language while referring us in an epiphanic moment to our interdependency and relatedness to the richer planet whose operations created and sustain us" (42).

The result of such affirmation and recognition is the sustainable poem: poetry that "presents nature as a separate and at least equal other," that "offers exemplary models of biocentric perception and behavior," and that "does not subordinate nature to a superior human consciousness or reduce nature to immanence" (78–79).

Scigaj suggests, at least, that the sustainable poem is largely the product of a contemporary poetic consciousness and poetics. His choice of ecopoets reinforces his sense that such poetry functions within and against the postmodernist sensibilities of the past thirty years or so and especially the "postmodern critique of language." Against charges that ecopoets are guilty of semiotic naiveté, Scigaj argues that ecopoets are not in fact "indifferent to language or to poststructural critiques of the function of language." Rather, ecopoets "argue the reverse of the poststructural position that all experience is mediated by language. For ecopoets language is an instrument that the poet continually refurbishes to articulate his originary experience in nature" (29). Specifically, ecopoets deploy "postmodern self-reflexivity to disrupt the fashionably hermetic treatment of poetry as a self-contained linguistic construct whose ontological ground is language theory" (11). The sustainable poem thus brings to bear some of the tools of the postmodern critique of language in order to break out of the prison house of language.

But as his own treatment of these contemporary poets suggests (and especially his work on Merwin and Snyder), the historical roots of ecopoetics run much deeper than the epoch claimed by postmodernism. These poets' encounters with Taoist and Zen ideology, practice, and aesthetics, explicitly acknowledged in their work, and exhaustively explicated by their critics, offer a much larger cultural context for ecopoetry.

In these affiliated but not identical traditions the ability to bracket language is cultivated, a discipline that allows for unmediated and often epiphanic experience. By quieting the mind, silencing the chatter of language, repudiating its propensity for attachment and discrimination, one experiences loss of self and a concomitant ecstatic synthesis in the world. Such an experience entails a radical shift in perspective, in the Zen tradition called satori (or *wu* in Chinese), which D. T. Suzuki has defined as "an intuitive looking-into, in contradistinction to intellectual and logical understanding . . . the unfolding of a new world hitherto unperceived in the confusion of a dualistic mind."[3] In terms of aesthetics, poetry written from this kind of experience serves as a record of the intuitive moment, the gesture toward presence, a reminder of what is possible. Satori achieves a measure of articulation in the language of poetry written by those who value such experience.

Consider, for example, the following poem written by Han-shan in the seventh century:

My mind is like the autumn moon
shining clean and clear in the green pool.
No, that's not a good comparison.
Tell me, how shall I explain?[4]

Here Han-shan reaches for a very traditional simile to describe the state of intuitive, nondualistic consciousness: the moon "shining clean and clear in the green pool." The first two lines capture the calm yet attentive aspect of intuitive awareness. Note that the poet's mind is identified with both the reflective surface of the pool and the autumn moon reflecting in it; no distinction is made between the "objects" of consciousness and the "medium" of consciousness. Or that might seem to be the ambition of these first two lines, but as the balance of the poem indicates, such a simile, albeit graceful and suggestive, cannot capture in language this state of nondualistic awareness. One is left with the autonomy of distinct nouns, the moon and the pool, and the syntactic tyranny of subject and predicate. Han-shan is moved to stop the figure in its tracks, criticizing his own simile. "Tell me," he asks, "how shall I explain?" At the edge of language, the poet arrests himself, inviting the reader to consider the dilemma at hand.

In this second poem Han-shan is much less hesitant to characterize the quality of meditative consciousness:

The clear water sparkles like crystal,
you can see through it easily, right to the bottom.
My mind is free from every thought,
nothing in the myriad realms can move it.
Since it cannot be wantonly roused,
forever and forever it will stay unchanged.
When you have learned to know in this way,
you'll know there is no inside or out![5]

Here the experience of the unencumbered mind is identified explicitly as a unique way of knowing, a meditative or contemplative epistemology. The poem emphasizes that this meditative epistemology serves to frustrate that most basic of dualisms, the distinction between inside and outside, ultimately between self and other, human and nature. As many ecocritics have noted, such a decomposition of the autonomous self leads us to discover a new sense of identity, the relational identity of the "ecological self" with implications that are epistemological, ethical, and political.[6]

A final poem by Han-shan reaffirms the distinction between the natural world and the world of books:

> My house is at the foot of the green cliff,
> my garden a jumble of weeds I no longer
> bother to mow.
> New vines dangle in twisted strands
> over old rocks rising steep and high.
> Monkeys make off with the mountain fruits,
> the white heron crams his bill with fish
> from the pond,
> while I, with a book or two of the immortals,
> read under the trees—mumble, mumble.[7]

In this poem the poet and his demesne have gone to seed, the poet having given up whatever ambition he might have had to domesticate the dynamic world around him, no longer bothering to mow his garden. In his retirement the poet witnesses the flourishing world that surrounds him: "New vines dangle in twisted strands / over old rocks rising steep and high" as "Monkeys make off with mountain fruits" and "the white heron crams his bill with fish from the pond." The final image of the poet sitting under the trees reading "a book or two of the immortals" is comically pathetic, the literary magnificence of the immortals' artifice is reduced to mere mumbles in the presence of "wild" nature. The poem asks, How can words, even the best words, compete with this green world?

The ninth-century poet Ssu-K'ung T'u poses a similar question in his prayer "Animal Spirits":

> That they might come back unceasingly,
> That they might be ever with us!
> The bright river, unfathomable,
> The rare flower just opening,
> The parrot of the verdant spring,

The willow-trees, the terrace,
The stranger from the dark hills,
The cup overflowing with clear wine. . . .
Oh, for life to be extended,
With no dead ashes of writing,
Amid the charms of the Natural,
Ah, who can compass it?[8]

What is writing but "dead ashes" in comparison to life, the natural world? And who can "compass" the beauty and fecundity of the world, especially in words? Moved beyond words, the poet leaves us with his gentle plea that such beauty bound by mystery might abide.

The explicit debt contemporary ecopoets owe to poets like Han-shan and Ssu-K'ung T'u might tempt us to look no further. Certainly the central place occupied by poets such as Merwin and Snyder in the ecopoetic canon focuses our attention on its Asian roots. But I would like to suggest that the Taoist and Zen influences observed in contemporary ecopoetry, although obviously important, offer only a partial context for understanding the poetics that underwrites it.

The ancient European contribution to both the linguistic skepticism and the meditative epistemology of contemporary ecopoetry has received scant critical attention. We have tended to view the European tradition as hopelessly logocentric, in love with the Word (not the World), hostile to unmediated experience, in short, antithetical to the ecopoetic aesthetic. The easy dismissal of the European tradition often rests on a simple-minded caricature of what is in fact an enormously diverse body of wisdom. While giving the devil his due, I would like to argue that the ancient European tradition, despite its historical biases, offers models of both linguistic skepticism and meditative epistemology.

Let us consider first of all Plato, the putative father of (phal)logocentric excess. As early as the *Phaedrus* Plato takes pains to underscore the limitations of language in both its written and spoken forms. Written language comes in for an especially tough time in the *Phaedrus;* Plato worries that relying overmuch on the written word serves only to atrophy the memory. He complains that one cannot ask questions of a written text as one can of a living interlocutor. Finally, he says that writing leads only to the "delusion" that we have wide knowledge and cripples our ability to make real judgments. Plato also argues that even the spoken word is functionally limited; having little merit on its own, it must be tailored to serve the ultimate end: the meeting of minds (especially the mind of one who knows with one who doesn't) in the realm of pure Idea.

In the *Cratylus* Plato refines his theory of language further by staging a showdown between the rival linguistic theories of his day. The conventionalist position of the Eleatic philosophers (and the sophist Gorgias) is presented in the person of Hermogenes, who confesses to Socrates that he

> cannot come to the conclusion that there is any correctness of names other than convention and agreement. For it seems to me that whatever name you give to a thing is its right name; and if you give up that name and change it for another, the later name is no less correct than the earlier . . . for I think no name belongs to any particular thing by nature, but only by the habit and custom of those who employ it and who established the usage. (384D)[9]

Plato then moves Socrates to refute Hermogenes' conventionalist position, arguing that "the giving of names can hardly be, as you imagine, a trifling matter, or a task for trifling or casual persons," and further, that Cratylus must be "right in saying that names belong to things by nature and that not every one is an artisan of names, but only he who keeps in view the name which belongs by nature to each particular thing and is able to embody its form in the letters and syllables" (390D).[10]

Although Plato is often taken to sympathize with the naturalist position of Cratylus in this dialogue, Plato's own position is rather more complex.[11] As we noted in the *Phaedrus,* the key to Plato's epistemology is that knowledge and language proceed on different tracks. Those tracks may diverge, as when the written word steers us away from real understanding. Alternatively, the tracks of knowledge and language may, in the best of all possible worlds, parallel one another. At the end of the *Cratylus* he fantasizes about a more perfect language in which words, or names, correspond more directly and with less ambiguity to their referents. Such an ideal language would ultimately facilitate knowledge by pointing directly and unproblematically to the only real manifestation of truth: the ideal Forms.

In developing his theory of language as an explicit alternative to conventionalist doctrine, Plato does not simply adopt Cratylus's rather naive naturalism. Indeed, Plato's naturalistic tendencies are strategic; even as it flirts with conventionalist heresy, Plato's embrace of language carries him beyond the ken of linguistic structures into a realm of knowledge subject to very different rules.

On this account the conventionalist attitudes of pre-Socratic intellectuals like Democritus and Gorgias, and in a very qualified way Plato's own linguistic theory, stake out positions at least sympathetic to the linguistic skepticism we have noted in latter-day ecopoetry. But before I stand accused of dyeing Plato green, I need quickly to acknowledge the signal reason why Plato does not generally receive good reviews in the ecocritical press. I refer, of course, to the transcendentalist bent apparent even in his treatment of language. For Plato's theory of Forms discounts the sensible, material world in ways that make lovers of nature cringe. Plato argued that the natural world that we labor to love is in fact nothing but a pale imitation of the really real, a shadow of ultimate Form that lies outside of space, time, and the vagaries of human perception and cognition.

Given the unfortunate and ultimately tragic way any such transcendentalism effaces the world on which all life, including the lives of philosophers, depends, it is easy to see how Plato and his ilk have come to serve as lightning rods for environmentalist ire. But again, the demonization of European (and American) transcendentalists tends to overlook the transcendentalism of other, ostensibly more earth-friendly traditions. Consider the case of Basho, the most celebrated of haiku poets. The choice is appropriate given that haiku is arguably the most quintessential of ecopoetic forms, parlaying as it does concise moments of unmediated perception grounded in actual time and place. Nobuyuki Yuasa, in the foreword to his translation of *The Narrow Road to the Deep North and Other Travel Sketches,* reminds us that before Basho set out on his many journeys, he suffered, and wrote about, the materiality of the so-called floating world (that is, the world of sensible, everyday objects) only with great dissatisfaction, eventually rebelling against it.[12] Yuasa describes what was for Basho a spiritual crisis, a longing for something in excess of the ordinary world before him. It was at this time that he began to practice Zen meditation in earnest. Yuasa writes, "Whether Basho was able to attain the state of complete enlightenment is a matter open to question, for he repeatedly tells us that he has one foot in the other world and the other foot in this one" (27).

What can we make of this talk of two worlds? We have reached the point where prudence dictates caution; even though the rhetoric appears to be similar, speculation concerning what Basho, or Plato, means by reference to realms that supplement or supplant the mundane must be deferred, at least for a moment.

Thus I will put aside, temporarily, the question of transcendentalism and turn to the status of meditative epistemology in the European tradition. Although every age may be said to harbor its mystics, for a complete elucidation of a meditative epistemology we inevitably turn to Augustine. As one critic has noted, Augustine is responsible for nothing less than redrawing the epistemological map.[13] For Plato the primary epistemological struggle is between certain knowledge *(episteme)* and mere belief or opinion *(doxa)*. One arrives at certain knowledge primarily by virtue of one's rational capacities. In contrast, Augustine's epistemological theory exploits the tension between reason and faith. According to Augustine, the power of rational understanding is essentially limited; *scientia,* or classical knowledge, is corrected and completed by divine or Gospel wisdom *(sapientia)*.

Augustine's meditative epistemology is invoked in the rhetoric of introspection, contemplation in the realm of silence. Rist points out that Augustine was not the first to advocate introspection as a legitimate way of knowing; such a position is in fact a common feature of Neoplatonic doctrine. The novelty of Augustine's approach is found in his claim that God is within, an assertion that has the effect of "anchoring" introspection.[14] Rist observes that

> a major objection to introspection, as Augustine knows, is that one cannot see within oneself without distorting what one sees, simply because the viewer is also the object of vision. But Augustine's idea that God is within us implies that one's inward eye is not merely looking at oneself as an object, and thus creating an image: it is also looking at something independent of the self, namely God, an ever present object which will always "resist" human misrepresentation. (89)

As in the meditative epistemology of Taoism and Zen, Augustine's path of knowledge through introspection serves to disintegrate and deprivilege the autonomous self. But what the inward turn anticipates, or discovers, is not Nature but God. Introspection, as a turn toward the indwelling God, is very explicitly a turning away from the natural world that is seen, as in Plato, as untrustworthy. For although "nature and the knowing mind are *informed* by God . . . the knowledge of nature does not necessarily disclose but may in fact obscure God."[15] *Sapientia* is opposed to *scientia* because the understanding of the rational mind is "limited to changing objects of knowledge in the external world."[16] For Augustine introspection affords us the opportunity to reach, "to some degree—a vision of Truth, that is of God, within ourselves though beyond ourselves. Hence we are able to reach something fixed and unchanging, something within us which is not an image constructed from our defective readings of ourselves and of the external world, but a meeting (which can be misunderstood and misinterpreted) with the unchanging God."[17]

We now confront the full force of the problem postponed only a moment ago: how do we account for epistemologies that, although similar, lead in radically different directions? That is to say, Why does Taoist and Zen epiphany, predicated on the bracketing of language and the cultivation of intuitive understanding, ground the self in the material world (for Basho, whatever his transcendentalist credentials, never shifts his focus from the material), whereas Platonic understanding and Christian epiphany, both predicated on the bracketing of language and the cultivation of intuitive understanding, lead one away from nature?

The answer is probably less mysterious than the question, and it is instructive. It demonstrates a fundamental truth that the field of environmental studies is particularly suited to articulate: ethics precede, and inform, epistemologies (and the poetics based on them). We should expect differing cosmologies, and the different social and environmental relationships they articulate, to structure ways of being and ways of knowing. Experience and knowledge are, in this sense, tautological. Plato comes to discover the Forms that he "knew" to exist independent of any kind of Being-in-the-World. As a theist Augustine "discovers" the God within, a divine presence that supercedes its own creations.

The idealist epiphany of Plato and the theist epiphany of Augustine both stand in stark contrast to what we might call the materialist epiphany recorded in Taoist and Zen literature. One might suppose that the materialist epiphany is underwritten by a basic pantheism (whether "theological" or "scientific") that can never stray too far from the sensible world.

The historical hegemony of idealism and theism in European and American experience served to direct understanding away from the material. But when our basic conception of the cosmos and our place in it began to change (egged on by industrialization and its excesses and a shift in our scientific thought from the Newtonian to the ecological) the meditative epistemology and linguistic skepticism that underwrite the aesthetics of ecopoetry, and that previously served only the transcendentalist fetish, finally appeared useful in forging a vital connection to phenomenal nature.

In a very real sense we (post)moderns who remain spellbound by the spirits called down by the traditions that claim us are just beginning to (re)discover worlds of wisdom well lost. The search for sustainable poetry, and more generally, sustainable cultural practices, is redirecting our attention in many directions simultaneously: toward the acumen of a diverse past, toward contemporary expressions of environmental discretion, and, ultimately, toward the insight made possible through our own experience of an interdependent and interanimating world. The real work at hand consists in cultivating the powers of judgment that will allow us to recognize the wisdom we need, wherever it dwells.

Notes

1. Charles Wright, from *The Southern Cross* (New York: Vintage/Random House, 1981), 43.

2. Leonard Scigaj, *Sustainable Poetry: Four American Ecopoets* (Lexington: University Press of Kentucky, 1999), 41.

3. D. T. Suzuki, "Satori, or Acquiring a New Viewpoint," in *The World of Zen*, ed. Nancy Wilson Ross (New York: Vintage/Random House, 1960), 41.

4. Han-shan, *Cold Mountain: 101 Chinese Poems*, trans. Burton Watson, 2nd ed. (Boston: Shambhala, 1992), 127.

5. Ibid., 115.

6. See Neil Evernden, "Beyond Ecology: Self, Place, and the Pathetic Fallacy." *North American Review* 263, no. 4 (winter 1978): 16–20; Freya Mathews, *The Ecological Self* (Savage, Md.: Barnes and Noble, 1991); George Sessions, ed., *Deep Ecology for the Twenty-First Century* (Boston: Shambhala, 1994), 226; Jack Turner, *The Abstract Wild* (Tucson: University of Arizona Press, 1996); Laird Christensen, "Spirit Astir in the World: Sacred Poetry in the Age of Ecology" (Ph.D. diss., University of Oregon, 1999), esp. chap. 5, "Always a Knit of Identity: Invoking the Ecological Self."

7. Han-shan, 100.

8. Ssu-K'ung T'u, in *Taoist Tales*, ed. Raymond Van Over (New York: Mentor/New American Library, 1973), 236.

9. Plato, in *Plato with an English Translation*, trans. H. N. Fowler (London: William Heinemann, 1926), 9–11.

10. Ibid., 31.

11. See Nicholas P. White, *Plato on Knowledge and Reality* (Indianapolis: Hackett, 1976), esp. 117–156.

12. Nobuyuki Yuasa, introduction to *The Narrow Road to the Deep North and Other Travel Sketches* (New York: Penguin, 1966), 25.

13. John M. Rist, *Augustine: Ancient Thought Baptized* (Cambridge: Cambridge University Press, 1994), 44.

14. Ibid., 89.

15. Robert E. Cushman, "Faith and Reason," in *A Companion to the Study of St. Augustine,* ed. Roy W. Battenhouse (New York: Oxford University Press, 1955), 293.

16. Rist, 89.

17. Ibid., 86.

Roger Thompson

Emerson, Divinity, and Rhetoric in Transcendentalist Nature Writing and Twentieth-Century Ecopoetry

In the fall of 1993 I attended a reading by W. S. Merwin at Baylor University. At the time I had had little contact with Merwin's writings and went to the reading on the advice of a professor who knew my interests well. I remember an intense excitement about seeing a *poet,* as though I were about to come into contact with a prophet who would utter profound and universal truths about nature and spirit. As Merwin began his reading, however, I was struck by what I considered (at the time) a lack of lyricism in his poems and a complete absence of soul-shattering, divine utterances. I left the reading feeling that I had gone to see an activist speak, not a poet.

Since that reading I have realized that my conceptions of poetry descended from the traditional curriculum in which I was educated: the poet was the romantic messenger of God, not civic spokesperson. Even so, I have never forgotten the discomfort I felt at Merwin's reading. In fact, a similar discomfort is often expressed by my students, who conceive of poetics as distinct from rhetoric, lyricism divorced from overtly persuasive appeals. The reason that the lines of demarcation between poetics and rhetoric are drawn so strictly is historical, wrapped in a lineage of criticism from the eighteenth century through much of the twentieth century that insists on a view of poetry as divine or romantic inspiration and rhetoric as materialist, sophistic persuasion. And although these differences obscure some shared traits between poetics and rhetoric, they also highlight the significant difference between nature poets of the nineteenth century and nature poets of the twentieth century; they indicate the fundamental differences between poets such as Whitman and Merwin or Emerson and Snyder.

For the nineteenth-century transcendentalists in particular, poetics and rhetoric are conflated as unique expressions of divine eloquence, and both arts prioritize the role of the individual in his or her connection to the divine. By the mid-twentieth century, the focus on the individual and his or her connection to divinity has slowly given way to a predominant view of poetry as a consciously rhetorical act, whose purpose is social change. In terms of contemporary environmental poetry this shift from a conflated poetry and rhetoric to an overtly rhetorical poetics highlights a fundamental shift in conceptions of self and social responsibility. Whereas the nineteenth century might be seen as an era of "nature as inspiration," or even "nature as divine metaphor," the twentieth century increasingly conceived of the environment, at least in part, as the location of revolution, as source of scientific inquiry, and as location of metaphoric connections among social classes. Indeed, transcendentalist nature poetry can hardly be called ecopoetry in the contemporary sense, the term *ecopoetry* being so deeply saturated with rhetorical purpose that it diverges significantly from the explicit purpose of transcendental poetics—the communication of the divine without regard to social action.

Transcendentalist writers conceive of nature as metaphor for the divine. As Emerson writes:

> 1. Words are signs of natural facts.
> 2. Particular natural facts are symbols of spiritual facts.
> 3. Nature is the symbol of spirit.[1]

Emerson constructs here the metaphorical value of nature by assigning spiritual power to all nature symbols. The transcendentalist nature poet, following from Emerson's formulation, takes as his or her subject divine immanence. Walt Whitman describes the poet's responsibility: "The land and sea, the animals, fishes and birds, the sky and heaven and the orbs, the forests mountains and rivers are not small themes . . . but folks expect of the poet to indicate more than the beauty and dignity which always attach to dumb real objects. . . . [T]hey expect him to indicate the path between reality and their souls."[2] With nature as divine subject, social activism is subjugated to fortunate by-product of poetry's ultimate goal: contemplation of spiritual essence. Nature, therefore, is the location of reflection and divine illumination, and the hope for any sort of social action remains secondary.

Because social action is secondary to contemplation of the divine, the usual art of civic activism, rhetoric, is conflated with poetry in order to ensure that spirituality remains at the center of the arts. Emerson articulates most clearly the nineteenth-century conflation of rhetoric and poetics through a reliance on divine insight. In "The Poet" he declares:

> This insight, which expresses itself by what is called Imagination, is a very high sort of seeing, which does not come by study, but by the intellect

> being where and what it sees, by sharing the path, or circuit of things through forms, and so making them translucid to others. The path of things is silent. Will they suffer a speaker to go with them? A spy they will not suffer; a lover, a poet, is the transcendency of their own nature,—him they will suffer. The condition of true naming, on the poet's part, is his resigning himself to the divine *aura* which breathes through forms, and accompanying that. (3:30)

Emerson configures poets as "liberating gods" (35) and "the true and only doctor" (14) because they have a special connection to the divine. In "Shakespeare; or the Poet" he explicitly seeks this connection through a "poet-priest, a reconciler," which betrays the transcendentalist hope for a unifying vision of the world through divine immanence (4:209).

Emerson's conception of the poet as the articulator of the divine parallels his conception of the orator as communicator of divine mission. In "Eloquence" Emerson defines the orator's power as overflowing spiritual power: "Thus it is not powers of speech that we primarily consider under this word *eloquence,* but the power that being present, gives them their perfection, and being absent, leaves them a merely superficial value. Eloquence is the appropriate organ of the highest personal energy" (7:81). For Emerson the "highest personal energy" results from self-reliance that has at its heart an immanent God. So to express the personal energy is to express universal laws and principles: the orator has "an immortality of purpose," and he speaks of "nothing less than the grandeur of absolute ideas, the splendors and shades of Heaven and Hell" (7:97, 61).

Emerson's twin conceptions of eloquence and poetry surface through the explicit conflation of the two arts throughout his work. For example, in "The Poet" he calls the poet "the true and only doctor" (3:14), and in "Eloquence" he labels the orator "the physician" (8:113). Perhaps more clearly, in "The Method of Nature" Emerson compares the eloquence of debaters and the literature of poets, describing both as "authoritative and final" (1:201), and in "The Poet" he lists the orator alongside the "epic rhapsodist" as among those artists who seek to express themselves "symmetrically and abundantly" (3:41). The power of the poet and the power of the orator are at root the same.

The significance of this conflation is that it situates the purpose of both poetry and rhetoric outside the realm of materialist and sophistic persuasion. Emerson denounces firmly that poetry and rhetoric whose purpose is simply persuasion. In "Eloquence" he argues that such rhetoric is base: certain levels of rhetoric are prioritized so that the top level, yoked to the divine, outstrips lower levels that involve only the day-to-day affairs of humankind. In the transcendentalist vision of poetry and rhetoric, persuasion is a result of divine workings in the world—social action a useful by-product of the divinely inspired poet. As he writes in "Shakespeare; or the Poet," "A poet is no rattle-brain, saying what comes uppermost, and, because he says every thing, saying, at last, something good; but a heart in unison with time and country" (4:181). Poets are connected to their place and time, but they ultimately transcend those times through universal expression. To conceive of an art that fails to invoke the divine is to fail to transcend the material realm that binds the artist, and transcendence ultimately has the persuasive force of a true rhetoric.[3]

In terms of transcendentalist nature poetry, then, the divine power in nature is prioritized over its rhetorical function; indeed, the rhetorical function is disavowed in favor of the configuration of nature as exclusively divine metaphor.[4] This disavowal can be most clearly seen in poems that concern obviously rhetorical topics but that shift the focus of rhetoric away from social action and back to reflection on the power of divine nature. For example, Charles Timothy Brooks's "Channing" constructs the outspoken and eloquent W. E. Channing in natural metaphors for spiritual power. Reflective of the life of Channing (who had secured a church position for Brooks and whom Emerson lauded as a preeminent orator), the poem self-consciously moves from nature-based, divine power to a suggestion to social change, but that call for change remains invariably tied to a conception of nature as metaphor for divine. The opening stanza ensures that the place of the divine in Channing's life is prioritized:

> *From* the pure upper world to-day
> A hallowed memory meets us here, —
> A presence lighting all our way
> With heavenly thoughts and lofty cheer.[5]

Channing's connection to the "pure upper world" has practical results in the material world in that he lights his parishioners' way. Even so, his guidance is couched in traditionally spiritual terms: "lighting our way" and "heavenly." As the poem progresses, it becomes clear that Channing's connection to divinity results from a unique connection to nature that allows an in-flowing of spiritual power:

> And in the broad blue sky above,
> In the large book of Nature, then

He felt the greatness of God's love
Rebuke the narrow creeds of men.

Communing there with Nature's word,
Beside the vast and solemn sea,
With awe profound his spirit heard
The holy hymn of Liberty.[6]

Here the power of nature as divine again leads to "Liberty" so that Channing's power as orator, preacher, even poet has concrete rhetorical results. Nonetheless, those results remain couched in terms of divine, natural metaphor. In fact, the rhetorical results depend on the connection to a spiritualized nature.

This interplay between social action and divine, natural metaphor is borne out in Emerson's poetry so that in "Ode, Inscribed to W. H. Channing" Emerson refutes social activism in favor of contemplation of divine laws. Although speaking of a different Channing from Brooks, Emerson situates his claims for social change, like Brooks, in the immediacy of divine power, not a base rhetoric. Emerson declares he cannot leave his "honied thought / For the priest's cant, / Or the statesman's rant," and he argues that his studying Channing's "Politique" angers his own muse and results in confusion. He argues, in a famous phrase, that "Things are in the saddle / And ride mankind," reflecting a belief in the primacy of natural power, a spiritual metaphor, over the political powers of the "blindworm." Ultimately, Emerson returns to his own place in nature to reject the appeals of an empty rhetoric:

Yet do not I invite
The wrinkled shopman to my sounding woods,
Nor bid the unwilling senator
Ask votes of thrushes in the solitudes.

The final stroke is that the universal law divides the world on its own accord, so to seek out action is to fail to connect to universal truths:

He who exterminates
Races by stronger races,
Black by white faces,—
Knows to bring honey
Out of the lion.

Action is literally the natural result of connecting to divinity in nature, and "The astonished Muse finds thousands at her side" because the spiritual power makes the division possible and supplies the muse with her might.[7]

Ultimately the rhetorical power of transcendentalist nature poetry is best called the power of the divine; spiritual movement may (or may not) result in civic action. This is not to say that nineteenth-century American nature poetry is not rhetorical; indeed, poems such as Emerson's "Ode" demonstrate clearly that a desire for radical change in social structures was desired by, in particular, the transcendentalists. The point here is that poetry and rhetoric are conflated because both are conceived of as issuing from the divine and as acting in accordance with universal principles and essences. When Whitman writes in "Song of the Redwood-Tree," for example, that he sees in the redwood tree "certain to come, the promise of thousands of years, til / now deferr'd, / Promis'd to be filfill'd [*sic*], our common kind, the race," he engages in an act of persuasion, but the force of the argument is in its appeal to universal laws that transcend sophistic appeals to social action; even the falling trees sound "of voices ecstatic, ancient and rustling," and echo across the world even "to the deities of the modern henceforth yielding."[8] The spirit of the work, the Poetic, is intended to move the audience to contemplation and, if properly moved, a reconfiguration of social structure. The purpose is ecstasy, the result, possibly, persuasion.

This prioritization of divine ecstasy is absent in most contemporary ecopoetry, and its absence bespeaks an entirely different worldview, one in which nature is seen as location of argument for social change and for dynamic center of revolutionary new visions of civic duty.[9] Indeed, the name *ecopoetry* highlights its rhetorical roots, deriving from environmentalist movements whose purposes are a cultural reconfiguration of the value of nature. Nature, even if vaguely divine for the ecopoet, needs social action to halt its rapid destruction; thus, poetry needs explicitly rhetorical movements to enact that action.

W. S. Merwin's ecopoetry (paralleling his outspoken opposition to the Vietnam War) illustrates how poetry becomes an increasingly overt vehicle for social change. In "For a Coming Extinction" nature might be lamented as lost heavenly host, but the power of the poem is in its direct appeals for change; in other words, persuasion is the purpose more than the contemplation of the spiritual force of nature. Hank Lazer suggests that the persuasive element of Merwin's poetry in *The Lice,* including "For a Coming Extinction," is at root political, closely tied to Merwin's opposition to the Vietnam War. For Lazer, however, Merwin transforms the political into a broad mythology reliant on spiritual themes.[10] This maneuver to the mythological, however, too easily leads to a reading of Merwin as a poet of contemplation; instead, the move to the mythological highlights the rhetorical function of the poem. The opening lines demonstrate the polemic:

> Gray Whale
> Now that we are sending you the End
> That great god
> Tell him
> That we who follow you invented forgiveness
> And forgive nothing.

The invocation of deity here is accusatory, immediately condemning humanity for breaking its own civic virtues. The gray whale represents nature and the future connection to divinity, but the certainty of the whale's extinction drives within the poem a call for reform. So in the final lines of the poem the condemnation culminates in an ironic request that the whale, at its death, tell the god "That it is we who are important." The irony that humanity is essentially the more significant of the creatures creates a shift of worldview and calls explicitly for change.[11]

Wendell Berry has driven to the heart of this call for change in terms of explicit rhetorical purpose by shifting the idea of morality and virtue from contemplation of transcendental signifiers to social action: "Moral value, as should be obvious, is not separate from other values. An adequate morality would be ecologically sound; it would be esthetically pleasing. But the point I want to stress here is that it would be *practical.* Morality is long-term practicality."[12] The conception of morality as practicality has a profound effect on conceptions of poetics and its role in social activism. Although Emerson and the transcendentalists might see morality as necessarily linked to experience of nature, that experience is not necessarily yoked to practical, social virtue; Whitman can declare with force that "the greatest poet does not moralize or make applications of morals. . . . [H]e knows the soul."[13] By contrast, Berry's morality insists on use, so that what is moral in terms of ecology must have some practical purpose. Poetry, then, if it is to be part of a virtuous ecological moral system, must have a practical purpose. In short, it needs to be rhetorical.

So with Merwin poetry becomes ecological rhetoric. The poem, shifting clearly from its romantic roots, enters the world of pragmatism so that in works such as "Witness" nature is tied to the practical world of language to ensure a clear signifier between language and nature: language must provide a persuasive message about a slowly ebbing environment:

> I want to tell what the forests
> were like
>
> I will have to speak in a
> forgotten language.[14]

Although the poem posits a lost language at the root of understanding nature, the poem's rhetorical turn projects a "forgotten language" if current conditions continue. In fact, the language of the poem attempts to capture that disappearing natural world and its lost language in order to suggest the need for change.

Merwin's rhetoric is not unique among ecological poets. Leonard Scigaj, in distinguishing between linguistic essentialism and referentiality, asserts that Wendell Berry "is deeply suspicious of those who sever language from its intimacy with action and referentiality."[15] Similarly, William Rueckert argues that in Gary Snyder's *Turtle Island* "[e]very poem is an action which comes from a finely developed and refined ecological conscience and consciousness. The book enacts a whole program of ecological action; it is offered (like *Walden*) as a guide book."[16] What both Scigaj and Rueckert approach, in vastly different theoretical analyses, is the rhetorical roots of ecopoets, their need for environmental reform. To suggest that *Turtle Island* is a "guide book" for "ecological action" illustrates the degree to which poetry becomes an overt rhetorical document.

Ultimately, the ecopoet might be called cause-centered, declaring the natural world as center to societal reform. Ecopoets are, in fact, ecocritics themselves, shelving notions of nature as solely metaphoric divinity in favor of a conception of nature as potential action, possible location of human reform. Whereas the nineteenth-century nature poet might self-consciously attempt to make the divine real through natural metaphors, and in so doing attempt to obscure the rhetorical act by calling it poetical, the twentieth-century ecopoet increasingly writes overtly rhetorical poems. The poem becomes the location of argument for social change and environmental awareness—not an argument embedded in conceptions of divine poetics and eloquence but an argument self-consciously rhetorical and openly persuasive.

Walter Jost has argued that Robert Frost's "Two Tramps in Mud Time" is a rhetorical document, and he suggests that to best understand the poem, scholars must use rhetorical criticism.[17] Jost's argument suggests distinctions between what is rhetorical and what is poetical while simultaneously attempting to break down those distinctions. The exercise is useful, not only because it shows the rhetorical vector of poetry (which is so often conceived of as nonrhetorical) but because it highlights how a culture's conceptions of the two arts has significant impact on ideas of selfhood and social responsibility. The distinctions between rhetoric and poetry are ultimately bound by different time periods, so to discuss poetry and its relationship to rhetoric depends largely on the era of literature. The difference between rhetoric and poetics of nineteenth-century environmental writing and twentieth-century ecopoetry highlights the shift from conceptions of nature as divine metaphor to nature as location of social responsibility and action. With this move the poet becomes a new kind of prophet: no longer is the poet messenger of God, but he or she is instead messenger of civic virtue. In this way the ecopoet might be called uniquely American or, at least, uniquely democratic, because ecopoetry is less about specialized, priestly incantations and more about accessibility to people whom the poet hopes to call to action, not simply contemplation.

Notes

1. Ralph Waldo Emerson, *The Complete Works of Ralph Waldo Emerson,* 12 vols., ed. Edward W. Emerson (Boston: Houghton Mifflin, 1903–1904), 1:31. Subsequent citations of this work will be referenced parenthetically in the text proper.

2. Walt Whitman, "Preface to 1855 Edition of 'Leaves of Grass,'" *Leaves of Grass and Selected Prose,* ed. Sculley Bradley (New York: Holt, Rinehart, and Winston, 1949), 458.

3. I see this "true rhetoric" as part of a tradition beginning with Plato and running through such figures as St. Augustine and Emerson. These rhetoricians distinguish between a "true" rhetoric and a false rhetoric based on rhetoric's referentiality to the divine. The contrast is most striking in Plato's *Phaedrus* and *Gorgias,* but it is also apparent in Augustine's *De Doctrina Christiana* and Emerson's "Eloquence" essays and "The American Scholar."

4. Stephanie Sarver has argued that Emerson advances a social agenda in his lecture essay "Farming," but she (rightfully, I think) indicates that "the farmer ultimately remains simply one entity among many within the larger natural cosmos" (162). Sarver indicates that commune with nature was the priority with Emerson, not social action, perhaps best illustrated by his skepticism of Brook Farm. Stephanie Sarver, "Agrarian Environmental Models in Emerson's 'Farming,'" in *Reading the Earth: New Directions in the Study of Literature and the Environment,* ed. Michael P. Branch, Rochelle

Johnson, Daniel Patterson, and Scott Slovic (Moscow, Idaho: University of Idaho Press, 1998), 155–164.

5. Charles Timothy Brooks, *Poems, Original and Translated. With a Memoir by Charles W. Wendte,* ed. W. P. Andrews (Boston: Roberts Brothers, 1885), 126.

6. Ibid., 127.

7. Emerson, 9:71–74.

8. Whitman, *Leaves of Grass,* 177, 176.

9. Ecopoetry often continues to rely on a type of spirituality for its power, especially the work of Mary Oliver, whose *American Primitive* is at root a call for a spiritualized nature. Even so, works such as those by Merwin demonstrate a tendency toward overt and activist poetry, and even Oliver's poetry emerges from a culture demanding political purpose within the spiritual struggle. In this way the spiritual angle of the work still moves toward persuasion rather than contemplation as an end to poetry.

10. Hank Lazer, "'For a Coming Extinction': A Reading of W. S. Merwin's *The Lice,*" *ELH* 49, no. 1 (spring 1982): 262–285.

11. W. S. Merwin, *The Lice* (New York: Atheneum, 1967), 68–69.

12. Wendell Berry, "Discipline and Hope," in *Recollected Essays: 1965–1980* (San Francisco: North Point Press, 1980), 217.

13. Whitman, "Preface," 460. This is not to say that Emerson does not recognize the value of practical ends of ethics. Indeed, "action" is one of the key features of *The American Scholar.* Even so, Emerson's conception of nature's relationship to social responsibility differs vastly from Berry's and those of many contemporary ecopoets largely because Emerson's culture of nineteenth-century New England saw little need for sweeping environmental reform. Current contingencies make Berry's rhetoric necessary in a way not possible in Emerson's time; specifically, the study of the destruction of the environment has been foregrounded in the contemporary media in such a way as to create a *kairos* for activist poetry.

14. W. S. Merwin, *The Rain in the Trees* (New York: Alfred A. Knopf, 1992), 65.

15. Leonard M. Scigaj, "Contemporary Ecological and Environmental Poetry: *Différence* or *Référance,*" *Isle* 2, no. 3 (1996): 7.

16. William Rueckert, "Literature and Ecology: An Experiment in Ecocriticism," in *The Ecocriticism Reader: Landmarks in Literary Ecology,* ed. Cheryll Glotfelty and Harold Fromm (Athens: University of Georgia Press, 1996), 116.

17. Walter Jost, "'The Lurking Frost': Poetic and Rhetoric in 'Two Tramps in Mud Time,'" *American Literature* 60, no. 2 (May 1988): 226–240.

Deborah Fleming

Landscape and the Self in W. B. Yeats and Robinson Jeffers

Although W. B. Yeats never met Robinson Jeffers, the two poets barely missed meeting each other several times. Yeats visited California in 1919 on a lecture tour to raise money for Tor Ballylee's new roof, the same journey during which he received messages from ghostly "instructors" through his wife's automatic writing that led to the creation of *A Vision.* Jeffers, meanwhile, was building Tor House in Carmel. The Jefferses visited Tor Ballylee in 1929, 1937, and 1948; on the first visit they sought out the house twice although Yeats was not there.[1] From Yeats's example Una Jeffers conceived the notion of her husband's building a tower in imitation of Tor Ballylee. The interesting similarity of their choosing towers as dwelling places informs their creation of the symbolism of landscape. Yeats bought and restored Thoor Ballylee, an eleventh-century Norman tower, in 1917; Jeffers helped build Tor House in 1919 and during the following decades built Hawk Tower. Gilbert Allan suggests that both tried to make their houses adequate symbols: "Yeats renovates, in order to reaffirm what strikes him as most admirable within the cultural past; Jeffers builds, in order to express in cultural terms a geological history that human beings habitually ignore."[2]

Both Yeats and Jeffers found it necessary to place their poetry in specific landscapes, and in doing so they challenged one of the fundamentals of modernism. Robert Zaller points out that at the heart of the modernist credo lies the primacy of aesthetic art or redemptive potential,[3] and Charles Altieri asserts that the two related modes of romanticism that helped to generate modernism were Wordsworth's "immanentist" mode and Coleridge's "symbolist" mode. Most modernists chose the symbolist mode with its allegiance to the "creative mind as the source of value."[4] Robinson Jeffers of course rejected the notion that art could possess independent or transcendent value; he embraced, on the other hand, the idea that artistic beauty could be derived only from natural beauty.[5] As Jeffers makes clear in "Love the Wild Swan," artistic beauty is in his view secondary to the natural. He did not ignore history and culture—his long narratives are testaments to his knowledge of them; rather, he valued history, society, and culture through their relationship to nature. He certainly rejected the modernist tendency to interpret nature poetically through human perception, as Wallace Stevens does in "The Idea of Order at Key West," where the setting exists only as the speaker interprets it through his artistic sensibility. For Jeffers poetry does not create the significance of place, as does, for example, the poetry of Stevens or William Carlos Williams; instead, for Jeffers place creates the significance for poetry.

W. B. Yeats, whose work more closely follows Coleridge's "symbolist" tradition, found it necessary nevertheless to locate his poetry in Irish tradition. Explaining his artistic choice in nationalistic terms, he wrote in 1888: "You can no more have the greater poetry without a nation than religion without symbols. One can only reach out to the universe with a gloved hand—that glove is one's nation, the only thing one knows even a little of." And in 1890: "The first thing needful if an Irish literature more elaborate and intense than our fine but primitive ballads and novels is to come into being is that readers and writers alike should really know the imaginative periods of Irish history."[6] To create this "elaborate and intense" Irish literature, Yeats knew that he needed to infuse his writing with a sense of place, the land from which the Irish ballads and mythologies had sprung. So although he, unlike Jeffers, embraced the symbolist mode of romantic poetry, he nevertheless insisted that art be grounded in place and tradition. Jeffers, on the other hand, although certainly peopling his narratives with extraordinary characters and describing the culture and traditions of the places he wrote about, nevertheless always valued the land itself more than any human construct.

William Nolte claims that both Yeats and Jeffers attempted "with unmatched success in this century—to give to their own locale an infinitely translatable meaning."[7] Critics have noted that Jeffers without Carmel is as "unimaginable as Frost without New England,"[8] but the same must be said of Yeats without Ireland. Furthermore, Jeffers cannot be identified with California merely but with the Big Sur coast[9]—not the sun-drenched south, the fertile valley of Steinbeck's writings, the wine country of Jack London, or the northern Cascades. Similarly, although Yeats places several important poems in different locations in Ireland (Dublin in "Easter, 1916" and "To a Shade"; the rock of Cashel in "The Double Vision of Michael Robartes," for example), when he wants to emphasize place he inevitably goes to Sligo (as, for example, in "The Lake Isle of Innisfree," "The Man Who Dreamed of Faeryland," and "The Hosting of the Sidhe") or to Galway ("The Tower," "Coole Park, 1929," "Coole and Ballylee, 1931, " and "The Wild Swans at Coole"). Some poems, for example "The Stolen Child," contain descriptions of the natural setting and folklore that clearly locate them in the west of Ireland even though the poet does not literally place them there. In fact, Jeffers's and Yeats's landscapes remain far more important to their aesthetic than the New England landscape does to Frost's. Any landscape would have served Frost's purpose. Jeffers, unlike Frost, takes his theme from landscape, celebrating the land as he does and creating it for the reader although at the same time making clear that the poem does not stand in the place of landscape. The poem is separate, and the landscape is the greater of the two.

For Yeats, on the other hand, the greatness of art stems from the richness of cultural tradition inevitably associated with place. Landscape also figures hugely in his aesthetic. Although readers may insist that Yeats recreated the Irish countryside (and people) to suit his own idea of what Irish literature and the Irish nation should have become, it is nevertheless clear that no other landscape and no other nation could have enabled him to write much of the work he did. Yeats found direction not only in his own aesthetic but also in the folk literature of his country. The poetry and the landscape are involved in a dialectic: the land speaks through the poems, and the poems speak through the land.

In the same way, Jeffers's landscapes established locale; Terence Diggory argues that Jeffers is one of several American poets to have found encouragement for his poetry of regionalism in Yeats's example.[10] Robert Zaller goes so far as to claim that landscape is Jeffers's abiding hero.[11] In "The Place for No Story," for example, the "place" is the hero:

> No imaginable
> Human presence here could do anything
> But dilute the lonely self-watchful passion.[12]

Jeffers describes the hills with their "scant pasture," a rock "shaped like flame," the cows grazing, the ocean beneath, and the air above, "haunted with hawks," as if they were spirits. The landscape itself is the hero: "This place is the noblest thing I have ever seen." "Gray Weather," moreover, although describing the Pacific coast as place, becomes a metaphor of landscape and the human. Watching the sea, Jeffers sees no shining or dark, just the essential; all emotion suspended, he "explores deeper than the nerves or heart," to the very bone:

> It is true that, older than man and ages to outlast him, the Pacific surf
> Still cheerfully pounds the worn granite drum;
> . . . .
> The stormy conditions of time and change are all abrogated, the essential

Violences of survival, pleasure,
Love, wrath, and pain, and the curious desire of knowing, all perfectly
suspended.
In the cloudy light, in the timeless quietness,
One explores deeper than the nerves or heart of nature, the womb or soul,
To the bone, the careless white bone, the excellence.[13]

Looking at the Big Sur coast and knowing it will endure far longer than human beings enables the poet to understand that he is part of nature, that his consciousness need not separate him from it.

In the same way, Ireland is a protagonist of sorts in Yeats's work as a whole, not only as landscape but also as a nation emerging from a past full of linguistic and political domination, gaining a sense of ethnic and historical nationhood. In "A General Introduction for My Work," for example, Yeats articulates the fact that everything he loved (mostly literature) had come to him through English and that his hatred tortured him with love:

> [N]o people, Lecky said at the opening of his *Ireland in the Eighteenth Century,* have undergone greater persecution [than the Irish], nor did that persecution altogether cease up to our own day. No people hate as we do in whom that past is always alive, there are moments when hatred poisons my life and I accuse myself of effeminacy because I have not given it adequate expression. It is not enough to have put it into the mouth of a rambling peasant poet. Then I remind myself that though mine is the first English marriage I know of in the direct line, all my family names are English, and that I owe my soul to Shakespeare, to Spenser and to Blake, perhaps to William Morris, and to the English language in which I think, speak, and write, that everything I love has come to me through English; my hatred tortures me with love, my love with hate.[14]

Thus deprived of his national language, lamenting his own fate as a writer in a colonial nation, and determined to revivify a sense of Irish nationhood, Yeats felt the necessity of creating a literature firmly imbued with the sense of place. In "The Celtic Element in Literature" he writes that the Irish poets' "natural music" stemmed in part from their ancient worship of nature and the certainty that beautiful natural places were visited by spirits:

> Men who lived in a world where anything might flow and change, and become any other thing; and among great gods whose passions were in the

> flaming sunset, and in the thunder and the thunder-shower, had not our thoughts of weight and measure. They worshipped nature and the abundance of nature, and had always, as it seems, for a supreme ritual that tumultuous dance among the hills or in the depths of the woods, where unearthly ecstasy fell upon the dancers, until they seemed the gods or the godlike beasts, and felt their souls overtopping the moon; and, as some think, imagined for the first time in the world the blessed country of the gods and of the happy dead. They had imaginative passions because they did not live within our own strait limits, and were nearer to ancient chaos, every man's desire, and had immortal models about them.[15]

Thus, the development of a vigorous folklore and mythology cannot be separated from the land.

The literary treatment of the landscape of a nation engenders questions about the separation of observer from the observed. Raymond Williams, in *The Country and the City,* emphasizes the idea of separation that he believes is fundamental to romantic pastoralism and to nature writing in general. Moreover, Williams continues, writing about landscape implies observation separate from the land.[16] Just as an observer of landscape must view it from a vantage point removed from the scene in order to appreciate it, the writer about landscape must achieve aesthetic distance from the subject in order to capture its beauty. Such distance necessarily implies objectivity.

We may ask how much of Yeats's and Jeffers's relationship to the land was a result of their distance from it. Jeffers constantly alludes to the separation he feels from the natural world (as in "The Answer," "The House," and "Consciousness") and longs to become part of it, whereas Yeats uses that separation to create aesthetic tension. He is not one of the swans in "The Wild Swans at Coole" that embody the youthfulness he longs for; the woods of Coole may hide the squirrels from old age, he says in "I walked among the seven woods of Coole,"[17] but they cannot work such magic on the poet. Although he can never be one with nature, however, he can achieve transcendence through the poem. Sometimes, of course, he wishes to escape from nature (or time) entirely as in "Sailing to Byzantium," but the famous last line asserts that even immortal art takes its form from nature. Yeats wishes to transcend mortality through the creation of art, yet he knows he can never escape nature in doing so; for Jeffers immortality lies in the permanence of nature and the natural cycles that include mortality.

Landscape, as pointed out by W. J. T. Mitchell in "Imperial Landscape," changes the way people see, as well as what they see. *Landscape* employed as a verb means to use the land in order to shape ideas, attitudes, and perceptions. Mitchell speaks of landscape painting, a recent and decidedly Western form of art, a "pseudohistorical myth" in which "the discourse of landscape is a crucial means for enlisting 'Nature' in the legitimation of modernity, the claim that 'we moderns' are somehow different from and essentially superior to everything that preceded us, free of superstition and convention, masters of a unified, natural language epitomized by landscape painting."[18] Yet landscape may also be used in the same way by poets to create artistic power. Yeats invents the idea of an Irish aristocracy by incorporating ancestors not his own (Burke, Grattan), raising the importance of his own real ancestors (George Pollexfen; his father, John Butler Yeats), and appropriating local landowners involved in art or politics (Lady Gregory, Hugh Lane, the Gore-Booths) to create an Ireland that existed primarily in his own mind. The poems express a culture that he believed should belong to Ireland. To find a tradition for himself, he restored Tor Ballylee and created a history for it out of both fact and legend, enabling himself to achieve poetic power.

Ironically, Yeats borrowed from British aristocratic values in order to establish his poetic and national traditions. The importance of the Pollexfens' Sligo estate, the Gore-Booths' Lissadell, and Lady Gregory's Coole Park issues from the idea of noble householder-landowners who are generous, courteous, and faithful, who fulfill expectations although their rank allows them to do otherwise, who preside over estates that are both beautiful and bountiful. Such an estate and landlord appear in Jonson's "To Penshurst," one of the first and certainly one of the most important landscape poems that itself affirms—perhaps even creates—the ideal it describes. To this tradition Yeats adds artistic patronage and patriotism.

Although it was Jeffers's purpose to describe landscape apart from the human and to emphasize his belief in separation of the land itself from the anthropocentric vision of it, there can be no doubt that the Big Sur coast and its human as well as geologic history empowered Jeffers not only to create but to sustain his poetic vision. His artistic power is founded in identifying himself with the landscape even as colonists occupy land and transform it to their own purposes. Location thus enables both Jeffers and Yeats to achieve their poetic purpose, but, in addition, their poetry in part creates the place they write about, for themselves and for the generations who succeeded them.

The most striking similarities between the two poets are Yeats's and Jeffers's identifying themselves with the mountainous, rocky west coasts of their countries—Yeats with Sligo and Galway, Jeffers with Big Sur. Because the rocky soil restricted agriculture, both locations afforded poor livings for most of their inhabitants before the dawn of tourism. These western locales were therefore sparsely inhabited (Ireland not having recovered from the population depletions of the nineteenth century) yet at the same time scenic and endowed with folk history and local culture. Both western coasts had the added advantage (for purposes of poetry) of being far from the civilized centers in the east. Yeats and Jeffers munificently describe their coastal regions' rocky slopes and forests, as well as the animals, both tame and wild, that inhabit them. Few poets have as keen an eye for bird life, partly because of the abundance of habitat that coastal regions afford: Jeffers names herons, pelicans, eagles, swans, grebes, gulls, sea parrots, vultures, sparrows, cormorants, and, of course, hawks. In the poem "Birds" alone he names sparrow hawks, seagulls, falcons, and hawks, whose flight he praises as "nothing gracefuller. . . . Their wings to the wild spirals of the wind-dance," because "a poem / Needs multitude, multitudes of thoughts, all fierce, all flesh-eaters, musically clamorous."[19] He implies that the poem lives only because of the natural world. W. B. Yeats, meanwhile, also chooses symbols from the natural world because without it a national poetry cannot exist. Nation, rather than nature, may be his ultimate concern, but, again, nation and place cannot be separated. Yeats's bird symbols include moor-hens, herons (cranes), linnets, stares (starlings), jackdaws, and especially swans. In addition, both poets describe the native inhabitants of their regions—not from an anthropologist's perspective perhaps but from the poet's view of those who live on and earn their living from the land. For Jeffers these are small farmers and ranchers of Big Sur; for Yeats they are peasants, small farmers, tinkers, and beggars of western Ireland.

Both Jeffers and Yeats, moreover, created themselves as protagonists in their own poetry and described themselves in the landscape. The earth was at the center of Jeffers's aesthetic, whereas the realization of a new Ireland created from the old traditions remained at the center of Yeats's. Winfield Townley Scott remarks, "Only Yeats in modern poetry could so powerfully make himself his own protagonist,"[20] as had Jeffers, Wordsworth, and Whitman. They all created a poetic voice so distinctive that one is never tempted to refer to a speaker other than the poet himself.

Terence Diggory argues that in order to become its own tradition, the self required a heroic dimension.[21] It was Yeats's tower that finally allowed him to explore fully the consequences of the tradition of the self. Although he had been incorporating autobiographical detail into his poetry for at least a decade, for the most part he could not express the self as fully as the tower—which was chosen and created—enabled him to do. The tower offered poetic authority, a seemingly traditional source but actually a new one that allowed

Yeats to claim spiritual ancestors.[22] Diggory explains that criticism of Yeats's identifying himself with ancestors who weren't his in fact misses the point; Yeats's claim to the tradition creates a new tradition.

Whereas Yeats adopted both personal and impersonal roles (the personal in, for example, "The Tower"; the impersonal in works such as "The Man Who Dreamed of Faeryland"), Jeffers decided, as Yeats had, that the personal role was the one that best defended against the modern world. Diggory argues, however, that in conceiving of himself as a tradition, Jeffers in fact preserves an impersonal aesthetic: "Tradition, as a dimension of the self, is a larger-than-life dimension such as Jeffers had sought to incorporate in the characters of his narratives and plays. As in his early lyrics, Jeffers is still playing a role, presenting a self that has been made, not born . . . a role based on his own life" (132). For Yeats the poetic individual must be created: "he is never the bundle of accident and incoherence that sits down to breakfast; he has been reborn as an idea, something intended, complete."[23] This is true for Jeffers as well. As Diggory remarks, "It is appropriate that Jeffers's first intimation of that role and his final recognition of it both involve the building of his house and tower, a symbolic act that can be traced directly to Yeats."[24]

From their respective towers Jeffers and Yeats project themselves and their imaginative beings onto the landscape. They created poetic roles and personae from the self and adopted their respective towers as symbols but also as real constructs. In "The Tower" Yeats takes fullest advantage of landscape; he "send[s] imagination forth / Under the day's declining beam" to call forth images to question: Mrs. French whose servant clipped an insolent farmer's ears; Mary Hynes, the peasant girl and legendary beauty; and Red Hanrahan himself, a character from Yeats's own stories who is patterned on the legendary Owen Rua O'Sullivan.[25] The landscape signifies the place where all this happens, where memory and present time coincide, where the tradition he created is ongoing.

Mary Hynes, a local peasant girl who lived long before ("Some few remembered still when I was young"), was so beautiful that she was "commended by a song." She lived "somewhere upon that rocky place" isolated and away from civilization. She became an emblem of beauty, and if she walked among the crowd at the fair, "[f]armers jostled," not so much because of Mary herself but because "[s]o great a glory did the song confer." And certain men, transported emotionally by poetry ("maddened by those rhymes") or else by their collective mythology ("by toasting her a score of times"), declared that they must "test their fancy by their sight"—find out the truth concerning her beauty. The vision, however, overwhelms them ("Music had driven their wits astray"), and one was drowned in "the great bog of Cloone." He had mistaken the moon's brightness (poetry) for the "prosaic light of day" (reality) and would never be able to "test his fancy" (imagination). Yeats compares blind Raftery, the poet who created the song about Mary Hynes, with Homer and Mary with Helen of Troy:

> Strange, but the man who made the song was blind;
> Yet, now I have considered it, I find
> That nothing strange; the tragedy began
> With Homer that was a blind man,
> And Helen has all living hearts betrayed.

He thus links the Irish and Greek folktales and hence, by means of the poem, the literature and traditions of Ireland with those of ancient Greece. The characters imagined from the top of the tower are not only isolated by their landscape but speak from it.

In the next section the poet recreates his own mythology: "And I myself created Hanrahan / And drove him drunk or sober through the dawn / From somewhere in the neighbouring cottages." It is significant for Yeats that his character emerges from among "the neighbouring cottages," that is, near the tower, in Yeats's immediate and imagined landscape. An enchanted old man shuffled cards and bewitched young Hanrahan, newly engaged to be married, so that he wandered witless into the night after a magical hare and hounds and so forgot his engagement. Doomed to wander for the rest of his life, Hanrahan is a figure of the hedge schoolmaster and wandering poet of eighteenth-century Ireland—persons inseparable from their landscape. Yeats thus establishes his own myth from the folklore of the place.

Yeats then recalls the ancient master of the house and his rough men-at-arms who once billeted in the tower and whose ghosts, playing with great wooden dice, disturb the current sleepers. They are types whose "images" are stored in the Great Memory just as are the farmers and beautiful peasant girl. Yeats desires to question them all—Oisin ("old, necessitous, half-mounted man"), Raftery ("beauty's blind rambling celebrant"), Mrs. French, and the man destroyed by the image of beauty itself who drowned "[w]hen mocking muses chose the country wench." Yeats's questions involve old age and love—that is, death and desire—and he needs their "mighty memories," the relationship to history and the land. The answers enabled him to write the powerful final section of the poem in which he "creates" an ancestry and tradition for himself. He chooses "upstanding men / That climb the streams" like the idealized fisherman of the poem of that title who has become the repository of an ancient culture of aristocracy and peasantry.[26] The poems following "The Tower" continue the theme of creation of tradition: "Ancestral Houses," "My House," "My Table," "My Descendants," "The Road at My Door." He continues to build and construct his "tradition," half imaginative, half taken from the history of the place.

Even in poems not as personal as "The Tower" Yeats turned to the Irish landscape to locate his images. Yeats's "The Man Who Dreamed of Faeryland" is a veritable map of Sligo, the man's experience taking place in the here and now and yet also within the timelessness of faery lore.[27] Lissadell, Toberscanavin (shortened to "Scanavin" in the poem), and Lugnagall are in Sligo, and Dromahair is immediately across the border in Leitrim.[28] Lissadell House, the home of Yeats's friends the Gore-Booths, is named for the barony of Lissadell in County Sligo. The well of Scanavin is in County Sligo, as is Lugnagall, "The Hollow of Foreigners," a town land in Glencar Valley in County Sligo. The dreamer, caught up in desire for the beauty and timelessness of faeryland, nevertheless has a good life: he is successful in love and commerce, and his celebrated fiery personality is "a country tale." Just as he achieves success, however, the faeries enter his life in the forms of common things—fish, lugworms, knot-grass, worms—in each stanza something lowlier than the last. The man achieves no happiness because he has been "glammoured"—his soul is paralyzed by the imagined beauty of faeryland, which he is never allowed to enter.[29]

In "The Wild Swans at Coole" the speaker identifies himself with the place, is careful to note exactly the number of years (nineteen) he has been visiting Coole and gazing on the swans, and even counts them as if the loss of a single one would bring some tragedy.[30] He asks among what rushes they will build—where they will be—when he "awakes" as if from slumber to find them gone. A poet may locate romantic allegory in any traditional, beautiful, or natural scene, but Yeats chooses Galway and the estate of his friend Lady Gregory in order to place the image in the land that holds for him the greatest significance. His dream of the creation of an Irish literature involved more than recalling the old legends and making them known to all classes in Ireland; it involved the poetic recreation of Ireland itself, which transcends the establishment of a merely political nation.[31]

Jeffers uses the same image of wild swans in "Love the Wild Swan" to express his Inhumanist philosophy. He declares in this poem that he hates his verses for not being as beautiful as the natural world:

Oh pale and brittle pencils ever to try
One grass-blade's curve, or the throat of one bird
That clings to twig, ruffled against white sky.
Oh cracked and twilight mirrors ever to catch
One color, one glinting flash, of the splendor of things.[32]

Calling it "The lion beauty, the wild-swan wings, the storm of the wings," he declares that better poets than he have failed to realize their imaginative vision. At least, he concludes, love your eyes that can see the majesty of nature: "Love the wild swan." In Yeats's poem the water itself "Mirrors a still sky" within the "October twilight," and the sound of the swans' wings is "clamorous," whereas with Jeffers it is "storm." Jeffers seems in fact to be "mirroring" Yeats's poem, providing this difference: Yeats laments the passing of romanticism and youth; Jeffers celebrates natural beauty exclusively, dismissing the value of any human construct.

Yeats's aesthetic, however, is not so very far from Jeffers's on the issue of the value of natural beauty. Lady Gregory's estate contained not only the wild swan lake but also seven woods, which Yeats carefully names in several poems, such as "In the Seven Woods" and "To a Squirrel at Kyle-na-no," in order to establish not only tradition but tradition associated with place. The introductory verses to *The Shadowy Waters* name all seven woods and the source of their distinctiveness:

Shan-walla, where a willow-bordered pond
Gathers the wild duck from the winter dawn;
Shady Kyle-dortha; sunnier Kyle-na-no,
Where many hundred squirrels are as happy
As though they had been hidden by green boughs
Where old age cannot find them: Pairc-na-lee,
Where hazel and ash and privet blind the paths;
Dim Pairc-na-carraig, where the wild bees fling
Their sudden fragrances on the green air;
Dim Pairc-na-tarav, where enchanted eyes
Have seen immortal, mild, proud shadows walk;
Dim Inchy Wood, that hides badger and fox
And marten-cat, and borders that old wood
Wise Biddy Early called the wicked wood:
Seven odours, seven murmurs, seven woods.[33]

Although the poet had not "enchanted eyes" he dreamed that "beings happier than men" moved in the shadows, and at night his dreams "were cloven by voices and by fires," and the images of *The Shadowy Waters* moved round him in those voices and fires. He asks, apostrophizing either the woods or waters that become the shadowy images with which he peoples the poem, "*How shall I name you, immortal, mild, proud shadows? / I only know that all we know comes from you, / And that you come from Eden on flying feet.*"[34] Thus, "all we know comes from you"—from woods, water, and the spirits that dwell there. All he knows comes from the earth, the tradition associated with place and created through human emotion and experience.

In *The Winding Stair* Yeats further examines the interrelationship of place and tradition in the companion poems "Coole Park, 1929" and "Coole and Ballylee, 1931." Certainly it is an interior landscape that Yeats describes in the former, although he is careful also to describe the western landscape amid trees and wildlife, "A sycamore and lime tree lost in night / Although that western cloud is luminous."[35] He celebrates Coole Park because of its notable visitors who have ensured the sacredness of the place even when they and the house are gone: "When all those rooms and passages are gone, / When nettles wave upon a shapeless mound / And saplings root among the broken stone" (423). Thus he envisions the future when traveler, scholar, and poet will visit the place and calls upon them to dedicate "A moment's memory to that laurelled head" (423). The writing of the poem itself creates the tradition that Yeats labored assiduously to create—one of nobility, art, and history in order to inform and enrich the culture.

"Coole and Ballylee, 1931" spiritually links the two locations in Galway. It may be spurious geology, but Yeats declares that the stream joins estate and tower, running beside Tor Ballylee and then underground:

> darkening through "dark" Raftery's "cellar" drop,
> Run underground, rise in a rocky place
> In Coole demesne, and there to finish up
> Spread to a lake and drop into a hole.[36]

The places are connected by the lives lived there: a solitary poet who seeks to establish tradition in his dwelling place and a playwright and essayist who brought talented people together to create the Irish Literary Theatre. The stream itself spiritually connects not only the two artists but also the two places that are imbued with history.

For Jeffers, on the other hand, history is natural history, of which the experience of individuals and cultures is a mere part. In "Granite and Cypress" Jeffers envisions the future as "one piece with the past."[37] In "Tor House" he imagines the future in which the poem's eponymous house and Hawk Tower have fallen (as Yeats envisioned the future in which Coole Park's house is "broken stone"). What remains, Jeffers says, will be the planted forest of eucalyptus or coast cypress, "haggard / With storm-drift." The foundation of "sea-worn granite" may remain after "a handful of lifetimes," but the traveler who visits after ten thousand years will find no foundation, only the

> granite knoll on the granite
> And lava tongue in the midst of the bay, by the mouth of the Carmel
> River-valley, these four will remain
> In the change of names.[38]

Passing time, which brings with it destruction of human creations, is not to be lamented; Jeffers celebrates the natural processes and what will remain—the rock, river valley, and water itself.

As Yeats in "The Tower" paced "under the day's declining beam" on the battlements and called forth images, Jeffers from the top of Hawk Tower recalls the story of Margrave:

> On the small marble-paved platform
> On the turret on the head of the tower
> Watching the night deepen . . .
> . . . .
> I lean on the broad worn stones of the parapet-top.[39]

No clearer allusion to Yeats exists in Jeffers's work. Like Yeats, Jeffers includes two related poems—"Point Joe" and "Point Pinos and Point Lobos"—in the same volume, *Tamar* (1920–1923). Point Joe is distinguished by fierce and solitary beauty: "Walk there all day you shall see nothing that will not make part of a poem."[40] The point has teeth (rocks) that have torn ships. Fog and light suffuse upward. Jeffers describes every detail carefully, the debris of shipwreck, desolate sea meadows riotous with flowers and wind-beaten pines, and the golden light beating upward. One other person moved there, a Chinese man who gathered seaweed and spread it on the rocks to dry:

> Permanent things are what is needful in a poem, things temporally
> Of great dimension, things continually renewed or always present.

. . . .
Fashionable and momentary things we need not see nor speak of. (90–91)

Grass that renews itself annually is as great as the mountains; moreover, the man "gleaning food between the solemn presences of land and ocean" (90) is as great as the mountain in past and future for he engages, like Yeats's fisherman,[41] in one of the timeless activities of human beings.

Separated by one poem, "Gale in April"—a song to the harsh beauty of nature—"Point Joe" and "Point Pinos and Point Lobos" both praise the beauty and permanence of nature and tradition, but the second poem identifies the presence of God in nature. Jeffers carefully locates the poem named for two sacred places:

A lighthouse and a graveyard and gaunt pines
Not old, no tree lives long here, where the northwind
Has forgot mercy. All night the light blinks north,
The Santa Cruz mountain redwoods hate its flashing,
The night of the huge western water takes it,
The long rays drown a little off shore, hopelessly
Attempting distance, hardly entering the ocean.
The lighthouse, and the gaunt boughs of the pines,
The carved gray stones, and the people of the graves.[42]

The poem, a philosophical meditation on God, is divided into three sections, the first describing the tortured Christ—the dying god who struggles still to redeem people—and section 2 contemplating the legacy of Buddha. The final stanza in this section, however, returns to place, even alluding to Jeffers's own creation, the girl Tamar, whose narrative is included in the same volume:

The evening opens
Enormous wings out of the west, the sad red splendid light beats upward
These granite gorges, the wind-battered cypress trees blacken above them,
The divine image of my dream smiles his immortal peace, commanding
This old sea-garden, crumble of granite and old buttressed cypress trunks,
And the burnt place where that wild girl whose soul was fire died with
her house. (97)

Finally, in the third section, Jeffers chastises both great teachers and religious founders, Buddha and Christ, "One striving to overthrow his ordinances through love and the other crafty-eyed to escape them / Through patient wisdom" (97). The poet banishes both love and wisdom as human constructs, almost as he imaginatively views both rocky points (Pinos and Lobos) as the real entities to be worshiped. Although these great teachers—Christ and Buddha—are wiser than other human beings, they are still more foolish than the "running grass" that "fades in season and springs up in season." God is not made manifest through love or wisdom:

> For the essence and the end
> Of his labor is beauty, for goodness and evil are two things and still
> variant, but the quality of life as of death and of light
> As of darkness is one, one beauty, the rhythm of that Wheel, and who can
> behold it is happy and will praise it to the people. (97)

God is manifest in nature's beauty, however fierce and violent it appears.

Just as Yeats visits the scenes where he had located his narratives and poems, Jeffers returns to the landscape of his earlier work. "The Loving Shepherdess" visits scenes from earlier narratives and observes characters from the perspective of time past. The coast itself, although beyond tragedy and human consideration, is so beautiful that it cries out "for tragedy like all beautiful places."[43] The opening stanza in "The Dead Man's Child" celebrates place: "The track across the desert runs vague toward the north star and then more firmly / Along the clipped butt of the mountain; it curves into a bay of the cliff, where natural cisterns / Keep the water in the streaked rock; the people call them *las tinjas altas*—the high water-jars—."[44] In "Bixby's Landing" the poet describes an abandoned mine and an iron car on a long cable. Although the laborers have gone, "a good multitude / Is here in return": lichened rocks, stone-crop, ocean voices, cloud-lighted space. In the broken boiler lizards lighten, and

> a rattle-snake flows
> Down the cracked masonry, over the crumbled fire-brick. In the rotting
> timbers
> And roofless platforms all the free companies
> Of windy grasses have root and make seed; wild buckwheat blooms
> in the fat
> Weather-slacked lime from the bursted barrels.
> Two duckhawks darting in the sky of their cliff-hung nest are the voice
> of the headland.

Wine-hearted solitude, our mother the wilderness,
Men's failures are often as beautiful as men's triumphs, but your
returnings
Are even more precious than your first presence.[45]

These last two lines demonstrate conclusively that for Jeffers, the human experience is a metaphor for the natural, not the other way around.

Jeffers creates a spiritual association with the Irish landscape in his series called "Descent to the Dead." "Oisin's Grave" compares the coasts of Antrim and Carmel and his own death with that of the hero, linking both coasts metaphorically. Jeffers is ambivalent about his return: "And I a foreigner, one who has come to the country of the dead / Before I was called, / To eat the bitter dust of my ancestors."[46] The poet of California, unable to feel the same sense of living tradition that Yeats does, recalls the spirits of dead heroes who lived more fully than contemporary people could. The ghost of Oisin says to the newcomer,

Oh but we lived splendidly
In the brief light of day
Who now twist in our graves.
. . . .
We dead have our peculiar pleasures, of not
Doing, of not feeling, of not being.
Enough has been felt, enough done, Oh and surely
Enough of humanity has been. We lie under stones
Or drift through the endless northern twilights
And draw over our pale survivors the net of our dream. (109)

All the survivors' lives are "less / Substantial" than even one of the heroes' deaths:

they cut turf
Or stoop in the steep
Short furrows, or drive the red carts, like weeds waving
Under the glass of water in a locked bay,
Which neither the wind nor the wave nor their own will
Moves; where they seem to awake
It is only to madden in their dog-days for memories of dreams
That lost all meaning many centuries ago. (109–110)

Jeffers responds with Oisin's refrain, "Oh but we lived splendidly / In the brief light of day," Oisin hunting on the mountains or drinking with princes, Jeffers living "on the western cliff / In the rages of the sun." Oisin lies "grandly" under stones, but Jeffers eats "bitter bread with the dust of dead men" in a country grown weak with too much humanity, "In a uterine country, soft / And wet and worn out, like an old womb / That I have returned to, being dead" (110). Oisin nevertheless insists that he lived "splendidly," that the mountains—Tievebuilleagh, Trostan, Lurigethan, and Aura—are alive, and that a few of the dead in fact live "A life as inhuman and cold as those" (110). Jeffers does not answer Oisin's last protest but instead follows "Oisin's Grave" with "The Low Sky," in which he compares the low (clouded) sky of Ireland with the lid of a tomb and concludes that because the sky is low and the earth old, he can lie down in its tomblike space and allow his mind to dissolve and his flesh to fall to the ground. As dead Oisin speaks of life-in-death, Jeffers's life in Ireland seemed to encompass death-in-life.

In old age Yeats returns to his Sligo landscape to ask fundamental questions about his poetry and nation;[47] Jeffers, describing in "An Irish Headland" the tragic events that took place there, concludes the poem as he does when he sees the California coast that cries out for tragedy "like all beautiful places."[48] In Ireland Jeffers recalls the massacre at Rathlin, saying it was "nothing; not a gannet-feather's / Weight on the rock; the mood of this black basalt has never turned since it cooled."[49] In the next stanza he recalls the tragedy of Drogheda:

> The most beautiful woman
> Of the northern world made landfall under this cliff when she came
> to the bitter end that makes the life shine,
> But the black towers of the rock were more beautiful than Deirdre.
> Weep for the pity of lovers and the beauty of bereaved men, the beauty
> of earth is too great to weep for. (172)

For Jeffers, the earth is greater and more beautiful than all human tragedy.

Thus, whereas Yeats turned to the landscape to create a new literary tradition for Ireland, Jeffers celebrated the earth primarily. Both poets were able to realize their artistic aims by locating their work in specific landscapes through which they could in part establish their poetic identities. At the same time, their choosing their dwelling places as emblems of those landscapes enabled them to delve more fully into the consequences of the activity of writing.

Notes

1. Robinson Jeffers, *The Selected Letters of Robinson Jeffers, 1897–1962,* ed. Anne N. Ridgeway (Baltimore: Johns Hopkins University Press, 1968), 155, 179.

2. Gilbert Allan, "Passionate Detachment in the Lyrics of Jeffers and Yeats," in *Robinson Jeffers and a Gallery of Writers: Essays in Honor of William H. Nolte,* ed. William B. Thesing (University of South Carolina Press, 1995), 62.

3. Robert Zaller, "Robinson Jeffers, American Poetry, and a Thousand Years," in *Centennial Essays for Robinson Jeffers,* ed. Robert Zaller (Newark: University of Delaware Press, 1991), 36.

4. Charles Altieri, *Enlarging the Temple: New Directions in American Poetry during the 1960s* (Lewisburg, Penn.: Bucknell University Press, 1979), 29.

5. Zaller, "Robinson Jeffers," 36.

6. W. B. Yeats, *Letters to the New Island* (Cambridge: Harvard University Press, 1934), 103–104, 107, 174.

7. William H. Nolte, "Robinson Jeffers as Didactic Poet," in *Critical Essays on Robinson Jeffers,* ed. James Karman (Boston: G. K. Hall, 1990), 218. First published in *Virginia Quarterly Review* 4, no. 2 (spring 1966).

8. J. S. Porter, "Robinson Jeffers and the Poetry of the End," *Antigonish Review* 92 (winter 1993): 27.

9. Ibid.

10. Terence Diggory, *Yeats and American Poetry: The Tradition of the Self* (Princeton: Princeton University Press, 1983), 124.

11. Robert Zaller, *The Cliffs of Solitude: A Reading of Robinson Jeffers* (New York: Cambridge University Press, 1983), 225.

12. Robinson Jeffers, "The Place for No Story," in *The Collected Poetry of Robinson Jeffers,* ed. Tim Hunt, vol. 2 (Stanford, Calif.: Stanford University Press, 1989), 157.

13. Robinson Jeffers, "Gray Weather," in Hunt, 2:485.

14. W. B. Yeats, *Essays and Introductions* (New York, Collier, 1961), 519.

15. Ibid., 178.

16. Raymond Williams, *The Country and the City* (New York: Oxford University Press, 1973), 120.

17. W. B. Yeats, introductory verses to *The Shadowy Waters,* in *The Collected Works of W. B. Yeats,* ed. Richard J. Finneran (New York: Macmillan, 1989), 405.

18. W. J. T. Mitchell, "Imperial Landscape," in *Landscape and Power,* ed. W. J. T. Mitchell (Chicago: University of Chicago Press, 1994), 13.

19. Robinson Jeffers, "Birds," in *The Collected Poetry of Robinson Jeffers,* ed. Tim Hunt, vol. 1 (Stanford, Calif.: Stanford University Press, 1988), 108.

20. Winfield Townley Scott, "Jeffers: The Undeserved Neglect," review of *The Begin-*

ning and the End (1963), in *New York Herald Tribune Books,* June 16, 1963, 10; repr. in Karman, 173.

21. Diggory, 122.

22. Ibid.

23. Yeats, *Essays,* 509.

24. Diggory, 132.

25. W. B. Yeats, "The Tower," in Finneran, 194–200.

26. W. B. Yeats, "The Fisherman," in Finneran, 148.

27. W. B. Yeats, "The Man Who Dreamed of Faeryland," in Finneran, 43–45.

28. Frank Kinahan, *Yeats, Folklore, and Occultism: Contexts of the Early Work and Thought* (Boston: Unwin Hyman, 1988), 66.

29. Ibid., 71.

30. W. B. Yeats, "The Wild Swans at Coole," in Finneran, 131–132.

31. Yeats, *Essays,* 517.

32. Jeffers, *Collected Poetry,* 2:410.

33. Yeats, *Shadowy Waters,* in Finneran, 405–406.

34. Ibid., 406.

35. W. B. Yeats, "Coole Park, 1929," in Finneran, 242–243.

36. W. B. Yeats, "Coole and Ballylee, 1931," in Finneran, 245.

37. Jeffers, *Collected Poetry,* 1:105.

38. Ibid., 408.

39. Ibid., 2:160.

40. Ibid., 1:90.

41. Yeats, "The Fisherman," 148.

42. Jeffers, *Collected Poetry,* 1:92.

43. Jeffers, *Collected Poetry,* 2:98.

44. Jeffers, *Collected Poetry,* 1:384.

45. Ibid., 388.

46. Ibid., 109.

47. W. B. Yeats, "Man and the Echo," in Finneran, 345–346.

48. Jeffers, "Apology for Bad Dreams," in *Collected Poetry,* 1:208–211.

49. Jeffers, *Collected Poetry,* 2:172.

Mark Long

William Carlos Williams, Ecocriticism, and Contemporary American Poetry

I could not be a poet without the natural world.
—Mary Oliver

Without the human, how would I ever know nature?
—Ansel Adams

Most readers come to William Carlos Williams by way of a red wheelbarrow. This indelible image has come to stand in for the significance and distinctiveness of Williams's literary project. "So much depends" upon the wheelbarrow, and the qualities sustained in the image—

glazed with rain
water
beside the white
chickens.[1]

Similarly, generations of readers have come to understand Williams's poetics through the phrase "No ideas but in things," those deceptively simple words found in the opening lines of the book-length poem *Paterson*. The phrase signifies a poetics predicated not on ideas but rather on things, underscoring a poetic project that seeks immediate contact with the world. But so much more depends upon "The Red Wheelbarrow" in its unexcerpted place in a twenty-seven-section poetic sequence imbedded within the prose of "Spring and All." A survey of critical accounts of Williams's poetics will show a surprisingly consistent acceptance of Williams's romantic quest for immediate contact. It will come as no surprise, then, that studies of the social implications of Williams's project have concluded that Williams's social aim, in the words of one contemporary critic—"to free his readers' imaginations so that they could experience the world with sensual immediacy—is profoundly apolitical, even asocial."[2]

This aim to free the imagination as the prior condition to experiencing the world with sensual immediacy has been instrumental in determining the critical conversation about environmental and ecological poetry.[3] Yet, as John Elder suggests in *Imagining the Earth,* nature poetry, at best, does not simply reflect but shapes our vision of nature. "Poetic form," writes Elder, "secures a plot where the fruitful decay of order and intentions may occur; an unsuspected landscape rises through the traces of a poem's plan."[4] Poetic form is, in this definition, an especially promising site for more than simply renewing awareness—"the fruitful decay of order and intentions" depends on encountering an alternative to our necessarily limited experiential and cognitive frames. A poem is understood here as not merely a site for reflecting on our limits but as a space in which we might learn to construct alternative ways of thinking and acting in the world. Seeking primary, preverbal experience, then, is perhaps a necessary but in no way sufficient end for the environmentally or ecologically inclined poet.

More recent studies of nature poetry develop this connection between the experiential and referential function of literature and the politically and socially inflected rhetoric of poets who explicitly seek to reorient language toward the biocentric laws of nature. Writers such as A. R. Ammons, Wendell Berry, Denise Levertov, W. S. Merwin, Gary Snyder, and Adrienne Rich have now been read as ecological poets whose vision of nature seeks to fashion alternatives to the anthropocentric consciousness of modern high culture.[5] This vision, as expressed by Leonard Scigaj in *Sustainable Poetry,* is informed by a belief "that language is a positive instrument that can promote authentic social and environmental relations between humans and their environment—relations that can lead to emancipatory social change."[6] These ambitions are, of course, part of a more general national and international strain that worked in twentieth-century modernism to change the direction of poetry and art, in the words of Jerome Rothenberg and Pierre Joris, "as a necessary condition for changing the ways in which we think and act as human beings."[7] Ecopoets, more specifically, work from the conviction "that poetry is a part of a struggle to save the wild places—in the world and in the mind—and the view of the poem as a wild thing and of poetry and the poet as endangered species."[8]

Theories of writing and reading poetry that underscore language as a function of *poesis* suggest the inadequacy of the view that language separates us from the world—the idea that all human patterns of thought, schemas, and generalizations are impositions on a preexisting state we call nature. Yet critical statements regarding the purpose of poetry will always risk parochialism or, more precisely, narrowing the purpose of poetry to promoting *authentic* relations between the aesthetic object and its extrapoetic referent. Indeed, the pragmatic rhetoric of promoting nature as it is apart from human culture risks underestimating the problem of representation. Ecocritics, Dana Phillips cautions, share "assumptions about the ontological gulf between culture and nature, and the metaphysics of representation supposedly required to bridge that gulf."[9] And if poetry is "a manifestation of landscape and climate, just as the ecosystem's flora and fauna are," in the words of Elder, then the determinative analogy between a poem and an ecosystem may narrow the role of ecocritics to arbiters of the authentic.[10]

The distinctive modernist project of William Carlos Williams provides an exemplary occasion for reflecting on contemporary American poets with ecological and environmental concerns. Williams can help us to reflect on the ambitious attempts to link a poetics of presence with an ecologically informed project for social change.[11] In fact, Williams may prove to be a significant figure as we explore the assumptions that link the craft of poetry with the crafting of ecological change.[12] Charles Olsen has made the case that a poet's "stance toward reality" is crucial to the structuring of a poem; and a better understanding of Williams's stance toward the world might prove especially relevant to enriching the premises and practices of contemporary ecopoetics. But although the critical consensus regarding Williams's quest for immediacy may appear congruent with ecocriticism, I will underscore precisely Williams's argument *against* the idea that poetry might help us reestablish a more immediate contact with the world. My intent is to suggest how Williams's acute critique of the view that poetic language offers a less-mediated relation to the world might contribute to expanding the range and power of environmental and ecological reflection in contemporary American poetry.

David Walker argues, I think rightly, that "Williams is primarily interested not in the physical world itself, but in the dynamic relationship between the world and the life of the mind as it apprehends and responds to that world."[13] This drama of relation energizes Williams's early poetics. In the opening lines of his 1923 text "Spring and All," for example, Williams concludes that "there is a constant barrier between the reader and his consciousness of immediate contact with the world."[14] This precise formulation does not rule out the reader's immediate contact with the world; at the same time, he cautions, we cannot be conscious of that immediate contact. We need not deny immediate contact because the very possibility of cognizing a relation to the world is predicated on the presence of the world. But Williams's formulation does not obscure the important fact that immediacy is logically equivalent to an absence of relation. Further, it needs to be understood in this context that the relation is not simply between matter and form or the mind and the world. Any attempt to *recover* immediacy (what Williams called "the reality that we feel in ourselves") requires a third term, a representational medium that will nevertheless prove once more to be "a covering over" or, in Williams's stronger terms, another "dangerous lie."[15]

Williams's 1925 book *In the American Grain* further explores the process of mediation required to come to terms with the world. American history has always been mediated by our attempts to know it, despite the fact, Williams adds, that the "productive ground . . . the common thing . . . is anonymous about us" (*IAG,* 213). Yet, Williams insists, historical intelligibility must always involve *re*establishing a "ground" by breaking through dead layers of understanding. To "break through dead layers" the writer must "have the feet of his understanding on the ground, his ground, *the* ground, the only ground that he knows, which is under his feet." This concern with placing "the feet" of one's understanding is to be understood in the fundamental sense of *poesis,* or having to do with the making, building, or constructing of something. For the poet the construction must take place in the structural body of the poem, as a question of language and structure. The revolution, Williams presses, must be in the poem. "There is no poetry of distinction without formal invention, for it is in the intimate form that works of art achieve their exact meaning . . . to give language its highest dignity, its illumination in the environment to which it is native."[16]

Williams returns to this problem of locating one's self in the environment in his 1934 essay "The American Background." Here Williams recounts the psychological condition of the English settlers who had come to the North American continent: "*They found not only that they had left England but that they had arrived somewhere else: at a place whose pressing reality demanded not only a tremendous bodily devotion but as well, the more importunately, great powers of adaptability, a complete reconstruction of their most intimate cultural make-up, to accord with the new conditions. The most hesitated and turned back in their hearts at the first glance.*" Strange and difficult, Williams continues, "*the new continent induced a torsion in the spirits of the new settlers, tearing them between the old and the new.*" The old was the existing European frame of reference; the new was the very environment that surrounded them. The conjunction of a "*pressing reality*" and the immigrants' lack of "*adaptability*" follows Williams's description of how the settlers of the continent "*saw birds with rusty breasts and called them robins.*" (They were thrushes. "*Meanwhile, nostalgically, erroneously, a robin.*") "*Thus, from the start,*" Williams concludes, "*an*

America of which they could have no inkling drove the settlers upon their past. They retreated for warmth and reassurance to something previously familiar." But at a cost.

The cost was—and is—a failure to understand that "the new and the real, hard to come at, are synonymous" (*SE,* 143). Here Williams presses us to consider the pedagogical function of our experience in constructing a relation to place. One does not learn (or does so only partially) by assuming that what one needs are more facts, more information, or a closer, more qualitatively precise relationship to one's surroundings. The problem in American history has been "the success of the unrelated, borrowed, the would-be universal culture which the afterwave has run to or imposed on men to impoverish them, if it has not actually disenfranchised their intelligence" (149). Instead, what one needs is a genuinely new means of representing one's experience of place—a means of rendering the world intelligible. In a 1950 letter to Columbia University professor Henry Wells, Williams explains that a poem is "an attempt, an experiment, a failing experiment, toward assertion with broken means but an assertion, always, of a new and total culture, the lifting of an environment to expression."[18] The imagination works with the "broken means" of language not simply through the difficult and consequential work of recovering experience but by moving from experience to its representation.

The new and the real, one might say, become possible. However, for Williams, "Americans have never recognized themselves. How can they? It is impossible until someone invents original terms. As long as we are content to be called by someone else's terms, we are incapable of being anything but our own dupes" (*IAG,* 226). Such an attempt at placement in the world as a necessary means of self-definition is exemplified in Williams's book-length poem *Paterson.* Williams understands well, with Blake, that the condition of the imagination is loss, and he is similarly dedicated to the productive or constitutive function of imaginative work within these limits. Williams's case is, more simply, that a "poetics of presence" is a flat contradiction in terms. Consider the opening lines of the preface to book 1 of the poem: "Rigor of beauty is the quest. But how will you find beauty when it is locked in the mind past all remonstrance?"[19] The phrase "rigor of beauty" leads to the suggestion that beauty cannot be found. The quest for beauty involves the rigorous task of its demonstration—in this case, in the structural body of the poem. Williams immediately follows his question with a solution. His answer begins as the poem breaks into measured lines of verse:

To make a start,
out of particulars
and make them general, rolling
up the sum by defective means— (*P*, 3)

As Williams elaborates, seeking beauty involves moving from a formal system of measurement to the constituent parts of a system, a movement "from mathematics to particulars" (4). The movement involves a quest into the language of the poem—an incursion rather than an excursion. As *Paterson* begins to exemplify this incursive process we come to experience the movement of the poem as it begins to accomplish what the controlling speaker is seeking to overcome: "the language! / is divorced from their minds, / the language . . . the language!" (12). Williams animates divorce as "the sign of knowledge in our time, / divorce! Divorce!" (17). The question of direction in such a condition is in fact a question. In fact, Williams says, "There is no direction. Whither? I / cannot say. I cannot say" (17). The divorce is also between the idea and the thing, despite the presence of

the roar of the river
forever in our ears (arrears)
inducing sleep and silence, the roar
of eternal sleep. (17)

Our estrangement from the language we need to represent the world is compounded, Williams suggests, by the ever-present "mass of detail" (19). The problem is "to interrelate on a new ground," and the difficulty "Divorce (the / language stutters)" (21). The drama of these opening sections of the poem is precisely the struggle with representation, as we are tempted to fall back on an outmoded formula. "A chemistry, corollary / to academic misuse, which the theorem / with accuracy, accurately misses" (36).

Williams identifies a crucial problem in the opening pages of *Paterson*. Poetry always and necessarily must attend to the problem of our separation from speech. Rather than being alienated from the world (we are always already in the world, Williams insists), we have not found our way to the resources of our native tongue. We need to begin, in the words of Gary Snyder, by recognizing how wonderful it is "to be born to be a native speaker, to be truly a native of something."[20] His insight does not suggest poetry as simply the place of sentimental attachments, the place of literal topographies. Rather "the place of poetry," to borrow an apposite formulation from Heather McHugh, "is nothing less than the place of love, for language; the place of shifting ground, for human song; the place of the made, for the moving."[21] We go nowhere when we seek to use poetry to transcend itself—to misuse language as a vehicle for a remedial course in immediacy. Not *so much,* but *everything,* depends on the responding sensibility. In this way we come to understand the content of a poem, in the words of Charles Bernstein, as "more an attitude toward the work or toward language or toward the materials of the poem than some kind of subject that is in any way detachable from the handling of the materials. Content emerges from composition and cannot be detached from it; or, to put it in another way, what is detachable is expendable to the poetic."[22] Otherwise there is no distinctive claim for the poem.

Williams emphasizes poetry as a condition for changing the way we think and act as human beings. He is a poet not a philosopher, yet he is confident that the world lies beyond our conceptualizations of it. And he is adamant that the idea of an external world is in fact necessary to the subsequent internal formation of a relation and the embodiment of the relation in the structural invention we come to know as the poem:

> Without invention nothing is well spaced,
> Unless the mind change, unless
> the stars are new measured, according
> to their relative positions, the
> line will not change, the necessity
> will not matriculate: unless there is
> a new mind there cannot be a new
> line, the old will go on
> repeating itself with recurring
> deadliness: (50)

Recall T. S. Eliot, who observed that "when I say 'invent' I should use inverted commas, for invention would be irreproachable if it were possible." The problem for the poet is *invention,* a term Williams uses to describe the need to break free from the repetition of the old. The poem continues:

> without invention
> nothing lies under the witch-hazel
> bush, the alder does not grow from among
> the hummocks margining the all

> but spent channel of the old swale,
> the small foot-prints
> of the mice under the overhanging
> tufts of the bunch grass will not
> appear: without invention the line
> will never again take on its ancient
> divisions when the word, a supple word,
> lived in it, crumbled now to chalk. (50)

For Williams invention begins where we are: with the materials at hand and within the symbolic complex we use to measure our place in the world. The loss of presence is indeed a result of how the already-been-formulated shapes the formulations that follow. The difficult problem is that we are habituated to receiving the presence of the world in the terms of what we already know. Invention thus begins with the recognition that invention is necessary but only with the knowledge that there are always more to the prototypes of experience than we have acquired. Invention, for Williams, begins with the figure of descent into the limited frames of perception and cognition we use to craft our experience. Invention then moves toward the need for a form or structure for that experience. For Williams invention restores both the world and the person using the resources of language and who is in constant struggle with the limits of those resources.

Although Williams may have been sympathetic to the idea that poems might offer us ways into the world, he insists that the problem of literary representation cannot be understood as an exchange between something outside the poem and the poet. Representation is demanding precisely because it requires the poet's imagination. But the imagination must find a way to free itself. If we agree that the imagination is a constructive power, simply freeing the perceptive faculties to imagine possible versions of experience does not account for the more difficult problem of constructing a form in which to make intelligible (and to offer for reflection) the formal dynamics of a particular set of relations. The crucial point is that Williams's poetics look not back at reestablishing a lost connection with the world because, as I have said, we are always already in that world. Rather the problem the poet faces is looking forward to the ways we are able to become present to the possibilities of the phenomenal world where we have been living all along. The poet must discover the dynamic substance of the world by representing it as intelligible in the originary structure of the poem. Williams demands a radical commitment to the distinctive human power of language use and to developing the resources of poetic structures. It follows that the ever-present risk of any poetic theory is to define a priori a vital cultural practice. In advocating the distinctiveness of the poem as a "field of action" Williams challenges us in the permanently transitional space between the already known and the as yet unrealized potential of our lives.

The breathtaking structural movement of Williams's best poems (the field of action is *in* the poem)—and his restless commitment to poetic innovation—offers contemporary environmental and ecological poets an inspiring commitment to poetic innovation. The genre of ecopoetry might find a place for Williams in its historical development by using his work to refine its most common assumptions and foundational beliefs. But in his study of the "sustainable" poem, Scigaj construes a more narrow definition of the distinctiveness of ecopoetry. The ecopoem, in Scigaj's definition, "persistently stresses human cooperation with nature conceived as a dynamic, interrelated series of cyclical feedback systems".[23] The tradition of nature poetry is in this way understood as distinct from the environmental poetry written in an age in which environmental concerns were becoming manifest in the poetic imagination. Thus his argument is historical in that it locates in the poetry of the past thirty years an increasing awareness of ecological crisis. Following up Elder's insights about the tradition of American poets whose work concerns the human relation to nature, Scigaj seeks further to "explore new ways of developing a *theoretical* position" for ecopoetry that would "critique poststructuralist language theory and provide an alternative" (xiii). Scigaj then admonishes, "We need a sustainable poetry, a poetry that does not allow the degradation of ecosystems through inattention to the referential base of all language. We need a poetry that treats nature as a separate and equal other and includes respect for nature conceived as a series of ecosystems—dynamic and potentially self-regulating cyclic feedback systems" (5).

In the face of environmental crisis, Scigaj concludes, we are no longer able to naturalize these ecosystems "into benign backdrops for human preoccupations or reduce them to nonexistence by an obsessive focus on language in our literary creations."[24] The theoretical framework provided by Scigaj here (which is different from the practice of the poets and poems he discusses) therefore potentially determines the kinds of thinking—the subject matter—that would qualify under the rubric of ecopoetry. If the concept of a sustainable poetry is articulated as attentive to the "referential base" of all human activity, ecopoetry would by design "refer" the reader's perception beyond the printed page. The poem is thus understood by the poet, and by implication the reader, as at once pointing to the world as well as to the possible transparencies of language. The affective power of poetry is, in this view, narrowly construed. Williams addresses the practical limits of such a position regarding the content and the affective domain of language in general and the poetic in particular in "The Poem as a Field of Action," his address to Theodore Roethke's students at the University of Washington in 1948. Williams insists that you "can put it down as a general rule that when a poet, in the broadest sense, begins to devote himself to the *subject matter* of his poems, *genre,* he has come to an end of his poetic means" (*SE,* 288). Williams's exemplary efforts to see poetry as a distinctive form of cultural practice underscore how the ecological poet must not be limited to a subject matter such as the environment or to the ideological shape of a belief such as saving the environment.

It will come as no surprise that among postwar American poets with environmental and ecological concerns, one finds a renewable source of interest in Williams's work. Denise Levertov's 1972 essay "Williams and the Duende," for instance, praises Williams's constant (and consistently changing) attempt to take "up the challenge to deal with his time and place"; and Gary Snyder comments in "The New Wind," an essay from the 1960s, that Williams "has been the largest single influence on the present generation of writers."[25] For poets, singular influence can often be traced to the urgent formal intensity of a single poem—an exceptional poem that lives in its demonstration of a new possibility in the art form. For critics, a poet's significance is often understood in terms of what Harold Bloom has called the revisionary ratios of poetic influence. But a poet such as Williams shapes a tradition more fundamentally than by simply providing exemplary poems or by influencing a single poet or poetic school. Williams creates a singular set of conditions for poetic innovation during the second half of the twentieth century.

Adrienne Rich's recent collections of poems attempt to experience and constitute a series of intelligible relations at the local level to reflect on existing patterns of self-knowledge within a larger sense of the social and political world in the process of unfolding. In her poem "Natural Resources," to take an example, Rich writes,

> My heart is moved by all I cannot save:
> so much has been destroyed
> I have to cast my lot with those
> who age after age, perversely,
> with no extraordinary power,
> reconstitute the world.[26]

Yet my interest is less in thematic concern than in Rich's breathtaking allegiance to her craft in these lines as a pledge to a poetics rooted in what Gary Snyder calls the common ground, our native place, of language. Her commitment to the confusing, disorienting, and painful location in and from which she writes reflects an abiding commitment to integrating the descriptive (personal, reflective) and persuasive (political, oratorical) functions of poetry. In *An Atlas of the Difficult World* Rich shows her readers where she is through a Whitmanesque catalog of failures ("These are the materials") and the necessity of the possibilities of personal and collective redemption ("What does it mean to love my country?"). Drawing inspiration from Muriel Rukeyser's example ("There are roads to take"), Rich admonishes us "to catch if you can your country's moment, begin."[27]

Rich's two essays on placement—"Blood, Bread and Poetry: The Location of the Poet" and "Notes Toward a Politics of Location"—elegantly and forcefully trace "the possible credibility of poetry" through her own personal evolution from a conviction of uniqueness as a young poet to her emerging "untutored and half-conscious rendering of the facts of blood and bread, the social and political forces of my time and place."[28] In her sequences of poems in *An Atlas of the Difficult World* Rich further displays her commitment to the aesthetic I have traced out of Williams. These poems demonstrate how personal and political relationships and territories can be mapped and how, in the words of James Baldwin that she uses as inspiration, "Any real change implies the breakup of the world as one has always known it, the loss of all that gave one an identity, the end of safety" (*BBP,* 176). Rich's distinctive commitment of the heart and mind to a poetics that calls into question our best version of self and world suggests a definition of the poetic arts "not as a commodity, not as a luxury, not as a suspect activity, but as a precious resource to be made available to all, one necessity for the rebuilding of a scarred, impoverished, and still-bleeding country" (*BBP,* 185). The rebuilding is accomplished, for Rich as a poet, with the materials of the poem.

Rich categorically rejects poetry as simply seeking, in the satiric words of E. E. Cummings, to "live suddenly / without thinking."[29] For imagining a state of mindless immediacy must suppose that we can depend on our senses, and intuition, to transport us back to a direct, if not more certain, place in the world. Nostalgia for the world in and of itself misses the fact that the world in and of itself is precisely what we already have. Williams can help us to understand that we can know the world, and we can know it differently; the thing in itself is precisely what we do experience and see. The problem will always be how we will come to an awareness of the thingness of the world we have in common by bringing it into form in a particular way. Everything depends, Williams demonstrates—and I think convincingly—on the relations that are established, as there can be no final categorical distinction between the real and the represented. Our representations, although self-sufficient, are never all-sufficient. There are, however, linguistic representations, always the product of an abductive process of inference, that do not prove "sustainable." As Robert Hass reminds us, metonymy is the characteristic form of the poetic image "because all our seeing is metonymic."[30] Yet the way to most fully experience the sudden moments in our lives is by reflecting on the meaning of their partiality and staying open to possible revisions of the meanings we make.

Williams's commitment to his art is grounded in his abiding faith in humanity. His restless attempts to refine the resources of his language can inspire poets and readers to live beyond their limits by discovering what they do not already know. In this sense Williams's aesthetics is *political*,[31] a term Robert von Halberg defines as making categorical thinking difficult. "Poets who are satisfied with rousing simplifications or confirmations of their audience's views sell short the possibilities of their art."[32] A passionate commitment to the environment is perhaps a necessary risk for a poet who wishes to challenge existing modes of human relation to the world. But Williams demonstrates that without a genuine commitment to language and its domain of human culture, a supposed poetics of presence will slide into its relatively insignificant place, unable to articulate other than its own already known and local point of view. This essay only begins to suggest how Williams's insights into the way language renews itself as a specific form of cultural practice might create a specific set of conditions for overcoming these limited forms of artistic practice, especially in poems that are intentionally addressed to the environment and environmental concerns. Williams suggests the limitations of using poetry to disclose phenomenological presence. To expand, not diminish, the affective range and power of poems requires not the mystical one of knowing the world, of seeking something before making. On the contrary, Williams reminds us that the practice of poetry is a part of the constant development of a cultural reality from the potentiality of experience through particular linguistic acts.

Notes

1. William Carlos Williams, *Imaginations*, ed. Webster Schott (New York: New Directions, 1970), 138.

2. David Frail, *The Early Politics and Poetics of William Carlos Williams* (Ann Arbor: UMI Research Press, 1987), 92.

3. Important critical studies in the American tradition of poetry include John Elder, *Imagining the Earth: Poetry and the Vision of Nature* (Urbana: University of Illinois Press, 1985); Guy Rotella, *Reading and Writing Nature: The Poetry of Robert Frost, Wallace Stevens, Marianne Moore, and Elizabeth Bishop* (Boston: Northeastern University Press, 1991); Terry Gifford, *Green Voices: Understanding Contemporary Nature Poetry* (New York: Manchester University Press, 1995); Gyorgyi Voros, *Notations of the Wild: The Poetry of Wallace Stevens* (Iowa City: University of Iowa Press, 1997). Also see Bernard W. Quetchenbach, *Back from the Far Field: American Nature Poetry in the Late Twentieth Century* (Charlottesville: University Press of Virginia, 2000); Jonathan Bate, *Romantic Ecology: Wordsworth and the Environmental Tradition* (New York: Routledge, 1991). Anthologies that have helped to define the field include Robert Bly, ed., *News of the Universe: Poems of a Twofold Consciousness* (San Francisco: Sierra Club, 1980); Sara Dunn and Alan Scholefield, eds., *Beneath the Wide Wide Heaven: Poetry of the Environment from Antiquity to the Present* (London: Virago, 1991); Robert Pack and Jay Parini, eds., *Poems for a Small Planet: Contemporary American Nature Poetry* (Hanover, N.H.: University Press of New England, 1993); John Daniel, ed., *Wild Song: Poems of the Natural World* (Athens: University of Georgia Press, 1998). Among the dissertations on the subject see David Gilcrest, "Greening the Lyre" (Ph.D. diss., University of Oregon, 1995) and Laird Christensen, "Spirit Astir in the World: Sacred Poetry in the Age of Ecology" (Ph.D. diss., University of Oregon, 1997).

4. Elder, 215. Elder is important as one of the first voices pointing the way toward recent developments in the field of ecocriticism in general and the study of ecopoetry more particularly.

5. See Rotella's historical and intellectual survey of the changes and continuities of American poets' attitudes toward epistemology, aesthetics, and nature that lead to the poems written in the period between the publication of Robert Frost's first book of poems in 1913 and Elizabeth Bishop's final collection in 1976. Also see *Green Voices*, in which Terry Gifford asks, "What, then, have emerged as the criteria for valuing one 'green language' rather than another?" (143). In his detailed and illuminating exposition Gifford identifies "connection," "commitment," and "responsibility" as the dominant constituents in the nature poetry of Kavanagh, MacLean, Heaney, Hughes, et al. For a comparable attempt to define a set of criteria for valuing ecopoetry, see Gyorgyi Voros's discussion of ecology in the poetry and poetics of Wallace Stevens, in which she describes Stevens's sense of relationships as ecological and defines a list of six familiar aspects of Stevens's work that "readily lend themselves to an ecological reading" (83–86).

6. Leonard Scigaj, *Sustainable Poetry: Four American Ecopoets* (Lexington: University Press of Kentucky, 1999), 33.

7. Pierre Joris and Jerome Rothenberg, eds., *Poems for the Millennium: The University of California Book of Modern and Postmodern Poetry,* vol. 1, *From Fin-de-Siècle to Negritude* (Berkeley: University of California Press, 1995), 2.

8. Pierre Joris and Jerome Rothenberg, eds., *Poems for the Millennium: The University of California Book of Modern and Postmodern Poetry,* vol. 2, *From Postwar to Millennium* (Berkeley: University of California Press, 1998), 12.

9. Dana Phillips, "Ecocriticism, Literary Theory, and the Truth of Ecology," in the special ecocriticism issue of *New Literary History* 30, no. 3 (summer 1999): 575–602. Phillips discusses the antitheoretical spirit of ecocriticism, pointing to examples of ecocritics who "treat literary theory as if it were a noxious weed that must be suppressed before it overwhelms more native and greener forms of speech" (579). He cites Lawrence Buell's seminal book *The Environmental Imagination: Thoreau, Nature Writing, and the Formation of American Culture* (Cambridge: Harvard University Press, 1995), in which Buell asks, "Must literature always lead us away from the physical world, never back to it?" (11). Phillips provides a generative critique of the theoretical assumptions behind Buell's project. Using Buell as a case study, Phillips observes that "the result is not so much a new kind of blessedly untheoretical discourse as it is a discourse propped up here and there by some distinctly shaky theory" (579). Phillips also provides an incisive set of observations regarding Elder's analogy between poem and ecosystem—an analogy, Phillips argues, that "is faulty on scientific as well as literary grounds" (581). For a brief response by Buell to Phillips, see "The Ecocritical Insurgency," *New Literary History* 30, no. 3 (summer 1999): 703, 711 n. 11.

10. Quoted in Phillips, 581.

11. I take the phrase "poetics of presence" from Charles Altieri, "Denise Levertov and the Limits of the Aesthetics of Presence," in *Enlarging the Temple: New Directions in Poetry during the 1960's* (Lewisburg, Penn.: Bucknell University Press, 1980), 26; repr. in Albert Gelpi, ed., *Denise Levertov: Selected Criticism* (Ann Arbor: University of Michigan Press, 1993). Altieri's exploration of postmodern poetics raises important questions regarding the philosophical adequacy of a poetics of presence. "Considered as metaphysical or religious meditation, the poetry of the sixties seems to me highly sophisticated; it takes into account all the obvious secular objections to traditional religious thought and actually continues and extends the inquiries of philosophers as diverse as Heidegger, Whitehead, and Wittgenstein. This very success, however, makes it disappointing that the poetry fails so miserably in handling social and ethical issues." For a critique of Altieri's assumptions more generally as exemplifying the limits of postmodern language theory, and specifically in reference to the second major period

of W. S. Merwin's poetry, beginning with the 1967 book of poems *The Lice,* see Scigaj, 18–28, 176–177. Scigaj sets the project of ecocriticism against poststructuralist language theory, arguing that environmental poetry *must* emphasize its referential ground and "contain an activist dimension to foreground particular acts of environmental degradation and degraded planetary ecosystems" (21, my emphasis). Scigaj argues for the phenomenological approach of Merleau-Ponty as the proper theoretical model to elucidate the value of such poetry. Yet despite Scigaj's trenchant insights regarding Altieri's assumptions, in targeting Altieri's "aestheticism" he effaces the specificity of Altieri's readings he chooses not to cite, such as his treatment of Levertov's struggles to adapt her poetics to the pressing political issues in the Vietnam era.

12. The demand for an ethical extension from the relation of individuals, and the relation of individuals to society, to the relation between individuals in a biotic community that includes human beings is predicated on Aldo Leopold's "land ethic," which provides practitioners in the field of ecocriticism with a "mode of guidance" that "changes the role of *Homo sapiens* from conqueror of the land-community to plain member and citizen of it" (Aldo Leopold, *A Sand County Almanac* [New York: Oxford University Press, 1949], 204). The study of literatures of the environment is significantly informed by the understanding that "current environmental problems are largely of our own making, are, in other words, a by-product of culture" (Cheryl Glotfelty and Harold Fromm, eds., *The Ecocritical Reader: Landmarks in Literary Ecology* [Athens: University of Georgia Press, 1996], xxi). The ethical and cultural implications of ecocriticism therefore demand more than simply a rigorous interdisciplinary study of environmental literatures precisely because the cultural rhetoric of environmentalism is practiced with an urgent and irrepressible desire for personal, political, and economic transformation.

13. David Walker, *The Transparent Lyric: Reading and Meaning in the Poetry of Stevens and Williams* (Princeton: Princeton University Press, 1984), 118.

14. Williams, *Imaginations,* 88.

15. William Carlos Williams, *In the American Grain* (New York: New Directions, 1956), 1 (hereafter cited in text as *IAG*).

16. William Carlos Williams, *The Collected Poems of William Carlos Williams: Vol. 2, 1939–1962,* ed. Christopher MacGowan (New York: New Directions, 1998), 55.

17. William Carlos Williams, *Selected Essays* (New York: New Directions, 1969), 134 (hereafter cited in text as *SE*).

18. William Carlos Williams, *The Selected Letters,* ed. John C. Thirlwall (New York: New Directions, 1957), 286.

19. William Carlos Williams, *Paterson,* rev. ed. (New York: New Directions, 1992), 3 (hereafter cited in text as *P*).

20. Gary Snyder, *No Nature: New and Selected Poems* (New York: Pantheon, 1992), v.

21. Heather McHugh, *Broken English: Poetry and Partiality* (Hanover: Wesleyan University Press, 1993), 1.

22. Charles Bernstein, *A Poetics* (Cambridge: Harvard University Press, 1992), 8.

23. Scigaj, 17.

24. Ibid. At its strongest the field of literature and environment provides formidable theoretical insight into the relation between language and the world. At its weakest the field risks limiting its inquiry by pursuing the desire to imagine a more primary mode of conscious experience. The "loss of the world"—its immediacy, its presence—leads to the desire to lose the word; and in response to this estrangement from what we call nature, including our own naturalness, we attempt a solution by seeking primary or unmediated experience—a wholly understandable desire, it is important to add, given the overwhelming evidence that such estrangement has led to environmental ignorance and ecological irresponsibility. To expand the theoretical insights of environmental literature and the prospects for the practice of ecological literary criticism requires much more than what Dewey called "eulogistic predicates," those structures of thought that seek nostalgic and sentimental attempts to overcome anthropomorphic versions of experience. Williams provides a means of conceptualizing the problem of nostalgically or sentimentally longing for a lost sense of place in the world. (Rather than the redemptive project Northrop Frye described as the myth of the good old days, when people were closer to nature and got their milk from cows instead of bottles, the fields of environmental literature and ecological literary criticism require the distinctly human power of constructing better versions of human experience.) The critical risk for ecopoetry is isolating a canon of poets that encourages our attempt to transcend the linguistic structure of our conceptual life and thereby take us away from that world we wish to feel, understand, indeed preserve. The determinate power of predication gives language the capacity to construct sustainable relations with a world we wish to know and be responsible citizens of rather than enacting the cyclical historical ritual Milan Kundera has called "man's longing not to be man" (Milan Kundera, *The Unbearable Lightness of Being,* trans. Michael Henry Heim [New York: Harper, 1984], 296). Williams argues, to the contrary, that poetry needs to be more human, which is not to say less natural, because we need not simply to reflect on our actions but the conceptual structures that determine how it is we determine what should be done.

25. Denise Levertov, "Williams and the Duende," in *New and Selected Essays* (New York: New Directions, 1992), 37; Gary Snyder, "The New Wind," in *A Place in Space: Ethics, Aesthetics, and Watersheds: New and Selected Prose* (Washington, D.C.: Counterpoint, 1995), 15.

26. Adrienne Rich, *The Dream of a Common Language* (New York: Norton, 1978), 264. Coincidentally, Scigaj refers to sections of Rich's *Atlas of the Difficult World* as "archetypal" ecopoetry (37).

27. Adrienne Rich, *An Atlas of the Difficult World: Poems 1988–1991* (New York: Norton, 1991), 12.

28. Adrienne Rich, *Blood, Bread, and Poetry: Selected Prose, 1979–1985* (New York: Norton, 1985), 171 (hereafter cited in text as *BBP*).

29. E. E. Cummings, *Complete Poems: 1904–1962* (New York: Liveright, 1991), 159.

30. Robert Hass, *Twentieth Century Pleasures: Prose on Poetry* (New York: Eco, 1984), 290.

31. The political aesthetic is his refusal to separate a concern with poetry and place from an inquiry into the place of poetry. A stronger way of putting this equation would be to subordinate the literal discussion of poetry and place to the place of poetry. For a more detailed treatment of the problem of Williams's political aesthetics, especially in relation to the early experimental writing, see my essay "'no confusion—only difficulties': William Carlos Williams's Poetics of Apposition," *William Carlos Williams Review* 23, no. 2 (fall 1997): 1–27. In a useful overview essay Robert von Halberg discusses the strengths and limits of Rich's and Snyder's political aesthetics in "Poetry, Politics, and Intellectuals," in *The Cambridge History of American Literature*, vol. 8, *Poetry and Criticism, 1940–1995* (New York: Cambridge University Press, 1996), 9–212. See especially 33–39.

32. Halberg, 26.

Contemporary Ecopoets

Terry Gifford

Gary Snyder and the Post-Pastoral

> . . . language as wild system, mind as wild habitat, world as a "making" (poem), poem as a creature of the wild mind.
>
> —Gary Snyder, *A Place in Space*

When Lawrence Buell describes American pastoral as "simultaneously counterinstitutional and institutionally sponsored," he is returning pastoral to its original Greek function.[1] The poet Theocritus wrote the *Idylls* in the third century B.C. in order to use the mode of shepherds' songs in his native Sicily to indirectly critique the sophisticated court in Alexandria. An apparent retreat into what has come to be known as the "idyllic" is, in fact, a device for subtly suggesting reforms to an urban audience. What was institutionally sponsored from the court poet produces a poetry that is counterinstitutional. Buell argues from the example of Thoreau that the critiques made by American pastorals have tended to be taken onboard institutionally—"dissent can get coopted as an aspect of consensus"[2]—and the artist is encouraged to retreat again to the wilderness, the frontier, or its representative landscape. Thus a cycle that not only endorses but demands the pastoral, in continuously changing forms for each era, is posited not only by Buell but by Leo Marx as "a dialectical mode of perception" that has evolved as an essential cultural tool that can help us find a right relationship with the earth.[3]

English critics tend to be more skeptical about the pastoral, pointing out that in English literature the idyll of *Arcadia* is not only a successful and attractive strategy, but it is also fundamentally flawed by its artifice and idealization. The function of pastoral poetry in England has been to endorse the status quo of a stable society, from Sydney's *Arcadia* (1590), to Pope's *Windsor Forest* (1713), to Isabella Lickbarrow's *Poetical Effusions* (1814), to the contributors to *Georgian Poetry* (1912–1922), and to George Mackay Brown's *Fishermen with Ploughs* (1971). In response there has grown a corrective literature of anti-pastoral poetry, from Stephen Duck's *The Thresher's Labour* (1736), to Mary Collier's *The Woman's Labour* (1739), to George Crabbe's *The Village* (1783), to Byron's *Don Juan* (1819), to Patrick Kavanagh's *The Great Hunger* (1942), to Ted Hughes's *Moortown Diary* (1979).[4] Perhaps American anti-pastoral poetry is produced by those writers J. Scott Bryson refers to in his introduction to this volume as "antiromantics": Frost, Jeffers, Stevens, Moore, Williams.

But even for American pastoral the dangers of idealization in what Buell now prefers to call "pastoralism" remain. The classical modes of pastoral—the eclogue, the paean to a patron's estate—may now be "obsolescent conventions," as Buell puts it;[5] but the dangers of idealization can undermine celebration, and a certain smug coziness can infect the poetics of the most "right-on" of the ecopoets who, in Leonard Scigaj's words, "distill ecological processes into aesthetic techniques to restore our lost sense of connectedness to the planet that bore and sustains us."[6] This is especially true for a celebrant such as Gary Snyder, recently described by the English critic Jonathan Bate as "the most ecologically self-conscious of twentieth century poets."[7] The primitivism of the "Hunting" poems of *Myths and Texts,* for example, might well be read as impossibly regressive for a twentieth-century California man who will not actually "drink sea-water" or "sleep on beach pebbles in the rain" in a shamanistic journey of penance for killing deer.[8] This may be a reference to coastal Salish practices, as Patrick Murphy suggests,[9] and may act as a metaphor for earning the right to take life in order to sustain life, but Snyder's learning from Native American and Zen Buddhist myths and disciplines can be too easy in its assumptions about the way readers might relate metaphors to practice. In pastoral poetry metaphors can remain aesthetic rather than conceptually challenging, endorsing complacency. Blakean celebratory poetry can function as pastoral escapism for, say, the Californian Web-site developer I met on her air commute to Chicago, whose way of marking the seasons was to program changes in her screensaver.

So over the last few years I have felt the need for a term that characterizes literature that transcends the closed circle of the pastoral and anti-pastoral modes. *Post-pastoral* started out as a parody of all those "post-" theories until I found that I needed to take it seriously because it worked to characterize literature, like the best of Gary Snyder's poetry, that avoids the traps both of idealization of the pastoral and of the simple corrective of the anti-pastoral.[10] Thus post-pastoral is not necessarily postmodern. The heart of Blake's work is post-pastoral, as is the prose of John Muir and of Rick Bass's *Fiber* (1998). Pre-twentieth-century post-pastoral work anticipates ecological poetry in the way that Muir's vision, embedded in the poetic style of his prose, is, as I have argued elsewhere, protoecological.[11] Of course, much myth and oral literature in many cultures is post-pastoral. Patrick Murphy's multicultural project for ecofeminism will reveal new dimensions to the range of post-pastoral literature.[12]

So what is post-pastoral poetry? Currently I think of it as poetry that implicitly raises six questions for the reader. But before I enumerate them by way of Gary Snyder's work I need to remind myself that I am not speaking of the way questions would be raised in philosophy, or ecology, or politics. This discourse has to work as poetry first. There is a danger that I may appear programmatic in my analysis, demanding a set of ideas from poets. To put it the other way around, as a poet myself I have to remind myself that the post-pastoral is not a manifesto but a reflection on a series of challenges to my own creative work. So in my present role as reader and learner responding to Gary Snyder's work, it is important that these six questions are not boxes to be ticked but implications embedded in the poetry to be pondered further. I quite expect other readers to reply to me that post-pastoral texts really raise twelve questions, or one, or that these are not questions at all. While waiting, however, I offer the present six-part definition of Gary Snyder's post-pastoral poetry. First I ought to explain my own sense of "poetry working as poetry."

Ted Hughes, the preeminent British ecopoet of the twentieth century, admitted to me in correspondence that when he tried to address ecological issues directly in his poetry, the poetry tended to suffer. In a poem titled "Lobby under the Carpet," published in the *Times* before an election, Hughes attempted to draw attention to "a 40% drop / in the sperm count of all Western males." This is an important indicator of insidious toxic pollution that threatens our species, but when I criticized this poem's quality as poetry, Hughes wrote, "I've tried to write sort of semi-protest pieces of verse about this sort of thing, but I don't think it works. It may work as propaganda for a little bit for some people, for some readers, but I don't think it can ever be the real thing."[13] Jonathan Bate has recently made much the same point about a poem by Gary Snyder. He says of "Mother Earth: Her Whales," "The poem has been written as an expression of a set of opinions, not as an attempt to transform into language an experience of dwelling upon the earth. In this respect it is not what I call an 'ecopoem.' . . . The language itself is not being asked to do ecological work."[14] Bert Almon has also said of this poem, "[It] strikes me as a good prose essay mysteriously incarnated as a bad poem."[15] Bate quotes as evidence the third, fourth, and fifth stanzas of a fourteen-stanza poem that deliberately moves among different discourses, including rhyming simplicity, an English ballad, lyric imagism, open field form, a public chant, and manifesto prose. The fourth stanza is a superb alliterative imagist celebration of whale behavior that is Snyder's poetry at its best, working with all the resources of heightened language, doing nothing but "transform into language an experience of dwelling upon the earth," as Bate demands of ecopoetry. It may be that both

Bate and Almon are failing to notice the complex nature of this poem: the way the language and forms in the poem might be deliberately raising questions about its content. But their anxieties emphasize the proper demand that post-pastoral poetry must work as poetry. And this must be remembered as the mode in which the six questions that define post-pastoral poetry are raised for the reader.

Fundamental to Snyder's Buddhism is a position of humility that emerges from a contemplation of the huge complexity behind the simplicity of the natural world we inhabit with the other species, forms, and energies. The history of Western Christian civilization has largely been one of exploiting the earth to the point that we have alienated ourselves from our home. In Britain we have been producing nuclear waste by reprocessing other countries' plutonium at Sellafield, a site that is notoriously leaky but that through the marketing of its Visitors' Centre now rivals Wordsworth's Dove Cottage as a tourist attraction in the Lake District. We do not know how to dispose of the toxic waste stored in surface tanks there, yet we go on producing more of it. We need to be reminded of our hubris by the Victorian Christian poet Gerard Manley Hopkins: "And all is seared with trade; bleared, smeared with toil; / And wears man's smudge and shares man's smell: the soil / Is bare now, nor can foot feel, being shod."[16] This devastatingly simple image of our species' ultimate alienation from the earth on which we tread demands that we learn again to tread lightly and sensitively on the soil by recognizing what Hopkins, in the poem's title, calls "God's Grandeur," whether it be the "bright wings" of dawn, or "the ooze of oil."

Gary Snyder's mode of learning whether he can gain the humility that comes from awe—the first question of post-pastoral poetry—is most obviously explored in his early "Cold Mountain Poems," first published in autumn 1958. More than simply translations from the first-century Chinese of Hanshan, these poems represent Snyder's process of absorbing the Asian influences that have dominated his work to the present day. Significantly, these poems were begun when Snyder was studying Oriental languages at Berkeley and revised at the beginning of his ten years of Zen studies in Japan. So it is with the irony of hindsight that we now read Snyder's translation of Hanshan: "In my first thirty years of life / I roamed hundreds and thousands of miles."[17] The experience summed up in the first few lines of the poem is clearly shared by both poets:

Walked by rivers . . .
Entered cities . . .

Tried drugs . . .
Read books . . . (25–26)

The next two lines clinch a deeply felt humility that is to be learned from tuning in to the energies of nature: "Today I'm back at Cold Mountain: / I'll sleep by the creek and purify my ears" (26). The asceticism by which purification comes through sleep on the ground of Cold Mountain is a learned discipline of openness toward the energy of the creek. The complex nature of creek energy might be examined by the second question posed by post-pastoral poetry: what are the implications of recognizing the creative-destructive cycles of the universe of which we are a part?

Blake's "Marriage of Heaven and Hell" attempted to provocatively ("by the infernal method of corrosives") cleanse "the doors of perception" in order to be able to celebrate the "infinite" in everything, even in the predators—the serpent and the tiger—so that the "fearful symmetry" of a creative-destructive universe could be accepted within the self.[18] It is not only with breathtaking awe, but with "fearful" respect for the implications that Blake asks of the tiger, "Did he who made the Lamb make thee?"[19] John Muir received the same revelation in the swamps of Florida: "although alligators, snakes, etc., naturally repel us, they are not mysterious evils. They dwell happily in these flowery wilds, are part of God's family, unfallen, undepraved, and cared for."[20] Muir wrote in the manuscript that was on his bed when he died that the great cold, crushing glaciers of Alaska actually create beauty in their destructiveness: "what we in our faithless ignorance and fear call destruction is creation finer and finer."[21] A recognition of the death process in nature so horrified Mathew Arnold in the poem "Dover Beach" that he sought refuge in the integrity of love,[22] not having listened to the "creek energy" in the conclusion of the folksong "The Seeds of Love": "And I gained the willow tree."[23] In the 1955 poem "Milton by Firelight" Snyder is happy to accept a universe without Christian purpose and to put his faith in the material reality of creative-destructive "weathering" and the flux of nature represented by the sky: "No paradise, no fall, / Only the weathering land, / The wheeling sky."[24] In a poem first collected in the 1992 *Selected Poems* Snyder is hiking "At Tower Peak" and learning directly from his glaciated environment: "A kind of ice age, spreading, filling valleys / Shaving soils, paving fields, you can walk it / Live in it, drive through it."[25] *Shaving* and *paving* are a characteristic pairing of symbolic verbs that are actually lived by the human species here, whatever their mode of activity. Growing and eroding is lived by each of us in what Ted Hughes called "the elemental power circuit of the universe."[26]

If it is the case that our inner lives echo the ebbs and flows of growth and decay in the natural world around us, how can we learn to understand the inner by being closer to the outer? This is the third question of the post-pastoral. It is why nature imagery has always been the thinking tool of poetry since before writing, as a traditional song like "The Seeds of Love" demonstrates. Why do hospital patients recover more quickly, with less need for medication, if they look out at a tree through the window rather than a concrete wall? Why was it thought good for children of my generation in England to keep a short-living hamster as a pet? "The woods decay and fall," observed Tennyson in "Tithonus," a poem that rejects the Christian desire for immortality and tries to understand the death process: "Man comes and tills the earth and lies beneath."[27] He might have continued, "And after many a summer dies the hamster." For Snyder all this is a source of joy, often caught in a simple but profound effect like "creek music, heart music" in the poem "For All."[28] The Gaelic post-pastoral poet Sorley Maclean recognized in his famous poem "The Woods of Raasay" that science knows much about woods ("The way of the sap is known"), but, he wrote, "There is no knowledge of the course / of the crooked veering of the heart."[29] The veering of the creek and the music of its flux are one way to understand the flux that is "heart music."

"For All" concludes with an acceptance of the poet's commitment to "the soil" and "the beings" with which he lives in the ecological community that Snyder calls "Turtle Island," preferring a Native American term for his native land:

> one ecosystem
> in diversity
> under the sun
> with joyful interpenetration for all.[30]

Much of Snyder's prose work has been exploring the implications of that interpenetration for human culture and for poetry in particular. More than any poet since Wordsworth, Snyder has been meditating on the fourth question of post-pastoral poetry: if we all live in one ecosystem of diverse cultures, isn't nature culture and culture nature? The modern version of this question is: how can we use our culture, our imagination, specifically our poetic imagination, as a tool for healing our alienation from nature?

Wordsworth believed that his poetry could mediate nature. Before deconstruction he could not say that nature poetry constructs nature for us, making, in a linguistic sense, nature culture. But in "Home at Grasmere" he made the rather breathless discovery that culture is nature in that human mind, which for the Enlightenment separated (they would say elevated) us from nature, in fact, is itself nature. Wordsworth said he was

> Speaking of nothing more than what we are—
> How exquisitely the individual Mind
> (And the progressive powers perhaps no less
> (Of the whole species) to the external world
> Is fitted; and how exquisitely too—
> Theme this but little heard of among men—
> The external world is fitted to the mind.[31]

Snyder says in the epigraph to this chapter that the mind is a wild ecosystem. This is why the leading American nature poet can title his selected poems *No Nature.* All products of the human mind are, in a sense, the products of nature, although obviously some are more destructive of holism than others. It follows that the imagination is the tool nature has given us to allow us, if we now choose to heal the wounds of the past, to reconnect our culture with the wider ecosystem of which it is a part. So the poetry of Gary Snyder is, in a sense, nature thinking us back into nature:

> This living flowing land
> Is all there is, forever
>
> We *are* it
> It sings through us.[32]

These lines from "Frazier Creek Falls" are deceptively simple. For further elaboration I would refer readers to Snyder's essays, where, in "Tawney Grammar" for example, he explores notions like "Wild nature is inextricably in the weave of self and culture," and conversely, "When humans know themselves, the rest of nature is right there."[33]

In the essay "Some Points for a 'New Nature Poetics'" Snyder follows up his statement that nature writing "has the potential of becoming the most . . . morally challenging kind of writing" by suggesting that ecological poets not only inform themselves from science, especially "the emergent new territories of science," but "go further with science."[34] His thinking here is confronting the fifth question implicit in post-pastoral poetry: if our evolved consciousness gives us conscience, how should we exercise our responsibilities toward our material home? Snyder is aware that new scientific evidence is continuously informing our revision of precisely what responsible behavior is. What was once good to eat becomes bad for us then becomes good again for different reasons. So it is with our relationship with the land. Because we are present in the land, some concept of land management seems responsible. If we have stopped suppressing natural forest fires, for example, should we also suspend our use of wood altogether and stop all logging?

Even sleeping on the ground out in the forest, Snyder catches the sound of the 4 A.M. log trucks interrupting his "dreaming of health": "The log trucks remind us, / as we think, dream and play / of the world that is carried away."[35] Snyder's "Little Songs for Gaia," of which this is a part, are an example of the way post-pastoral poetry reminds us of the complexities of our responsibility toward the biotic community we inhabit. How can we live in it without in some manner "carrying away" some of it? What does it mean to "carry away" the world? Is our health, or the health of the world, ultimately served by logging? What, then, are our dreams? What is our healthiest manner of "play"?

All these difficult and necessary questions bring us to the sixth and final question that post-pastoral poetry asks: how can we best address the issue that ecofeminists in particular have helped us understand better—that our exploitation of our environment has emerged from the same mind-set as our exploitation of each other? In Europe around the time of the collapse of the communist states it was fashionable to declare that radicalism had moved "from red to green." Ecofeminists have shown us that this was dangerously mistaken thinking, especially, for example, for those women in the world whose quality of life as women is directly linked to the quality of their environment. Blake knew this too in the mode of his own time. In his poem "London" the harlot's curse is heard in the final line, "blight[ing] with plagues the Marriage hearse"; the first stanza tells us, "Near where the charter'd Thames does flow."[36] In a short poem Blake does not include such detail for background color. What begins and ends the poem are images of the unnatural causing, his audience cannot fail to know, physical and moral ill health. A river that is a "charter'd" sewer is produced by the same society that has fouled marriage and the individual lives of infants, chimney-sweepers, soldiers, and youthful prostitutes.

To find Gary Snyder's global exploration of this issue we have to return to "Mother Earth: Her Whales" and what Jonathan Bate sees as embarrassingly unpoetic discourse:

Solidarity. The People.
Standing Tree People!
Flying Bird People!
Swimming Sea People!
Four-legged, two legged, people![37]

Snyder's playfulness can mislead the earnest literary critic. It should be clear by now that his sense of play is both light and thoughtful, joyous and serious. His play with discourses in this poem extends to a ridiculously long single line: "North America, Turtle Island, taken by invaders who wage war around the world" (237). One could argue that this is an outpouring of heartfelt rage to justify this long line and one can point to the alliteration to justify it as poetics. In fact, this apparently prosaic line is one extreme in the poem's pushing at the whole range of what poetry can do on the page. What is important is its easy comprehension that war is being waged by America on both land and people, both within and without the continent that once was a sacred land called "Turtle Island." Such complex content can only be achieved by the playful seriousness of Snyder's poetry commanding the full resources of poetics.

In his introduction Scott Bryson defines ecopoetry as informed by—and responding to—modern ecological knowledge and concepts. This clearly is the agenda that Gary Snyder has been urging on us in his essays and exploring in his poetry. The advantage of placing Snyder's work within the broader frame of post-pastoral literature is to see its continuities back to Blake and across to the prose of John Muir. It also helps to establish the ways in which Snyder's poetry has transcended the traps of the pastoral to imaginatively, playfully, confront the difficult questions of our time—as he urges other poets: "be crafty and get the work *done.*"[38]

Notes

1. Lawrence Buell, *The Environmental Imagination* (Cambridge: Harvard University Press, 1995), 50.
2. Ibid.
3. Leo Marx, *The Machine in the Garden* (New York: Oxford University Press, 1964), 44.
4. See Terry Gifford, *Pastoral* (New York: Routledge, 1999).
5. Lawrence Buell, "American Pastoral Ideology Reappraised," *American Literary History* 1, no. 1 (spring 1989): 23.

6. Leonard M. Scigaj, *Sustainable Poetry: Four American Ecopoets* (Lexington: University Press of Kentucky, 1999), 12.

7. Jonathan Bate, *The Song of the Earth* (London: Picador, 2000), 246.

8. Gary Snyder, *No Nature: New and Selected Poems* (New York: Pantheon, 1992), 50.

9. Patrick Murphy, *Understanding Gary Snyder* (Columbia: University of South Carolina Press, 1992), 33.

10. I first developed the notion of the post-pastoral in relation to the poetry of Ted Hughes. See Terry Gifford, *Green Voices: Understanding Contemporary Nature Poetry* (New York: St Martin's Press, 1995).

11. Terry Gifford, introduction to *John Muir: The Eight Wilderness-Discovery Books* (Seattle: Mountaineers Press, 1992).

12. Patrick D. Murphy, "'The Women Are Speaking': Contemporary Literature as Theoretical Critique," in *Ecofeminist Literary Criticism,* ed. Patrick D. Murphy and Greta Gaard (Chicago: University of Illinois Press, 1998), 23–48.

13. Quoted in Gifford, *Green Voices,* 132.

14. Bate, 200.

15. Bert Almon, "Buddhism and Energy in the Recent Poetry of Gary Snyder," in *Critical Essays on Gary Snyder,* ed. Patrick D. Murphy (Boston: G. K. Hall, 1991), 87.

16. Gerard Manley Hopkins, *Poems and Prose* (Harmondsworth: Penguin, 1953), 27.

17. Snyder, *No Nature,* 25.

18. *William Blake: The Complete Poems,* ed. W. H. Stevenson (London: Longman, 1971), 114.

19. Ibid., 215.

20. *John Muir: The Eight Wilderness-Discovery Books,* 148.

21. Ibid., 841.

22. See Gifford, *Pastoral,* 117–120.

23. A. L. Lloyd, *Folksong in England* (London: Lawrence and Wishart, 1967), 183.

24. Snyder, *No Nature,* 7.

25. Ibid., 373.

26. Ted Hughes, interview in *London Magazine,* January 1971, 9.

27. *The Poems of Tennyson* (London: Frowe, 1904), 614.

28. Snyder, *No Nature,* 308.

29. Sorley Maclean, *From Wood to Ridge* (Manchester: Carcanet, 1990), 183.

30. Snyder, *No Nature,* 308.

31. William Wordsworth, "Home at Grasmere," in *The Oxford Authors: William Wordsworth,* ed. Stephen Gill (Oxford: Oxford University Press, 1984), 198.

32. Snyder, *No Nature,* 234.

33. Gary Snyder, *The Practice of the Wild* (San Francisco: North Point Press, 1990), 68.

34. Gary Snyder, *A Place in Space* (Washington, D.C.: Counterpoint, 1995), 172.
35. Snyder, *No Nature,* 289.
36. *William Blake: The Complete Poems,* 213–214.
37. Snyder, *No Nature,* 237.
38. Snyder, *A Place in Space,* 172.

Gyorgyi Voros

Earth's Echo

Answering Nature in Ammons's Poetry

> . . . nothing here shows me the image of myself.
>
> —A. R. Ammons, "For Harold Bloom"

> Eros is an issue of boundaries. He exists because certain boundaries do. In the interval between reach and grasp . . . the absent presence of desire comes alive.
>
> —Anne Carson, *Eros the Bittersweet*

Although much ecocritical analysis in recent decades has focused on the Western attitude of domination toward physical nature, the model of conquest and exploitation describes only one (albeit prevailing) stance toward nature. Carolyn Merchant has shown that this version itself arose when "a mechanistic world view in which nature was reconstructed as dead and passive, to be dominated and controlled by humans" replaced an earlier conceit of an "organic cosmos with a living female earth at its center."[1] Yet other versions of nature have endured alongside the domination model, even if as undercurrents in the culture, occasionally burbling to the surface to cleanse the old metaphors, refresh and challenge the life of the imagination, and redirect human energies. One alternative construction that has held sway since the Book of Job, and with which the poet A. R. Ammons has spent a career grappling, is nature as unattainable Other, unanswerable to human need or desire, with whom the human exists in a state of awe, fear, or, as is most often the case in Ammons, erotic longing. Ammons frames questions of how to live with, and within, the vast inhuman Otherness of nature in two recurring tropes: mirror and echoing voice. Where mirroring and the ocular metaphors related to it fail poetically to effect a sustainable ecological relation between human and nonhuman Other, tropes arising from acts of voicing—speaking, singing, echoing—realize a provisional equilibrium.

Early on, the theme of the futility of seeking any semblance of the human in nature gains expression in certain moods of the English romantics and American transcendentalists. For Shelley this is the nature that "dwells apart in its tranquility / Remote, serene, and inaccessible";[2] for Thoreau, it is the "Earth, of which we have heard, made out of Chaos and Old Night . . . the home, this of Necessity and Fate."[3] In twentieth-century American poetry the consciousness of nature's Otherness strongly colors the work of several significant postromantic American nature poets before Ammons: Robinson Jeffers, Robert Frost (in his "Once by the Pacific" humor), and Wallace Stevens. Of these, Stevens struggles most ardently with the issues of the proper human relation to nonhuman nature and with the role of language and poetry in a nonverbal universe. Stevens lays the groundwork for a deliberately nonanthropocentric poetry. Always adamant in his rejection of the pathetic fallacy and every other humanizing tendency, Stevens from the first dismisses the notion that physical nature emulates the human: "The world? The inhuman as human? That which thinks not, / Feels not, resembling thought, resembling feeling?"[4] Recognizing that any "response" from the natural world can only be human projection, Stevens petitions the world for silence: "If there must be a god in the house, let him be one / that will not hear us when we speak."[5] The most valuable function for human imagination, in Stevens's view, is the decreative one of *imagining* the world without the encrustations of human imagination (that is, without layers of human conceptualization): "Let's see the very thing and nothing else. . . . // Trace the gold sun about the whitened sky / Without evasion by a single metaphor."[6]

A. R. Ammons is Stevens's successor in both linguistic and ecological concerns. The heir apparent, schooled in the sciences, deft in incorporating both the language and methods of biology, astronomy, and ecology in the poems, witty and innovative in his poetic demonstrations of higher mathematics at work (Marjorie Perloff applies both fractal geometry and chaos theory to Ammons's poems, and Roger Gilbert likens *Glare* to a Möbius strip),[7] Ammons seems even less inclined than Stevens to impose correspondences between physical nature and human mind. Yet the central paradox for both Ammons and Stevens is that the condition of unrequited love does not preclude love itself. Stevens professes devotion for what he calls his "ultimate inamorata": "the indefinite, the impersonal, atmospheres and oceans and, above all, the principle of order."[8] Ammons frames his love in homier terms when he harks back to his early years on a farm: "I love the land and the terrible dependency on the weather and the rain and the wind. . . . That's where I got my closeness and attention to the soil, weeds, plants, insects and trees."[9] This sense of intimacy with natural phenomena and processes that cannot respond in kind is a driving force in both poets' work. However, where Stevens achieves a sort of resolution within his imagination/reality dialectic, concluding that "Poetry is a nature created by the poet,"[10] Ammons's work remains charged with alternating currents of despair and rapture.

These poles of feeling in Ammons's poetry derive from the fundamentally erotic nature of his linguistic pursuits. Whenever the poet's role is to woo, mirror, embrace, or seek to be subsumed within a nature that appears to have within it no trace of the human, and that the savvy poet refuses anyway to anthropomorphize, that is at best "communicative, but not with human sound,"[11] then the relation between the poet and nonhuman nature is inherently erotic. Anne Carson writes that "the Greek word *eros* denotes 'want,' 'lack,' 'desire for that which is missing.' The lover wants what he does not have. It is by definition impossible for him to have what he wants if, as soon as it is had, it is no longer wanting"[12] Or more succinctly: "A space must be maintained or desire ends."[13] This lack, or space, or desire for that which is missing—namely, congruence between human experience and nonhuman nature—informs the ecopoetry of A. R. Ammons, who himself renders the observation in more dispassionate terms: "a poem is a linguistic correction of disorder. . . . The disorder may be sensed as an incongruence between our nonverbal experience or reality and our language reflection of it."[14] Either way, incongruence—the space that must be maintained—lies at the heart of the poetry.

Consider a small poem, "Reflective," a linguistic sleight-of-hand that at least initially appears to depict a state of perfect congruence between human and nonhuman worlds. "I found a / weed," begins the poet, "that had a // mirror in it." He slyly suggests at the outset a natural world capable of reflecting the human. The next lines continue buoyantly to blur the distinction between subject and object: the weed itself looks at

> a mirror
> in
>
> me that
> had a
> weed in it."[15]

The poem's surface charm evokes a sprightly optimism: how wholesome and satisfying that the speaker can see in nature his perfect counterpart. And how right that he should perform the same affirmative function for nature, itself matched in the speaker's visage. On closer inspection the odd fact emerges that it isn't speaker and weed communing in a mutually transfixed gaze; it's mirror reflecting mirror:

> that
> mirror
>
> looked in at
> a mirror
> in
>
> me.

Instead of mutual affirmation, a veritable funhouse hall of mirrors tunnels toward an infinity of hollowness. As Herbert Grabes baldly puts it, "It is the fact that the mirror has no image of its own which makes it a mirror."[16] In this light the poem's beatific smile extolling harmony between humans and nature congeals to a mocking leer: clearly, all sentient beings trapped in their own perceptions are destined to see nothing but themselves reflected in the shards of a fragmented world.

Mirror imagery is in itself multivalent and contradictory: in Grabes's typology mirrors may reflect things as they are, show things the way they should or should not be, show things the way they will be, or show what exists only in the mirror or the beholder's imagination.[17] *Reflection* contains at least the first and last of these implications within its lithe structure. The title—a pun connecting the act of thinking with the visual phenomenon of mirroring—contains, too, the central epistemological problem described by Richard Rorty in *Philosophy and the Mirror of Nature.* Rorty ascribes to "the historical phenomenon of mirror-imagery . . . the story of the domination of the mind of the West by ocular metaphors. . . . Without the notion of mind as mirror, the notion of knowledge as accuracy of representation would not have suggested itself."[18] Mirror imagery, by extension then, is also the story of the domination of nature by the West.[19] When Eve makes air the mirror of herself in Stevens's "Notes toward a Supreme Fiction," she assures that humanity will forever seek its own face in nature, remaining blind to what is already "Venerable, articulate and complete."[20]

Ammons both employs and critiques ocular metaphors throughout the poems, although his strongest bent is toward shattering them. "Laser," for example, anguishes over the exclusionary function of the mind's eye-beam (an image for the sort of focused, fragmented knowledge that makes Western positivism possible): "the mind's light," as kinetic and unstable as "surf / or ocean shelves," voraciously consumes all in its path, "gathers up, / parallelizes, focuses / and in a rigid beam illuminates the image."[21] One wants to read "paralyzes" for "parallelizes." The poem goes on to narrate how

> the head seeks in itself
> fragments of left-over light
> to cast a new
> direction

but is unable to do so; "any found image falls / back to darkness" (58). It seems the mind's function in this poem is to rend and dissect; fixed on one spot, it is unable to assimilate any other direction or "contradicting image." Fittingly, the light emanates from a detached head. Having created a paralytic order, the mind seeks its opposite in an image of natural orders open to flux, repeatedly shattering and bursting out of order: "mountain / rapids shattered with sound and light" or "wind fracturing brush." The powerful beam, though, "folds all energy in: / the image glares filling all space" (58). The human image obscures whatever reality was there before. A glare suggests reflected light so bright as to blind; in "Laser" it grows into a black hole sucking "all energy in" (58).

Elsewhere, too, Ammons links the act of reflection with a disarticulated world. "Gravelly Run's" mirror imagery leads the poet to "look and reflect, but the air's glass / jail seals each thing in its entity."[22] The same poem turns the human aspiration toward knowledge on its head by qualifying the great Delphic injunction to "Know thyself!" More important to Ammons than knowing the self is knowing it

> as it is known
> by galaxy and cedar cone,
> as if birth had never found it
> and death could never end it. (11).

In later poems as well Ammons repeatedly shatters the mirror of anthropocentric human knowledge *and* self-knowledge. *Sphere,* the poem inspired by the first NASA images of the planet Earth floating in space like a great eyeball and witness to human activity, asks "when we have made the sufficient mirror will // it have been only to show how things will break: know thyself // and vanish!"[23] In his last book, *Glare*—a disgruntled, curmudgeonly work in which the poet's countenance assumes just the expression the title suggests—Ammons asserts that he is ready to "fracture the mirror" of human perception because it "has no truth to see except its own, / its own splits and deflections."[24] The poem goes on to argue that when human vision seeks, and sees, only its own visage projected onto nature, it loses touch with the very mystery that is key to fully experiencing the world's complexity.

Vision in Ammons, then, expressed in tropes of looking, seeing, and mirroring, is most often the mechanism for failed negotiations of the incongruence between human and nonhuman worlds. For a poet as receptive to flux, process, and motion as Ammons is, the sense of sight entails all that an ecological consciousness of nature eschews: it is spatial, atemporal, privy only to surfaces and exteriors, fragmented in that only one of many angles is available to view at a given time, and it emphasizes separation between subject and object.[25] Another class of tropes centered on poetic voice and related acts of listening, speaking, and singing serves Ammons in creating still problematic but more often satisfying resonances, however provisional, between human experience and nonhuman nature.

This is not to say that tropes centered on voice do not themselves engender incongruities within Ammons's oeuvre. In one instance, for example, the poet's recollections of his solitary woodland wanderings as a child in North Carolina portend the adult's respect for and curiosity about otherness, a seemingly uncharacteristic (anthropomorphizing) longing for "speech" from and "presence" in that inhuman Other, and the concurrent recognition that that speech is but a "rhetorical device": "One can search out another's 'presence' for its otherness or for its sameness. I was alone enough as a child to want to know something besides myself. It was easy for me later to adopt the rhetorical device of 'speaking' mountains and winds: I recognized them as presences and wondered, if they spoke, what nature they would speak out of."[26]

One passage in *Glare* addresses the same longing poetically, attributing a moral, parental, and paternalistic authority to a nature that suggests a soon-to-be-lost paradise. When he was young, "under the apple trees," the poet writes, "the very whispering of the / breezes" *seemed* to him "parental (and / societal) authority," a situation that led him to become "hooked on the nature of things."[27] Even here, the attribution of authority is put in terms of "seeming," not being. Ammons, it is true, imputes these anthropomorphizing tendencies to a younger self. The earliest works in which Ammons speaks fully in his own adult poetic voice—the Ezra poems—show him in a much more Jobian frame of mind. When the poet announces himself to the sea with a booming "I am Ezra," there are "no echoes from the waves," and "The words were swallowed up / in the voice of the surf."[28] "So I Said I Am Ezra" falls within the tradition of the stoical anti–pathetic fallacy poem (Stevens's "The Snow Man" is another example). In contrast to the rather passive dismay of this Ezra poem, the later long poems, *Garbage* most explicitly, express anxiety and rage that language is not only futile when one is seeking dialogue with nature but may itself be a wasteful by-product of twentieth-century consumer society, cluttering up the cultural landscape, embalming ideas (as landfills mummify material waste), adding to the junk heap of culture: at worst the poem "becomes a relic . . . // a real stick in the fluencies: a leftover light that hinders the light stream."[29]

Long before venting his spleen at poststructuralist sophistry and language's obstructionist capabilities, though, Ammons laments a voice subsumed by nature's vastness. One of Ammons's figurations for the place of human voice in nature—"The Pieces of My Voice"—evokes the myth of Echo and Narcissus. Echo, in love with an unattainable self-enclosed, self-reflexive otherness in the person of Narcissus, eventually attenuates down to a pile of bones and a disembodied voice. In Ammons's poem the poet's voice, like that of the nymph Echo, has become mixed with the elements: "The pieces of my voice have been thrown / away," cries the poet. Canvassing hedgerows and ditches, he asks, "Where do the pieces of / my voice lie scattered."[30] Although it could be said that this poetic voice has achieved its goal of becoming integrated with nature, oneness comes at the cost of losing all individual identity (a problematic that itself forms another of Ammons's major themes throughout the work). The eventually recovered scraps of voice in the poem accrue to a silence much emptier than the "unwasting silence" of the surrounding hills: "I am broken over the earth— / so little remains / for the silent offering of my death," mourns the poet.[31]

As Ammons's poetic inquiry into the place of the human voice within nature deepens and develops, he grows more, not less, like the mythic Echo who exists as a voice in air. For one thing several of Ammons's most characteristic poetic moves—the chiasmus,[32] repetends, and other forms of wordplay—simply *sound* very echo-y. To wit (to offer some wholly random examples): "turbulence / livens our passion for clearing, clearing for / turbulence"[33]; "the tiniest kiss / at the world's end / ends the world"[34]; or the lovely poem "Small Song," in which

the reeds give
way to the

wind and give
the wind away.[35]

In view of the negative connotations of Ammons's mirror imagery, it is interesting to note that the chiasmus, in its reversal of linguistic elements in a line or a phrase, registers as a sort of aural mirroring. Mirroring, as has been argued above, connotes an anthropocentric, detrimental relation to nonhuman nature. Crucial differences exist, though, between the ocular and aural tropes. Unlike an image in an ocular mirror, chiasmic phrases occur in time; the rhetorical inversion's temporality assures that the completion of the poetic utterance is processive. Moreover, the echoing voice doesn't pretend to congruence; it follows, and is dependent on, the original, as human productions follow and derive from the natural world. The second phrase of the figure, then, modifies the first, changing the meaning of the whole. Thus it might be said that the figure of speech is an aural rendition of a processive, mutually defining interrelationship between human beings and nonhuman nature. As Leonard M. Scigaj has persuasively argued, the chiasmus in Ammons signifies a "characteristic crisscrossing of inner and outer energies in the moment of perception and artistic composition that constitutes the heart of Ammons's ecological poetic."[36]

Echo, the mythic embodiment (or disembodiment, rather) of the kind of speech acts under consideration here, has herself usually been regarded as pitiable: destined always to mimic, her love a lost cause. However, as the Jungian psychologist Patricia Berry demonstrates in her archetypal reading of the Echo and Narcissus myth, even Echo's circumscribed condition models a way of being in the world, and not a wholly unsatisfactory way of being at that. Although it is true that Echo has no "identity" of her own, Berry suggests that the merits of *identity,* as that term is understood in our culture, are vastly overrated: "Self-identity implies an entity distinct from surroundings and other persons. It implies an essential sameness, oneness, and internal unity of personality."[37] Narcissus has plenty of self-identity. Echo, by contrast, "needs surroundings in order to speak."[38] She is relational; she has, according to Berry, loose boundaries; she is context dependent. (One thinks of Wallace Stevens in "Theory": "I am what is around me."[39] And elsewhere: "The world is myself."[40]) In this regard her status may be seen as ecocentric.

Ammons's poem "Identity" addresses the same valence between fixedness and formlessness personified by Echo: in the poem the point of equilibrium is a spiderweb, trope for both poetry and for the human relation to the nonhuman world. The spiderweb is "beyond destruction / because created fully in no

/ particular form." Were its shape preset, it might not fit into its environment; were it "perfectly adaptable, / if freedom and possibility were without limit," it would "lose its special identity."[41] As the web is the spider's expression of itself, so is the human voice in general and the poet's voice in particular the medium of interplay and interaction with what Kant (and Stevens) called the "enormous a priori." Both the mythic Echo and Ammons's spiderweb taken as tropes for manners of speaking (being) in the world urge creativity through adaptability to the given. Berry again:

> The echo of what one means is not literally what one says but could in nuance and situation . . . be any or everything, depending on the shape of what's around, the shape of the line, the stanza, the situation. . . . So imitation is a mode of creating and shaping psychic heat. The psyche is in this way an artist—a shaper, maker, a creator of beauty within itself. . . . But important to this shaping of heat is also the shape of surroundings. As Echo shapes, she is shaped by what's around her.[42]

The condition of mutuality suggested by the myth of Echo remains, of course, ultimately unconsummated: her voice is destined never to be wholly congruent with the surroundings that give rise to it (she never wins Narcissus), just as no poetic voice ever fully articulates the world it seeks to express. ("It was she and not the sea we heard," says Stevens in "The Idea of Order at Key West."[43] And Ammons: "keep this / poem, this reminder not of keeping but of not keeping."[44]) However, precisely because "Echo's passion requires a distance, a space between her and her beloved,"[45] she remains a figure for erotic connection: her voice configures a bridge spanning the space between her and her beloved. To invoke Carson again, "A space must be maintained or desire ends."[46] Paradoxically, space assures the connection by ensuring desire.

Ammons at his most sanguine both acknowledges the disjunction between human utterance and that which it seeks to articulate, and affirms that human language may nevertheless perform a necessary function—if not necessary to nature then necessary to creating the proper, that is, ecologically right and binding, human relation *to* nature. An excerpt from *Glare* sounds a cautionary note about human attentiveness and the dangers of its lack but also wryly asserts the practical value of language. Material reality may "communicate" itself in its own, nonhuman way: hills, for example, "communicate / by abrupt concretions, not words"—an uncomfortable state of affairs for the poet, given that hills' "concretions / are roughish."[47]

In a later passage *Glare* concedes that human response is a wholly different category of experience from whatever it might speak to or represent but posits that the dialogue—"queries and responses"—encourages circulation (blood flow) between human and nonhuman Other. Although "an answer is not the same thing as a / mountain falls or rose," it is possible that "queries and responses give / circulation to the things that sit still and / be."[48] The human voice, in Ammons, then, however impervious nature is to "hearing" it, remains the best expression of the desire that connects human to nonhuman Other.

Nowhere does Ammons model a way of lending human voice to nature's already articulate silence more than in section 13 of *Garbage.* The passage below follows a diatribe against exploitive forms of language—"surface-mining words"[49]—spoken by the "blabbermouth" who crashes through "sophistic woods . . . verbal provinces of pure dissemblance" (78). Having spent his venom, the poet subsides into a state of profound attention to the things of the world, even as those things often communicate their unwillingness to communicate: the rocks, the poet writes, "came up to me in a wall saying they would say / nothing"; tree tops sway into silence; a brook babbles unintelligibly. The poet discovers, as he always does, that in nature there is "no saying / and no listening either." The task he finally designs for himself—to derive "the nature / of each thing from itself" and to make "each derivation / speak"—is Echo-like in that what he produces is not originative but derivative. Yet in honoring "each derivation," the poet creates, in Patricia Berry's words, the "echo that completes the word to itself." When Ammons describes, in the poem, giving tongue to adder's tongue, periwinkel, and jimminycricket, and writes that the "tongues rang in my head / as in a chanson delicate of essence and point,"[50] he not only suggests an erotic act but also the act of making music. If the music rings only in his own head, if that *as* in the last quoted line carries the Stevensian burden of a necessary fiction, so be it: only through this mediation of human voice can human desire for relation with the nonhuman be consummated.

This essay began by alluding to different metaphoric constructions of nature, channeling human energies and actions toward nature in different ways. A mechanical conception of the physical world implies very different values and uses than an organic one does. Where are those metaphoric constructions born and nurtured if not first in the body and then the body's issue—the breath: poetry? Words, names, images, utterances, even the rhetorical architecture of a figure like the chiasm, all frame different relations to the Otherness in which we dwell as human beings. Ammons's poetry, in the way it transmutes ocular metaphors of mirroring to aural metaphors of echoing, and in the ways it makes human voice resound among the resonances of natural phenomena, shows how poetry can effect an ecological relation to the world. And it discloses how human desire can create the relation it needs to live in the world soundly and, at moments, fulfilled.

Notes

1. Carolyn Merchant, *The Death of Nature: Women, Ecology, and the Scientific Revolution* (New York: Harper and Row, 1982), xvi.

2. Percy Bysshe Shelley, "Mont Blanc," in *John Keats and Percy Bysshe Shelley: Complete Poetical Works* (New York: Modern Library), 573.

3. Henry David Thoreau, *The Maine Woods,* ed. Joseph J. Moldenhauer and Edwin Moser, with Alexander C. Kern (Princeton: Princeton University Press, 1975), 71.

4. Wallace Stevens, *The Collected Poems* (New York: Vintage, 1982), 493.

5. Ibid., 328.

6. Ibid., 373.

7. See Marjorie Perloff, "'How a thing will / unfold': Fractal Rhythms in A. R. Ammons's *Briefings,*" in *Complexities of Motion: New Essays on A. R. Ammons's Longer Poems,* ed. Steven P. Schneider (Madison, N.J.: Fairleigh Dickinson University Press, 1999), 68–82; Roger Gilberg, "Mobius Meets Satchmo: Mixed Metaphors, Form, and Vision in *lare,*" in Schneider, 183–213.

8. Samuel French Morse, introduction to *Opus Posthumous: Poems, Plays, Prose by Wallace Stevens* (New York: Vintage, 1982), xxxii–xxxiii.

9. A. R. Ammons, "An Interview," by William Warsh, in *Set in Motion: Essays, Interviews, and Dialogues,* ed. Zofia Burr (Ann Arbor: University of Michigan Press, 1996), 60.

10. Wallace Stevens, *Opus Posthumous: Poems, Plays, Prose,* new ed., revised, enlarged, corrected, ed. Milton J. Bates (New York: Alfred E. Knopf, 1989), 192.

11. A. R. Ammons, *Garbage* (New York: Norton, 1993), 84.

12. Anne Carson, *Eros the Bittersweet: An Essay* (Princeton, N.J.: Princeton University Press, 1986), 10.

13. Ibid., 26.

14. A. R. Ammons, "A Note on Incongruence," in Burr, 8–9.

15. A. R. Ammons, *The Selected Poems: Expanded Edition* (New York: Norton, 1986), 53.

16. Herbert Grabes, *The Mutable Glass: Mirror-Imagery in Titles and Texts of the Middle Ages and English Renaissance,* trans. Gordon Collier (Cambridge: Cambridge University Press, 1982), 111.

17. Ibid., 39.

18. Richard Rorty, *Philosophy and the Mirror of Nature* (Princeton, N.J.: Princeton University Press, 1979), 12–13.

19. On the metaphoric implications of sight, see Walter J. Ong, *Interfaces of the Word: Studies in the Evolution of Consciousness and Culture* (Ithaca, N.Y.: Cornell University Press, 1977); Hans Jonas, "The Nobility of Sight," *Philosophy and Phenomenological Research* 14 (1954): 507–519; Evelyn Fox Keller and Christine B. Grontkowski, "The Mind's Eye," in *Discovering Reality: Feminist Perspectives on Epistemology, Metaphysics, Methodology, and Philosophy of Science,* ed. Sandra Harding and Merrill B. Hintikka (Boston: D. Reidel, 1983), 207–224.

20. Stevens, *Collected Poems,* 383.

21. Ammons, *Selected Poems,* 58.

22. Ibid., 11.

23. A. R. Ammons, *Sphere: The Form of a Motion* (New York: Norton, 1974), 31.

24. A. R. Ammons, *Selected Poems,* 74.

25. For discussions of the metaphor implications of the senses of sight and hearing, see Jonas; Keller and Grontkowski; and Ong.

26. Quoted in Scigaj, 88 (from Shelby Stephenson, "An Interview with A. R. Ammons," *Pembroke Magazine* 18 [1986]: 196–202).

27. Ammons, *Glare,* 21.

28. Ammons, *Selected Poems,* 1

29. Ammons, *Garbage,* 109. For a full discussion of Ammons's language = garbage metaphor, see Gyorgyi Voros, "Wallace Stevens and A. R. Ammons as Men on the Dump," *Wallace Stevens Journal* 24, no. 2 (2000): 161–175.

30. Ammons, *Selected Poems,* 3.

31. Ibid.

32. For a detailed discussion of the ecopoetic implications of Ammons's chiasmic constructions, see Leonard M. Scigaj's chapter "Homology and Chiastic Energy in the Lived Body: A. R. Ammons," in his invaluable study, *Sustainable Poetry: Four American Ecopoets* (Lexington: University Press of Kentucky, 1999), 83–127.

33. Ammons, *Garbage,* 99.

34. A. R. Ammons, *Brink Road* (New York: Norton, 1996), 138.

35. Ammons, *Selected Poems,* 69.

36. Scigaj, 89.

37. Patricia Berry, *Echo's Subtle Body: Contributions to an Archetypal Psychology* (Postfach, Switzerland: Spring Publications, 1982), 113.

38. Ibid.

39. Stevens, *Collected Poems,* 86.

40. Stevens, *Opus Posthumous* (1989), 192.

41. Ammons, *Selected Poems,* 28
42. Berry, 120–122.
43. Stevens, *Collected Poems,* 129
44. Ammons, *Brink Road,* 111.
45. Berry, 123.
46. Carson, 11.
47. Ammons, *Glare,* 30.
48. Ibid., 238–239.
49. Ammons, *Garbage,* 74.
50. Ibid., 81–82.

J. Scott Bryson

"Between the Earth and Silence"
Place and Space in the Poetry of W. S. Merwin

In his short poem "Utterance" W. S. Merwin writes of sitting "over words" and hearing a sound, "a kind of whispered sighing," that transcends language. This sound exists somewhere beyond the earth and the poet's ability to convey it but still not in the realm of silence, where it cannot be heard—it is "spinning its one syllable / between the earth and silence."[1] Merwin's dilemma is to communicate his experience with the unarticulable sound that has so moved him, while still honoring its ultimate unattainability. From his earliest work Merwin has repeatedly explored this tension, attempting to address issues of consequence while highlighting the ineptitudes of the very language he employs. Like many other ecopoets, he deals with this conflict by offering a vision of the world that values the interaction between two interdependent and seemingly paradoxical desires. In the words of cultural geographer Yi-Fu Tuan, these two desires are (1) to create *place*, making a conscious and concerted effort to know the more-than-human world around us and (2) to value *space*, recognizing the extent to which that very world is ultimately unknowable. In other words, most of the project undertaken by Merwin falls somewhere within these two objectives: to know the world and to recognize its ultimate unknowability. But whereas many ecopoets find a way to balance these two concepts in their work, Merwin's poetry displays a consistent uneasiness when it comes to finding this equilibrium. Because of his skepticism concerning human language and its ability to communicate something meaningful about the world, Merwin often displays a reluctance toward offering finalizing statements, even about matters for which he feels intensely passionate. Instead, his poetry consistently tends toward silence.

To flesh out this claim, I am going to rely heavily on the work of Tuan, who in his landmark *Space and Place: The Perspective of Experience* explains, "'Space' is more abstract than 'place.' What begins as undifferentiated space becomes place as we get to know it better and endow it with value."[2] For example, a neighborhood "is at first a confusion of images to the new resident; it is blurred space 'out there.' Learning to know the neighborhood requires the identification of significant localities, such as street corners and architectural landmarks, within the neighborhood space" (17–18). Thus, says Tuan, "Enclosed and humanized space is place" (54).

When viewed through Tuan's framework, Merwin can be perceived as a place-maker, attempting to move his audience out of an existence in an abstract space, where we are simply visitors in an unknown neighborhood, and into a recognition of our present surroundings as *place* and thus as home. Like most ecopoets, Merwin attempts to depict the world as a community founded on reciprocity between human and nonhuman nature. As he commented in a 1998 interview, "I think that it's a great delusion to feel that we are separate from the world. I mean, what we see on the outside and what we are on the inside, we can't tell where the one starts and the other one goes on, and if we damage one we damage the other. We can't make that separation."[3] Throughout his career Merwin has looked to articulate this relationship with the world around him, as in "Burning Mountain" from *Drunk in the Furnace,* where he personifies a mountain, highlighting its mutual bond with the humans around it and emphasizing its "heart" and "veins."[4] And in a poem from *Rain in the Trees* he writes, "by the tree touching the tree I hear the tree / I walk with the tree / we talk."[5] Merwin has repeatedly stressed this interdependent quality of the relationship between himself and the nonhuman world around him, asserting that the earth "is still a very beautiful place; it's seldom enough that it's seen [in and of itself]. It's seen as an object of exploitation, rather than as something of which we are a part. We are neither superior nor inferior, we are a part of it. It is not different from us. So when we treat it with contempt and we exploit it, we are despising ourselves."[6] This attitude demonstrates the essence of a Tuanian sense of place, one that assigns a high priority to viewing the world as a community connected in a symbiotic web.

It follows, then, that Merwin's awareness of the reciprocal relationship between himself and a more-than-human world would result in a sincere attachment to that world. His lyrics consistently return to this affection. Notice, for example, the attention to details and the appreciation of place in "Sheep Passing," from *The River Sound,* where the poet images "Mayflies hover[ing] throughout the lone evening" and tells of a winding lane in which

> the stream of sheep runs among shadows calling
> the old throats gargling again uphill
> along known places once more and from the bells
> borne by their predecessors.

The music from these bells is "dull as wood" and "clonk[s] to the flutter of all / the small hooves over the worn stone."[7] In Tuanian terms this description—of the lane, the sheep, the hooves, the worn stone, the sound of the bells worn by generation after generation of sheep—is not a confusion of images to a new resident but a significant locality endowed with value by one familiar with the neighborhood.

Especially in *The River Sound,* a collection largely devoted to the past, Merwin frequently returns to a nostalgia about his former places. The centerpiece of the collection, the long poem "Testimony," focuses particularly on this affinity for place. Speaking to his wife, Paula, for instance, about their experiences with the land around them, Merwin describes the two of them listening to

> the long notes of those nightingales
> . . . .
> as we lie watching the moonlight
> that has remembered everything
> the stones of the old house shining
> the cloud of light veiling the hill
> and the river below shining upwards as though it were still."[8]

The details Merwin presents in this depiction of the experience, along with the quiet but fervent emotion he attaches to it, communicate his place-awareness. His connection to his place is manifested through the details he describes and the emotional attachment with which he describes them.

Just as often, though, we see the flip side of this issue, as Merwin's poetry laments the "placelessness" of modern society, whose members often seem completely unaware of the bond between themselves and the rest of the world. One of the best examples appears in "Native Trees," which begins with the lines "Neither my father nor my mother knew / the names of the trees / where I was born."[9] The poet tells of asking, as a boy, the names of the trees around him, but his parents failed even to look where he pointed. The poem concludes in the voice of the child, asking whether trees existed where his parents were children and whether they had seen them. The parents' answer typifies the placelessness Merwin condemns in this and many other poems, for he knows that "when they said yes it meant / they did not remember" (6). The boy asks the names of those trees, "but both my father and my mother / said they never knew" (6). The fact that they cannot name each species or the individual trees is not, of course, the issue for Merwin. Rather, it is the lack of attention to and awareness of the more-than-human world around us that he laments in this poem.

He takes up the issue of placelessness again, albeit less subtly, in "Airport." In this poem the airport is described as "devoted to absence in life," in that "the building is not inhabited it is not / home except to roaches / it is not loved it is serviced"; the airport "is not a place / but a container with signs / directing a process."[10] Then, after describing the building, the poet turns to its consumers and, in first person, concludes the poem by saying, "we travel far and fast / and as we pass through we forget / where we have been" (55). The implication is clear: by delivering ourselves up to such a placeless lifestyle, we lose a sense of ourselves, as well as an awareness of our past, of "where we have been," and thus of who we are.

Consequently, this placelessness can lead to a lack of connection to the nonhuman world. Some of Merwin's best-known poems deal with the disappearance of species that results from this lack of place-awareness, like the shore birds he references, which, "While I think of them . . . are growing rare."[11] The opening lines of "Orioles" underscore the same issue: "The song of the oriole began as an echo / but this year it was not heard afterward."[12] And as he points out in "The Asians Dying," the exploitation and destruction of parts of the nonhuman world offer serious consequences for the human world as well, for "When the forests have been destroyed their darkness remains."[13] Jane Frazier explains that for Merwin "the epistemological and physical distance between ourselves and nature that we have increasingly created has divided us from our most important psychic resource and the basis of our being. Humans are a part of a collective universe, and by shaping the world to accommodate our immediate desires we have gone far to eliminate the original conditions that we need for a complete, healthy environment."[14] Clearly, much of Merwin's poetry works from this assumption that a commitment to place helps prevent such physical and psychological disasters, whereas placelessness has the potential to produce them.

Simultaneously, though, Merwin's writings encourage readers to appreciate and even revere *space.* Although most critics readily discuss place in nature writing, we often denigrate space rather than value it, primarily because we typically interpret it as the opposite of place and thus as placelessness. As Tuan puts it, "Spaciousness is closely associated with the sense of being free. . . . Being free has several levels of meaning. Fundamental is the ability to transcend the present condition."[15] Based on this explanation, "spaciousness" would indeed appear to be a value that environmentally minded poets would deemphasize and even criticize, arguing that the *last* thing we should do is attempt to transcend our present situation. Rather, we have to learn to live in and with our environment.

Yet Tuan's explanation of spaciousness does not stop with the idea of transcendence; in fact, Tuan goes on to argue that this supposed ability to "transcend the present condition" is actually fool's gold in that the freedom associated with spaciousness only *appears* to offer the means to master the world beyond us. As we move into space, it ironically demonstrates for us the extent of our limitations, rather than our freedom: "Imagine a man . . . who learns first to ride a bicycle, then to drive a sports car, and eventually to pilot a small aircraft. He makes successive gains in speed; greater and greater distances are overcome. He conquers space but does not nullify its sensible size; on the contrary, space continues to open out for him."[16] Thus the more we move into space, the more we recognize its vastness as it expands before us, helping us to understand our own smallness and producing an attitude of humility.

Although the process of place-making is a crucial activity in the work of Merwin, that process is often overshadowed by a space-conscious awareness of the limitations of human insight, language, and even poetry itself. This ever-present Tuanian space-consciousness, perhaps the most prominent characteristic of Merwin's poetry, is much different from the placelessness discussed above, for it is based on a fundamental humility in terms of what we can and cannot know, can and cannot control. Space-consciousness emerges from a mindful relationship with place because a deep knowledge of place produces a humble awareness of our own limitations.

In Merwin's work this awareness of Tuanian space results in a prizing of ignorance, which represents the path to wisdom. Merwin makes this case in his interview with Folsom and Nelson, where he references Thoreau's essay "Walking" and argues that

> a real poem comes out of what you don't know. You write it with what you know, but finally its source is what you don't know. There's a passage where Thoreau says, "How can someone find his ignorance if he has to use his knowledge all the time?" The arrogance would be the assumption that what you know has some kind of final value and you can depend on it, and it will get rid of a whole world which you will never know, which really informs it.[17]

This appreciation of ignorance guides Merwin's verse, resulting in lines where he speaks of "the beam of some / star familiar but in no sense known" or where he hears the song of a wren but makes sure to point out that he hears it "without understanding."[18]

"The Saint of the Uplands" takes ignorance as its primary theme. The speaker of this poem, the saint himself, tries to explain to his followers that the ignorance of humanity is a gift to be appreciated. He states that his supporters' devotion to and reliance on him have actually cost them an understanding of themselves, explaining to the reader, "I gave them / Nothing but what was theirs."[19] He describes the people's eyes as "empty" and says that for them vision "[m]ight not come otherwise / Than as water" (20). He then metonymically links this vision-bringing water with ignorance and mystery as he tells of teaching the people that they have their own streams of water, their own ignorance:

> I took a single twig from the tree of my ignorance
> And divined the living streams under
> Their very houses. I showed them
> The same tree growing in their dooryards.
> You have ignorance of your own, I said.
> They have ignorance of their own. (20)

Here New Testament language such as "living streams" suggests a theme of redemption. With tree images calling to mind both the tree of good and evil and the crucifixion, and vision being "divined" from under these trees of ignorance, the speaker implies that the ignorance that brings vision, understanding, and redemption comes as a result of acknowledging the mystery that exists within everyone.

The poem concludes with the saint despondent over his ultimate inability to teach the people anything at all:

> I taught them nothing.
> Everywhere
> The eyes are returning under the stones. And over
> My dry bones they build their churches, like wells. (20)

Instead of understanding the ignorant vision the saint speaks of, the followers forsake their own streams of ignorance and build churches over the "dry bones" of the dead teacher. In their efforts to understand the religion and achieve salvation, the people have actually lost their own truth. By searching for the light, they have missed the meaning in the darkness.

Merwin's work continually returns to this theme, reminding readers to value ignorance and recognize that experience cannot be captured, even by the poet. The Heraclitus quote Merwin chose as the epigraph to *The Lice* is a prime example: "All men are deceived by the appearances of things, even Homer himself, who was the wisest man in Greece; for he was deceived by boys catching lice: they said to him, 'What we have caught and what we have killed we have left behind, but what has escaped us we bring with us.'"[20] In his reading of this passage Thomas B. Byers says that the epigraph sets up "a poetics not of self, but of self-restraint."[21] For Merwin, writes Byers, "[p]oems must not consent to the catching and killing of final statement or formal closure. Rather, they must 'escape' authority—go beyond the poet's largely delusive powers to fix and order—if they are to accompany the self on its journey" (81).

Allowing the subjects of his poems—for Merwin, both human and nonhuman nature—to "escape authority" is a fundamentally space-conscious act. He stressed this idea in a 1983 interview:

> I think that poetry, and maybe all writing, certainly everything we do to some degree, does not come out of what you know, but out of what you don't know. And one of the great superficialities of positivistic thinking is the assumption that things really evolve out of what you know. Nothing evolves out of what you know. You don't move from what you know to something else you know. And it's the unknown that keeps rendering possibilities.[22]

To accept that the unknown renders possibilities is to practice the appreciation of space.

What often appears in ecopoetry, indeed, what most ecopoets strive for, is a harmonization of place and space. Merwin also seems to find this goal attractive, if sometimes impossible. As he put it in a 1988 interview with David Elliot, a lack of place-awareness leads to a deprivation of reverence for the nonhuman world, which could potentially lead to the destruction of the earth:

> If we're so stupid that we choose to destroy each other and ourselves, that's bad enough; but if we destroy the whole life on the planet! And I'm not talking about a big bang; I'm talking about it—the destruction of the seas, the destruction of species after species, the destruction of the forests. These are not replaceable. We can't suddenly decide years down the line that we made a mistake and put it all back. The feeling of awe—something that we seem to be losing—is essential for survival.[23]

What is necessary, in other words, is a space-conscious "awe" combined with and resulting from a place-centered commitment to the world itself.

Often Merwin is able to achieve such a synthesis in his verse. Consider, for example, the title poem from *The Vixen,* in which the poet expresses his wonder at his encounter with the fox. The vixen becomes representative of the larger, nonhuman world Merwin loves, and the poem serves as something of a paean to the animal as Merwin prays that his words "find their own / places"[24] in the silence that follows his exposure to the world beyond him. We hear his enthusiastic fondness for the fox as he addresses her: "even now you are unharmed even now perfect / as you have always been now when your light paws are running / on the breathless night on the bridge" (69). Coupled with this sense of connection to the nonhuman world is Merwin's customary wonder at the ultimate unknowability of the vixen, whom he describes as an "aura of complete darkness,"

> keeper of the kept secrets
> of the destroyed stories
> the escaped dreams the sentences
> never caught in words. (69)

In this lyric Merwin presents us with a model for a balanced combination of place and space: proceeding out of his passionate attachment to the vixen is an intense appreciation for the fox's dark, secretive, uncatchable nature.

This combination surfaces frequently in Merwin's verse. The first line of the first poem of *The River Sound,* which fittingly uses bridges as one of its primary symbols, establishes the volume's place-space theme. In "Ceremony after an Amputation" the poet addresses "Spirits of the place who were here before I saw it."[25] With this line he asserts a point he repeatedly revisits in the collection: that his "place," the world around him, existed long before the individual speaker arrived to describe it or address it or even care for it.[26] This lone sentence articulates both Merwin's dedication to a Tuanian sense of place, as can be heard in the reverence with which he addresses the spirits, and his recognition of the "spaciousness" of the larger world, in that it is greater than his ability to understand or communicate it. This space-consciousness remains present throughout the opening stanza; the speaker goes on to tell the spirits of place, "You have taught me without meaning," and he describes them as "unpronounceable as a face."[27]

Take as another example a stanza from "Testimony," where Merwin narrates (in third person) a moment from childhood when he looked from a hilltop over "a green valley that shone / with such light all the words were poor / later to tell what he had known."[28] It is the very wonder he feels regarding this experience with place that convinces him that the feeling is not articulable—"the words were poor." But notice that it is merely the articulation that is marred by the linguistic limitation; the lack of sufficient words does not color or undermine the experience itself. Rather, the words are simply inadequate to render "what he had *known.*" There is no uncertainty here. The space-consciousness is certainly present, but it coexists with the poet's commitment to place.

Merwin often, however, is unable to present such a harmonizing vision in his poems, as his space-consciousness threatens to override his place sensibilities. Consider, for instance, the famous "For a Coming Extinction," in which Merwin addresses a gray whale that "we," humans, are sending to "The End." In this poem we see clearly the primary tension informing most of Merwin's ecopoetry. On one hand, the poet displays a postmodern awareness of language and its inability to communicate something important. He tells the whale, "I write as though you could understand / And I could say it."[29] Coupled with this is the absence of moral imperatives that results from a stripping away of transcendent foundations. The speaker commands the whale that when it meets "That great god" at "The End," it must

> Tell him
> That we who follow you invented forgiveness
> And forgive nothing.
> . . . .
> Tell him
> That it is we who are important. (123)

Yet on the other hand, this postmodern skepticism regarding language and morality is problematized by an ecologically minded belief that there is something important that must be conveyed, that a real world, not just a mere poetic construction, is at stake. A real-life species is near extinction, and its eradication will "Leav[e] behind it the future / Dead / And ours" (123). The other casualties of this dead future include the "irreplaceable hosts ranged countless / And foreordaining as stars," creatures like "The sea cows the Great Auks the gorillas" (123).

Awareness of these sometimes conflicting issues places Merwin, along with other ecopoets, in a difficult situation. For he is well aware of the linguistic and epistemological issues that have now come to bear on the current generation of poets and other thinkers, issues that call the very existence of "knowledge" and "truth" into question. Yet simultaneously, he is also intensely aware of the importance of communicating *something*, and of the impending loss if he does not speak. These two sets of issues—both postmodern and ecological—form the crux of Merwin's difficulty in writing as a contemporary ecopoet. Jonathan Bate explains this tension: "Postmodernity proclaims that all marks are textmarks; ecopoetics proposes that we must hold fast to the possibility that certain textmarks called poems can bring back to our memory humankind's ancient knowledge that without landmarks we are lost."[30] And much of the evocative power of "For a Coming Extinction" and other Merwin poems stems from the fact that we hear both a place-consciousness and a space-consciousness; but in these poems, unlike the poems discussed above, a discord exists between place and space.

The problem for Merwin is not that his sense of place is overcome by his space-consciousness. In other words, it is not that he loses sight of his devotion to the nonhuman world and what takes place around him. Rather, his awareness of Tuanian space, that is, the humble awareness of his own and humanity's limitations, sometimes prevents him from fully articulating that devotion to place; thus, in his poems the harmony is not always apparent. We know from his other writings, and from many of his poems, that an attachment to place is crucial to his poetics. But his skepticism regarding human language, human intentions, and human knowledge is so great that he becomes extremely dubious regarding our ability to fully interact with, commit to, and communicate our place in the world as a home.

Most of this skepticism centers on language and its inability to articulate accurately and fully the poet's experiences with the world. The words and their objects do not match up. Frustration with this linguistic difficulty appears throughout the Merwin canon. He speaks of "having a tongue / Of dust" and elsewhere calls the tongue "[t]he black coat that fell off the wall / With sleeves trying to say something."[31] He also depicts himself as an inept describer of the world: "My blind neighbor has required of me / A description of darkness / And I begin I begin. . . ."[32] Cheri Davis offers what she calls "the basic existential, linguistic, and spiritual problem Merwin faces in his poetry":

> This is Merwin's parable for our time: After God created Adam and Eve, He instructed them to give names to the animals. He brought the animals to them one by one, and they were named. The names were magical in that they had rapport with the spiritual being of each animal, but unfortunately since then language has lost its original symbolic function. It, like man, fell. Call a wild animal by its name today. What happens?[33]

The problem is that the poet comprehends the communal nature of the world and the connection that exists between himself and the animals, whom he regards as "the very embodiment of the miraculous in the common";[34] yet he feels that no language exists with which to assert the reality of this connection.

Merwin conveys this frustration in the three-line poem "The Old Boast," from the aptly titled *Writings to an Unfinished Accompaniment:*

> Listen natives of a dry place
> from the harpist's fingers
> rain[35]

In this complex lyric the poet indicates his awareness of his own limited powers. Although his poetry may approximate an individual version of reality, it is ultimately no more an accurate reproduction of reality than a harp's note is of actual rain. Thus we hear Merwin repeatedly bemoaning the fact that language (along with human understanding in general) is not up to the task of rendering an experience he has undergone. As he puts it, "the words I say / sometimes are heard another way / as nothing is dependable."[36] Each experience is, in the words of the title of Merwin's fifth collection of poems, *The Moving Target.*[37]

This issue is highlighted throughout Merwin's verse, so much so that the very form of his poems acknowledges the impossibility of "capturing" the poet's experience with the world around him. The poems' maze-like enjambment, turning virtually each line of each poem into something of a riddle; the almost complete lack of punctuation and capitalization; the often-cryptic titles; the difficult syntax; the abandonment of what Peter Davison calls "the devices of journalism—the who-what-when-where-why" that traditionally provide context for the poem's subject:[38] All of these qualities reinforce the concept that experience surpasses the signifiers we ascribe to it, that the world itself is greater than the words with which we attempt to articulate our understanding of and connection to it. Put simply, the very *form* of the poems distances the reader from their content, thus emphasizing disconnection.

Therefore, in response to this feeling of disconnectedness, Merwin's poems exhibit a fervent appreciation for silence, so much so that the conclusion of many poems finds the speaker sitting in silence, listening, waiting, not speaking. For decades Merwin critics have discussed his use of silence, darkness, and absence in his poetry. As Richard Howard has said, "a silence lines his speech."[39] And Byers points out that this silence is "made literal in the poems' appearance on the page, with their short, halting lines, wide margins, frequent stanza breaks, and vast amounts of white space after the last word."[40] In Tuanian parlance, this silence proceeds out of a deep devotion to place and a resultant space-conscious humility in the face of the poet's inability to communicate or fully understand that place.

Take, for example, Merwin's narrative poem "Finding a Teacher," which opens with the speaker coming on "an old friend fishing,"[41] to whom he asks a question. The friend answers only, "Wait" (285). The speaker tells us that it was

> a question about the sun
> about my two eyes my ears my mouth
> my heart the earth with its four seasons
> my feet where I was standing
> where I was going

and that "it slipped through my / hands as though it were water / into the river" and flowed away (285–286). The closing lines emphasize the lesson the speaker learned from the nonanswer he received from the fisherman: "I no longer knew what to ask / I could tell that his line had no hook / I understood that I was to stay and eat with him" (286). We see here the rational intellect being replaced by a respect for waiting and silence. The reason-based question appears, disappears, then dies away; then night falls, bringing with it the lesson of waiting and, symbolized by the unbaited hook, a voluntary surrender of control. And ultimately, even the lesson learned goes unexpressed.

At times another form of silence, darkness, is employed by Merwin. "By Day and by Night," from *The Moving Target,* suggests that the shadow, the "index of the sun," is in fact superior to the light in that it is omnipresent, whereas the light is transitory. Addressing the shadow itself, Merwin writes that it sets up the sun's absence "like a camp. / And his fire only confirms you. And his death is your freedom."[42] In this preference for darkness over light Merwin affirms that it is often better to remain in shadow and silence than to make pronouncements concerning issues about which we cannot have more than limited knowledge.

In "Finally" the poet relates the moment he decides to confront his own darkness, which he calls "[m]y dread, my ignorance, my / Self." He recognizes this unseen Self as his own identity, saying "Come, no longer unthinkable. Let us share / Understanding like a family name." The speaker goes on to demonstrate his hope in the meaning that lies in this darkness:

Come. As a man who hears a sound at the gate
Opens the window and puts out the light
The better to see out into the dark,
Look, I put it out.[43]

The speaker decides to confront and acknowledge his own "no longer unthinkable" and to accept that often the only authentic response to an experience with the world is to embrace and take refuge in the mystery of darkness and silence.

The alternative is to ignore the mystery, the shade, the absence, the silence. In "Native Trees," discussed above, when the young Merwin asks his parents about the place they live and the names of the trees, they do not hear his questions, in fact do not even look where the boy points. The reason is that their attention is held by their present, familiar surroundings so much that they no longer acknowledge the world's mystery:

across the room they could watch
walls they had forgotten
where there were no questions
no voices and no shade.[44]

The absence of questions, voices, and shade means that frightening mystery is no longer acknowledged there, a mystery that of course appeals to the young Merwin but frightens the parents who look to avoid such unknowns. The poem therefore highlights the fact that a lack of a space-consciousness that embraces the unknown can lead to a lack of connection to place as well.

Ultimately, then, as in most ecopoetry, place and space interact in Merwin's verse. The interaction leads to harmony at times, but more often the best the poet can do is to take refuge in silence. Still, the question for Merwin is how to honor his experience with the more-than-human world and still recognize his ultimate inability to communicate that experience. Leonard Scigaj writes that Merwin's poetry's

> self-reflexiveness is very postmodern, but the thrust is not centripetal, toward the world of words as a self-contained synchronic system. It mourns the loss of a naïve encounter with nature as it foregrounds the impedence [*sic*] of language and conceptuality. It wishes it could recover something more from the silence, to convey the quality of a silent apprehension of the

> earth, and therefore the thrust is centrifugal, towards the nature that lies beyond the power of language.[45]

This reading lines up well with the closing lines of "Testimony." As the autobiographical poem concludes, Merwin recounts the story of his mother showing him, as a boy, the Empire State Building. She instructs him to view the entire height of the building "as the time the earth existed / before life had begun on it,"[46] telling him that the lightning rod on the roof would then represent the short amount of time since life began. Switching metaphors, his mother then compares the entire structure to a large book, explaining to the young Merwin that "the whole age when there had been / life of the kind we knew which we / came to call human and our own" would rest on top of "that closed book" "as thick as one stamp that might be / on a post card" (108).

The poem then closes with Merwin's characteristic questioning acceptance of mystery, as he and his mother walk along the street "over the stamp I had not seen":

> where would the card be going to
> that the stamp was to be put on
> would I see what was written down
> on it whenever it was sent
> and the few words what would they mean
> that we took with us as we went (108)

The poem thus concludes with a question, and an unanswered one at that. Once again, mysterious silence reigns over Merwin's verse. Yet as he said in the Folsom and Nelson interview, "The human can not exist independently in a natural void; whatever the alienation is that we feel from the natural world, we are not in fact alienated. . . . We're part of that whole thing."[47] This place-centered conviction that "we're part of that whole thing" pervades Merwin's writings. But because he can never move beyond his mother's space-conscious lesson of the postage stamp, his poetry continually tends toward silence.

Notes

1. W. S. Merwin, *The Rain in the Trees* (New York: Knopf, 1992), 44.

2. Yi-Fu Tuan, *Space and Place: The Perspective of Experience* (St. Paul: University of Minnesota Press, 1977), 6.

3. W. S. Merwin, "'This *Absolutely* Matters': An Interview with W. S. Merwin," interview by J. Scott Bryson and Tony Brusate, *Limestone* (1998): 1–2.

4. W. S. Merwin, *The First Four Books of Poems: A Mask for Janus, The Dancing Bears, Green with Beasts, The Drunk in the Furnace* (New York: Atheneum, 1975), 254–255. Sandra M. Guy provides a fuller reading of this poem, along with an examination of Merwin's use of the four elements, in "W. S. Merwin and the Primordial Elements: Mapping the Journey to Mythic Consciousness," *Midwest Quarterly* 38, no. 4 (summer 1997): 414.

5. Merwin, *Rain in the Trees,* 7.

6. W. S. Merwin, "W. S. Merwin: An Interview," interview by Michael Clifton, *American Poetry Review,* no. 4 (July-August 1983): 22.

7. W. S. Merwin, *The River Sound* (New York: Knopf, 1999), 120.

8. Ibid., 88.

9. Merwin, *Rain in the Trees,* 6.

10. Ibid., 55.

11. Merwin, *The River Sound,* 124.

12. Ibid., 117.

13. W. S. Merwin, *The Second Four Books of Poems: The Moving Target, The Lice, The Carrier of Ladders, Writings to an Unfinished Accompaniment* (Port Townsend, Wash.: Copper Canyon Press, 1993), 118.

14. Jane Frazier, *From Origin to Ecology: Nature and the Poetry of W. S. Merwin* (Madison, N.J.: Fairleigh Dickinson University Press, 1999), 41.

15. Tuan, 52.

16. Ibid., 53.

17. W. S. Merwin, "'Fact Has Two Faces': Interview," interview by Ed Folsom and Cary Nelson, in *Regions of Memory: Uncollected Prose 1949–82,* ed. Ed Folsom and Cary Nelson (Urbana: University of Illinois Press, 1987), 335–336.

18. Merwin, "The Wren" in *The River Sound,* 114.

19. Merwin, *Second Four Books,* 20.

20. W. S. Merwin, *The Lice* (New York: Atheneum, 1967), epigraph.

21. Thomas B. Byers, *What I Cannot Say: Self, Word, and World in Whitman, Stevens, and Merwin* (Urbana: University of Illinois Press, 1989), 81.

22. W. S. Merwin, "Possibilities of the Unknown: Conversations with W. S. Merwin," interview by Jack Myers and Michael Simms, *Southwest Review* 2 (spring 1983): 168.

23. W. S. Merwin, "An Interview with W. S. Merwin," interview by David L. Elliott, *Contemporary Literature* 39 (spring 1998): 6.

24. W. S. Merwin, *The Vixen* (New York, Knopf, 1996), 69.

25. Merwin, *The River Sound,* 3.

26. See, for instance, "Harm's Way," "Wanting to See," and "Chorus" for other poems that highlight this theme.

27. Merwin, *The River Sound,* 3.

28. Ibid., 52.

29. Merwin, *Second Four Books,* 123.

30. Jonathan Bate, *Song of the Earth* (Cambridge: Harvard University Press, 2000), 175.

31. W. S. Merwin, *Second Four Books,* 83.

32. Ibid., 99.

33. Cheri Davis, *W. S. Merwin* (Boston: Twayne, 1981), 42.

34. Merwin, *Second Four Books,* 43.

35. Ibid., 233.

36. Merwin, *The River Sound,* 87.

37. Leonard M. Scigaj makes this point in his discussion of Heidegger, explaining that "even the most successful poetic quest leaves the quester cognizant of the fact that language does not reveal its origins, and Being conceals as it reveals glimpses" (*Sustainable Poetry: Four American Ecopoets* [Lexington: University Press of Kentucky, 1999], 181).

38. Peter Davison, "Merwin Hears the Immortality of Echo," review of *The River Sound,* by W. S. Merwin, *Boston Globe,* January 24, 1999, sec. G, p. 3.

39. Richard Howard, *Alone with America: Essays on the Art of Poetry in the United States since 1950* (New York: Atheneum, 1971), 380.

40. Byers, 109.

41. Merwin, *Second Four Books,* 285.

42. Ibid., 14.

43. Ibid., 24.

44. Merwin, *Rain in the Trees,* 6.

45. Scigaj, 183.

46. Merwin, *The River Sound,* 108.

47. Merwin, "Fact Has Two Faces," 323.

Leonard M. Scigaj

Panentheistic Epistemology
The Style of Wendell Berry's *A Timbered Choir*

After inventorying 1980s environmental disasters such as the mercury contamination of the Rhine River and poisoned fish in the Mediterranean, the Christian theologian Matthew Fox concluded in *The Coming of the Cosmic Christ* that "the killing of Mother Earth in our time is *the number one ethical, spiritual, and human issue of our planet.*"[1] Fox attributed the root cause of our planetary environmental degradation to a loss of faith in the living cosmology articulated throughout the New Testament and in the texts of medieval mystics.[2] Fox followed the work of Jaroslav Pelikan[3] in arguing that, since Augustine and the fourth-century patristic writers, Christianity has gradually lost that sense of a living cosmology by excessively focusing on guilt and personal salvation. The rationalism of the Enlightenment tolled the final death knell; according to Fox and Pelikan, it split the Western religious psyche into a dualistic preoccupation with objective fact, sexual guilt, and the search for the historical Jesus.[4]

To heal that split and forestall planetary environmental catastrophe, Fox followed Pelikan and Teilhard de Chardin[5] in asserting that we must reinvigorate a belief in the living cosmology articulated by the earliest Christian writers in the Gospels, the Acts of the Apostles, and St. John's Revelation—a cosmology last revived by the medieval mystics. In these works we find a Cosmic Christ whose *metanoia* or new insight is the nondualistic, compassionate, often mystic apprehension of the panentheistic divine wherein, as Sehdev Kumar once stated, "God is in all things and all things are in God."[6] The Cosmic Christ is for Fox "the *divine* pattern that connects."[7] He fosters a sense of environmental interdependence that we can find in Old Testament prophets (Jeremiah 23:23–24—"Do I not fill heaven and earth?" says the Lord), and most New Testament writers (see, for instance, God as "all in all" in 1 Corinthians 15:28 and St. John's vision of God as "Alpha and Omega," who creates a "new heaven and a new earth" in Revelation 21).

One finds similar statements of visionary interdependence in the majority of the medieval mystics, especially in St. Francis of Assisi's "Canticle of Brother Sun," Hildegard of Bingen's *Illuminations,* Dante Alighieri's *Divine*

Comedy, Meister Eckhart's *Meditations,* and Mechtild of Magdeburg's *Meditations.*[8] Ten years after Fox's *Cosmic Christ,* we find the same cosmological *metanoia* in the Sabbath meditations of Wendell Berry's *A Timbered Choir.*[9] Berry began writing his Sabbath poems in 1979, and he published two earlier volumes of these meditations in 1987 and 1992.[10] Berry and Fox were following the same historical zeitgeist, responding similarly, although from different disciplines, to the same problem: what Berry characterized in *A Timbered Choir* as "the destruction of the world / in our own lives that drives us / half insane, and more than half."[11] Why did this destruction occur so quickly, and what can we do to rectify the problem?

Berry's Christian environmental vision developed gradually, in part as a direct response to the medieval historian Lynn White Jr.'s essay about the negative environmental effects of Christianity. Thirty years ago White startled environmentalists and traditionalists alike with his argument that the roots of our ecological crisis concern the assumptions of medieval Western Christianity about the dominance of humans over the natural world. According to White, Christianity fostered dualism and a linear technology, both of which eroded an individual's reliance on sensual participation in nature in the present moment. Moldboard plowing, which "attacked the land with such violence that cross-plowing was not needed," illustrations of human mastery over nature on medieval Frankish calendars, the Genesis account of Adam's domination over the creatures he named (1:26–28), the attribution of religious motives for the investigations of New Scientists such as Leibnitz and Newton, and the extirpation of pagan animism by Christians—all of this evidence indicated to White that "Christianity made it possible to exploit nature in a mood of indifference to the feelings of natural objects."[12]

Christianity was not, of course, the only religion that resulted in the despoliation of nature, and the economics and power politics of individuals and nations throughout human history have certainly bent and in many cases subverted religious doctrine to underwrite environmentally suspect goals. Yet White's challenge remains; given that "no creature other than man has ever managed to foul its nest in such short order," it is certainly worthwhile to consider his point that "human ecology is deeply conditioned by beliefs about our nature and destiny—that is, by religion."[13]

Of the many direct responses to White's argument concerning the ecological effects of Christianity, Wendell Berry's in the title essay of *The Gift of Good Land* is one of the most eloquent and most incisive.[14] Berry argued that, although Adam *was* given dominion over other orders of nature, the Bible nowhere says that he was given power to destroy the land or any of the creatures living on it. Berry points us to Genesis 2:15, where Adam, newly exiled from Eden, is given the earth that he may "dress it and keep it" by the sweat of his brow. This for Berry implies a stewardship role for humans, and Berry reads the subsequent historical books of the Old Testament as the Israelites' slow growth to an understanding of how to acquire the Promised Land and keep it responsibly. Berry asserts that a story that begins in dark rapacity gains a "vein of light" that "still accompanies us": "this light originates in the idea of the land as a gift—not a free or a deserved gift, but a gift given upon certain rigorous conditions." The Bible explicitly presents the Promised Land as "a divine gift to a *fallen* people," and continuing to enjoy that gift depends on "ecological discipline"—on (1) their "faithful, grateful, and humble" memory, so that they continue to "bless the Lord thy God for the good land which he hath given thee" (Deuteronomy 8:10); (2) on their neighborly honesty and generosity; and (3) on the daily practice of good stewardship or sustainable husbandry, in preserving the health of the land for future generations, for "all Creation exists as a bond," an interdependent whole within which humans function as just one of many dependent parts.[15]

In the poems of *A Timbered Choir* Berry explores his belief that we must respond to the gift of good land with sustainable stewardship. Berry's latest volume of poetry collects the two earlier volumes, *Sabbaths* (1987) and *Sabbaths: 1987–90* (1992), and adds seven more recent years of Sunday meditations. The 1987 volume contained a helpful two-page appendix of notes, unfortunately not reprinted in *A Timbered Choir,* that chronicle many of the deliberately placed biblical echoes in poems dated from 1979 through 1986. In his preface to *A Timbered Choir* Berry calls himself an "amateur poet": he shuns the experimental, following traditional forms such as the quatrain and stanzas of rhymed couplets, with an occasional sonnet or use of terza rima. The real artistry exists in the drama of perception, where Berry complicates the spareness and directness of his presentation with overlays of imagery that achieve the complexity of a fugue.

For rest from weekday farm and literary labor Berry developed a habit of hiking into the hilly woods above his Port Royal, Kentucky, home, to compose austere, meditative poems. From 1979 through 1997 Berry completed one to twelve poetic meditations per year. Frequently in *A Timbered Choir* he refers to the land as the Creator's free gift.[16] God's "unabused // Gift that nurtures and protects" joins "the Giver and the taker" (14). Harmony occurs when humans respond to that gift with labor and caring for other orders of sentient nature. This is the land that humans were "given / in trust" (98), but in "our unraveling century" (14) greed and exploitation can make the slow leaf-growth of soil disappear very quickly: "The growth of fifty thousand years undone / In a few careless seasons, stripped to rock / And clay" (16).

Light, darkness, tree, seed, work, and song imagery knit the poems of this lengthy sequence together with fugal complexity. Light imagery appears on almost every page of *A Timbered Choir;* it often functions as a symbol of the continual bestowal of God's grace, his free gift, as the all-important transfer of energy that ensures the continued life of ecosystems, and as the slow coming of illumination in humans concerning the wisdom of stewardship, where humans assist in the drama of renewal within creation. Frequently light imagery oscillates dialectically with imagery of darkness, which can signify either a positive potential for new creation, as in Lao Tzu (1, 20, 21)[17] and in the soil cycle, or negatively as the limits of human understanding that artificially enclose God's creation in concepts and machines. Trees are the living intersections of divine light and dark soil and are thus emblematic of all created beings. Work imagery affirms that the best course of action for fallen humans is to respond to the energy that God continually invests in creation with labor and good stewardship. Seed imagery in consort with light and darkness imagery celebrates the God-ordained cycles of husbandry and the slow growth to illumination in humans who learn to see cosmologically. Song imagery, especially birdsong, is most cosmological in that it suggests the harmony of all creation that humans can perceive only by courting the state of silence, where human ratiocination evaporates and one listens attentively to nature's sounds.

We believe in these poems in part because Berry has lived his life deliberately, complicating his academic life as a university professor with an even more demanding life—living sustainably on a farm in Port Royal, Kentucky, where he has plowed and tended his fifteen arable acres, grown most of his family's food, cared for his lambs and sold them locally, and cut his own firewood for the past thirty-five years. The long poem "The Farm" in *A Timbered Choir* catalogs the cycle of labor-intensive tasks that Berry completes each year to keep his farm productive and nearly self-sustaining. Another reason that readers may believe in these meditations is the graceful calm of presentation where Berry often suffuses his perceptions, diction, and imagery with a cosmology borrowed in part from the same Christian scriptural and mystical traditions that Fox championed. The source of the cosmological design concerns Berry's perception, ubiquitous in the poems, that God's animating energy inhabits all creation and that humans can perceive how creation, unless fouled by humans, sings the praises of its Creator through a harmonious interconnectedness. Fox calls this mystic perception of God's animating energy suffusing all creation *panentheism.*[18] Fox prefers *panentheism* to *pantheism,* because pantheism, heretical to Christians, robs God of transcendence by equating his essence with his material creation—hence "everything is God and God is everything." Adding the Greek *en* results in the acceptable assertion that "God is in everything and everything is in God."[19] Lines celebrating God's animating spirit as light-giving energy and sustenance occur with noticeable frequency in Berry's Sabbath meditations:

> What are we but forms
> of the self-acknowledging
> light that brings us
> warmth and song from time
> to time?[20]
> . . . . .
> A richness from above,
> Brought down, is held, and holds
> A little while in flow.
> Stem and leaf grow from it. (57)
> . . . . .
> the Presence that we come into with song
> is here, shaping the seasons of His wild will. (73)
> . . . . .
> The dark
> Again has prayed the light to come
> Down into it, to animate
> And move it in its heaviness.
>
> So what was still and dark wakes up,
> Becomes intelligent, moves, names
> Itself by hunger and by kind,
> Walks, swims, flies, cries, calls, speaks, or sings.
> We all are praising, praying to
> The light we are, but cannot know. (75)

In *The Prose of the World* Merleau-Ponty argued that style concerns the process of individual human perception, as unique and distinctive as one's handwriting, especially the ability to create a "system of equivalences," for our glances explore or "prospect" our surroundings because our corporeal bodies express themselves prereflectively in the very act of establishing contact with that lived space.[21] Hence style is not a set of techniques but a mode of perception, the *way* the persona habitually interlaces the objects and events presented in poems or paintings. The more we investigate Berry's use of light, darkness, tree, seed, work, and song imagery in *A Timbered Choir,* the more we notice an epistemological process in which the poet's darting perceptions interrogate his world, only to reverse direction and let a biocentric viewpoint develop where he lets those elements of the natural world instruct him about how to live. The more he sees the more he realizes that he is "Seen by more than I see."[22]

The purpose of Berry's reversals of epistemological inquiry within his "system of equivalences," seen especially in the most recent group of Sabbath poems, 1991–1997, is to learn to inhabit the world so deeply that he comes to know his own mortality and thereby lose as much as possible his selfish ego in a spirit of giving in response to God's charity. Berry's style, his continual emphasis on perception and his ability to interlace light, darkness, tree, seed, work, and song imagery, gradually coaxes his readers to see as he sees and thus praise God's panentheistic energy, his continual gift that animates all created matter.

More than thirty years ago, in section 15 of "Window Poems," from his 1968 volume *Openings,*[23] Berry offered clues to his epistemological style. Here he meditates on one of the two sycamores that bookend his "long-legged house" or writing cabin on the Kentucky River. He hopes to "see beyond his glances," with their "distorting geometry / of preconception and habit." He wants fervently to know that sycamore "beyond words," yet "All he has learned of it / does not add up to it."[24] To know that sycamore "beyond words" Berry must be "of it," as Merleau-Ponty suggests in *The Visible and the Invisible*[25]—he must lose his anthropocentric bias and inhabit the earth, not dominate it. Of his residence in Port Royal, Kentucky, since 1964, Berry once said, "If I belonged *in* this place it was because I belonged *to* it."[26] Thirty years later, in *A Timbered Choir,* Berry time and time again shows his readers how to perform perceptual reversals where we learn of our humanity by enacting environmental versions of the Christian paradox that one must lose oneself to find oneself (Luke 17:33). Inhabiting the nonhuman world and learning values *from that nonhuman world* becomes a reliable guide to self-knowledge and self-conduct.

The volume title refers not only to line 4 of the first 1986 poem, but to poem VI in 1979, in which Berry in his 1990 North Point edition notes refers us to 1 Chronicles 16:32–33, where the trees sing the praises of the Lord. To gain an appreciation of this harmony, one must "leave behind / the six days' world," and come alone, without weapon, tool, or preconception, into the biocentric world of the woods. In this world one finds, as Berry echoes St. Francis, "the ease of sight, the brotherhood of eye and leaf."[27] Berry's emphasis on sight, accentuated throughout his meditations, suggests that seeing the "new heaven and a new earth" is a matter of revising one's perceptions. Berry refers to Revelation 21:1 in his notes to the 1987 edition as a gloss on line 6 of poem VI in the 1979 group. In the woods one might exist in such a state of biocentric harmony with nonhuman nature that one might encounter a deer "face to face,"[28] as God spoke to Moses—"as a man speaketh unto his friend" (Exodus 33:11).

Although Berry's lines seldom sustain the taut, clairvoyant visionary stare or exalted emotional outpourings of the writings of the medieval mystics, in both imagery and thematic substance many similarities exist. Both stress the potential of mystical moments to occur at any time within the ordinary everyday. Meister Eckhart wrote that "God is here—in this very place—just as much incarnate as in a human being long ago."[29] Similarly, Berry writes that the farmer must be aware, when he opens the barn door in the cold before daybreak, "that we / Ourselves are living in the world / It happened in when it first happened," for mortals can have visionary encounters with the manger scene, and the Christ child en famille, bathed "in light / That lights them from no source we see."[30] Even the winter wren "Breathes in the great informing Breath,"[31] with Berry in his biblical notes pointing out an allusion to Job 34:14–15: "If he set his heart upon man, *if* he gather into himself his spirit and his breath; All flesh shall perish together, and man shall turn again unto dust."

Many New Testament writers and medieval mystics use light imagery to signify both the continual outpouring of God's power and glory, or *doxa,* that promises a Second Coming[32] and his grace, his continuous gift that illuminates the world, grants us the wisdom to discern his workings and sustains every living creature. Such is the case, Fox notes, in the majestic opening of St. John's Gospel and in Christ's assertion in John that "I am the light of the world" (8:12, 9:5), in the risen Christ's return in St. Mark's Gospel (8:38), and in St. Paul's image of how God's spirit is at work every moment, transfiguring us into a glorious radiance that surpasses his appearance to Moses (2 Corinthians 3:18). For Hildegard of Bingen Christ is the illuminating, animating intelligence of the world—"Every creature becomes illuminated by the brightness of his light"—and for St. Francis Christ is "the light who enlightens all who have life"; for Dante Christ is the "Eternal Light" that reflects light from the Creator.[33]

Frequently in these Christian authors light imagery also conveys a mystic apprehension of panentheism, the nondualistic belief that God's animating energy suffuses all living creatures. Meister Eckhart stated that "God is in all things. The more divinity is in things, the more divinity is outside of things." Mechtild of Magdeburg wrote that "The day of my spiritual awakening I saw all things in God and God in all things." Mechtild believed that "God's word is in all creation, visible and invisible. / The Word is living, being, spirit, all verdant greening, all creativity."[34]

Compare Mechtild's belief with the following moment in *A Timbered Choir,* when Berry seeks nature and a reversal occurs. In the Merleau-Pontyian "system of equivalences" of *A Timbered Choir* the intersections of major imagery clusters and the reversals of perception that constitute his style in these meditations, Berry habitually perceives light displaying a panentheistic animating energy. When he relinquishes his egocentric preoccupation with tasks and schedules, he can concentrate on the activity of perception, and he soon realizes that "There is no vision here but what is seen: / White bloom nothing explains / But a mute blessedness" wherein "The fresh light" is "stained a hundred shades of green."[35] Immediately the spiritual dimension of this moment of perception opens for Berry, and he recognizes that "This is no human vision / Subject to our revision; / God's eye holds every leaf as light is worn" (11).

When Berry relinquishes his human dominance, he gains an intimacy with all of Being. Here he specifically refuses to identify this quiet mystical moment as *his* vision; he has relinquished his anthropocentric ego to achieve a perception of biocentric relatedness, where he fuses with the entire natural world, the "what is seen." The emphasis on God's sustaining presence as a perceptual process, an "eye" that "holds" all creation within its animating energy, underscores the panentheistic vision of *A Timbered Choir.*

Berry's panentheistic theme begins and ends with light. Early in his meditations Berry perceives the "light-filled leaves," and this reminds him of the original Sabbath, when God rested and took pleasure in his creation—a time when, before Adam's fall, "the Maker's radiant sight / Made radiant every thing he saw" (8). The "Art" of the "First Sabbath light" is an art that "makes new again and heals"; it is especially illuminating in Christ's redemptive pattern, "The light made flesh and blood" (27)—Fox's "*divine* pattern that connects." All earthly creatures are leaves that use light, fall into the dark, and return to light again in the renewal of the carbon cycle. This "calling of all creatures is design" (19), and Christ's travail in the dark of death for three days (analogous to winter and the underground germination of seed) is the original "seed," the pattern of work and growth for all creatures to once again "fill with light / Like opened eyes. He rests in rising" (25). Love's energetic craving, the "yearning of body for body" that dies and is renewed, is "unending light" (177), for it expresses the Divine Plan. Light is the guarantee of heaven's "forever" that a brass bowl can hold "for a while" (189). The spiritual light residing in humans is more important than the willful machinations of the human ego or the lights of sprawling cities; but "if we will have no light / but our own," we will "make illusory / all the light we have" (198).

The woods where Berry meditates contain old trees that are themselves "weighty creatures made of light" (73), plants created by sunlight and photosynthesis. These woods are evidently virgin forest, never clear-cut (89), and reside in an area whose soil type Berry tells us in his notes to the 1987 volume consisted of "Eden Shale." Here he finds the wild—nature undomesticated by human use—"where, in their long dominion, / The trees have been left free" (9). Once again we have a biocentric reversal. Humans were given dominion over other orders of nature before Adam's fall (Genesis 1:26–28), but according to Berry's biocentric light or understanding the trees are elders, older and longer-lived on this planet, who will remain after humans have made their exit in the march of geologic time. Once again the accent is on perception, on recognizing *human limits* within a less limited, biocentric whole. Speaking to himself, Berry acknowledges the trees as his "seniors." "Acknowledged in [his] eyes," the trees stand as his "praise and prayer." His "rest" or contentment is "in this praise / Of what you cannot be / And what you cannot do" (147). These trees supply a sense of permanence, of continuity, and they stand in perpetual praise of nature's ecocycles of renewal (21). They sing the praises of their Maker, with branches pointing upward like arms outstretched in praise or prayer (83).

Like the tepee center pole or the Cosmic Tree of many early cultures,[36] trees in *A Timbered Choir* hold together Berry's religious cosmology. These "Apostles of the living light" are "Uprisings of their native ground, / Downcomings of the distant light."[37] Berry's style is most epistemological as his perceptions of trees accrete in significance throughout the volume. Merleau-Ponty argues in *The Visible and the Invisible* that all our views of nature are necessarily perspectival.[38] We cannot see into the flesh of trees or see what exists behind trees, for instance, for the trees preexist our contemplation: they are a part of nature's density and independent of our conscious scrutiny. So Berry conveys dozens of darting glances at trees to assess what they mean for ecosystems as well as humans and how they provide clues to an apprehension of God's cosmological purpose. In another panentheistic passage of *A Timbered Choir* Berry reminds us of John 20:15, where Mary Magdalene, the first to see the risen Christ, mistakes him for a gardener. Here the light, darkness, tree, seed, work, and song imagery find their origin (once again Fox's "*divine* pattern that connects") in the risen Christ's redemptive labor, to which the poems of *A Timbered Choir,* another "figured cloth of song," stand as testament and praise:

> A man who seems to be
> A gardener rises out of the ground,
> Stands like a tree, shakes off the dark,
> The bluebells opening at his feet,
> The light a figured cloth of song.[39]

Several times in *A Timbered Choir* Berry bemoans the rampant clear-cutting of ancient trees that proves the myopia of humanity's "controverting will" (29). The destruction of the ancient forests in our time "is our madness" and a visible judgment upon us; one can only pray for Christ's forgiveness (97–98). But even in "the lamed woods," where the great trees fell, "The shadow of old grace returns," and "Beams reaching down" soon "animate" the dark, creating maples. Berry voices his panentheistic faith in the "light" that all living creatures are, but we "cannot know" this light, for its operations defy our limited understanding (75). At another Sabbath moment, when his darting interrogation of the trees takes another turn, Berry distances himself from the getting and spending of the workday week, and the trees of the woods instruct him to relax his analytic intellect, reverse his inquiry, and see himself as part of a larger harmony, a biocentric whole, rooted in a distinct bioregion. A paradox reinforces the contrast. By resting "apart" from the workday week, Berry finds himself "a part of the form / of the woods always arriving / from all directions home," a form that includes birdsong and "the hush of the trees" in a single "cell of wild sound" (101).

This soon leads to a meditation on a field that once was plowed but has now returned to forest. The reappearance of trees gives Berry more than a reassurance of nature's power of renewal; it also conveys a perspectival apprehension of elemental Being at the heart of the visible: "Where human striving ceased / The Sabbath of the trees / Returns and stands and is" (106). Even when Berry clears thickets for planting, he is careful to "spare the seedling trees" (120) and thus hasten the conversion back to forest after his death. Following nature's pattern brings peace to Berry, but the reader should not derive from these poems the Pollyanna belief that nature's bounty will heal all industrial wounds, for in his essays Berry is fully aware of how urban sprawl, suburban parking lots, and industrial exploitation may soon create ecological catastrophe. Like Fox, Berry rails several times in *A Timbered Choir* at our post-Enlightenment proliferation of machines and bureaucracies that create inefficiency, waste, and pollution. The human intellect, "blind in what it sees," detaches the mind from the body, and lets it rest in abstractions and machine logic that darken the light.[40]

Seed imagery, on the contrary, teaches us to believe in the God-ordained work of germination in the soil, where we trust that the darkness will one day bear light. Just as Christ's travail in death, "pent in seed," leads to a rising that fills all creation with light, so seeds must rest in darkness in order that the "dark come to light."[41] After the twinleaf blossoms fall, "the hinged capsules of seed // grow big" to ensure a cyclic renewal. And in the "resurrection / of bloodroot" one finds a flower that is also "a lamp," an illuminating guide (154–155). Reworking a theme from his seventies poetry, Berry considers marriage analogous to the growth of plants in the soil. He celebrates his twenty-fifth wedding anniversary to his wife, Tanya, as "Two kernels folded in one shell" that over the years have loved and learned to move "Darkly . . . toward light" (50). When Tanya travels without him, Berry feels "Dark in the ground" but is ready to "rise up alive" when she returns (157). Humans have their best chance at comfort and satisfaction when they trust in God's panentheistic energy and live in harmony with his cyclic pattern.

God's energy is most visible in his continual work of remaking creation. Because humans have "unmade" creation through the Fall, we are "fallen like the trees, our peace / Broken." But the outpouring of God's grace in the cyclic pattern of creation is where "The Maker comes to His work" (74). Our best path is to "join our work to Heaven's gift" and thereby continue creation's "song," the "old light held in soil and leaf" (49). Our joyous visions of harvest can be realized only through "our ten thousand days of work" (18, 136). Work in creating a clearing to plant crops "bind[s] the mind" to creation's seasonal cycle, creating a work of art that creation reclaims with forest after our death (17, 59, 119). Human work can "make / A harmony between forest and field," thus realizing "The world as it was given for love's sake" and leaving "unabused" the Giver's "Gift that nurtures and protects" (14). Meditations in the woods can restore an understanding of how "the world's being made" (35) without human hand, nurtured by the living light of God's gift. By responding to God's grace through work at home, one becomes so married to Fox's "*divine* pattern that connects" as to be almost invisible, like the Amish farmer (28, 146, 190–191). Our six weekdays of work culminate in a Sabbath that itself is God's gift: "We cannot earn or buy it" (29). Berry's greatest satisfaction lies in a silent appreciation of his house and farm—all that his vision and work have joined (108).

Song imagery abounds in *A Timbered Choir.* It testifies to the possibility of living in harmony with the earth. More important, birdsong regularly initiates biocentric reversals where Berry's gaze leads him to quiet his mind and listen to nature's speech. Here the birds in their singing are most at one with nature. Birdsong heard in the quiet is "Best of any song," but "first / you must have the quiet" (207). Berry's farm flowers in the spring when all the fields are mowed and fresh with dew. With "bird music all around" Berry experiences a Sabbath vision of harmony by realizing "The possibility / Of human life whose terms" are not those of anthropocentric humans but "Heaven's and this earth's" (136). If we wish a portion of eternal life, we must give up the "known life," the little light that the human will and decision making can produce, and court the dark that, like the Tao, "conceals all possibilities." By following the birdsong, we will experience a biocentric reversal: "As the known life is given up, birdcall / Become the only language of the way, / The leaves all shine with sudden light, and stay" (21). Stalwart trees, in harmony with their environment and bending as the wind blows, express a faith in their biocentric fate. "Birdsong / Is all they wanted, all along" (134).

On at least two occasions in *A Timbered Choir,* birdsong reveals the bird so intimately at one with its environment that Berry's perception approaches a mystic vision of unity with the earth. The first occurs at the opening of a Sabbath meditation, when Berry visits his "woodland never felled." Here the birdsong that suffuses everything becomes a living expression of panentheistic energy pervading creation. While climbing through a thicket, Berry hears "a bird's song somewhere within it" and reflects that not only is the "singer unfound within the song" but also that the song might come from "anywhere / from everywhere." The song permeates all creation, and the "whole air" is "vibrant with it, every leaf a tongue" (89). A similar instance occurs later in the volume, where "A bird the size / of a leaf" (202) fills the entire evening with its song, and the song becomes the entire poem.

As Merleau-Ponty continues his discussion of style in *The Prose of the World,* he recounts a story of a chimpanzee to suggest that desire works through visual means in a living body engaged in a task. A body working through the visible, tactile world creates new connections with its faculty of sight to achieve one's goal:

> The chimpanzee who learns to use a branch to reach his goal ordinarily does so only if the two objects can be seen in a single view, if they are within "visual contact." This means that the *new meaning* of the branch is a bundle of practical intentions which join it to the chimpanzee's goal. The

> meaning lies in the immanence of a gesture, that is, in the index of the manipulation. The new meaning is born in the circuit of desire between the chimpanzee's body and what it seeks. . . . [Thus] the signification which develops in objects . . . is a signification only for a body engaged at a given moment in a given task.[42]

Wendell Berry's task in *A Timbered Choir* is to offer a vision of biocentric harmony in his virgin woods meditations through a Christian "system of equivalences." The intersections of light, darkness, tree, seed, work, and birdsong imagery move with panentheistic fluidity throughout the text and with such a regular insistence on the process of perception that before long the reader sees the connections through Berry's own eyes—and with such luminance that the reader almost replaces Berry himself, walks in his worker's coveralls, so to speak. Like the chimpanzee using his vision to connect branch to banana, means to goal, Berry uses his panentheistic vision to create so many intersections of his basic imagery patterns that we move as he does toward the goal of a Christian biocentric harmony.

The imagery is most casual and paradoxically most intense in the last sections of *A Timbered Choir,* the poems from 1991 to 1997 that did not appear in either early volume of Sabbath meditations. Here Berry, entering the autumn of his life, practices what Lao Tzu called the art of "losing" (20, 48), a process of gradually eliminating conventional analytical knowledge to enter a quietude and tranquility where, according to Chung-Yuan Chang, "one strives to return to the deep root of his being and become aware thereby of the deep root of all things. It is a process of seeing and delving into the maternal depths of nature." This leads to an awareness of "a Heavenly radiance within. It is light in darkness."[43]

Often in this last section Berry loses himself in visions of biocentric wonder at creation, as in the frequent imagery of seed and resurrection,[44] or birdsong, or meditations on how the Maker's grace, "Spirit in love with form," is at work daily since the Fall, resurrecting the forest "Where the great trees were felled" (133). Sleeping well at times becomes a problem in one's mature years, but after nights when Berry sleeps well he experiences a Sabbath in selfless unity with his environment: "I rest in unasking trust / Like clouds and ponds and stones and trees" (187). The tall trees that really want only birdsong direct Berry's perceptions beyond self-interest and teach him to lose himself in praising creation (147). At other times Berry recognizes that in his golden years he has achieved nearly all the potential he had. He realizes that "Less and less you are / that possibility you were." This recognition of loss leads to a biocentric reversal in a moment of almost mystic unity with a tree: "And so you have become a sort of tree / standing over a grave." This perception teaches him to lose himself in further moments of biocentric unity with whatever happens in each day: "Every day you have less reason / not to give yourself away" (167). Berry finds in marital love another "longing of the self to be given away" (149). Conversely, Berry remembers a moment in his early adulthood where a strong sense of place, a moonlit moment of unity with the land of his forebears, gave him such a sense of "selfless / happiness" that he lost himself in that moment and for that moment forgot "the misery of a boy's love / inevitably selfish" (200).

In the poems that recount the last seven years of Sabbath meditations in *A Timbered Choir,* the theme of losing the self appears most directly in Berry's meditations on the Amish and on the death of his mother. In "Amish Economy" Berry recounts comments from his Amish friend David Kline: "We Amish, after all, don't try / To find ourselves. We try to lose /Ourselves" in daily labor and familial love (190). Deaf and infirm, Berry's mother delighted in telling her son before her death (March 14, 1996) that "finally you lose / everything"—"parents, husband, and friends, youth, / health, most comforts, many hopes" (211). Best is to merge with maternal nature, as Lao Tzu advised, to become that tree standing over a grave, wanting only birdsong. To do so is to merge with the root of maternal nature, especially with its pattern of eternal recurrence, in a mystic moment, a paradoxical unity of opposites, a moment when one perceives "dark within light, light / within dark" in the penultimate poem about the stone carving that "doubles / the superficial strip of Mobius" (214–215). In such moments Lao Tzu's "way" becomes a "place," as in the final poem—the place where the Kingdom of God resides (within you—Luke 17:21), as well as at one's home (Port Royal, Kentucky). But Berry's final resting place is also the book wherein his poetic praise of creation stands shining as a timbered choir.

One final question remains. To what extent must the reader accept Christianity in order to appreciate the poems in *A Timbered Choir?* For many Christian readers of this writer's generation, the failure of most denominations of Christianity to condemn the Vietnam War during the years of America's active engagement resulted in permanent disaffection. Many denominations still do not offer women equality in the celebration of religious services, and the strong stance against abortion and contraception in many denominations makes Christianity impossible to accept for environmentalists concerned with overpopulation. But Berry himself was an early and staunch critic of the Vietnam War (see, for instance, "Against the War in Vietnam" and "Window

Poems" in Berry's 1968 volume *Openings*), and he expressed his strong dissatisfaction with institutionalized Christianity in a 1993 essay, "Christianity and the Survival of Creation."

In the essay Berry asserted that "organized Christianity" has no idea of what economic and social practices would foster "the holiness of life" and that "the certified Christian seems just as likely as anyone else to join the military-industrial conspiracy to murder Creation" because "Christian organizations to this day, remain largely indifferent to the rape and plunder of the world and of its traditional cultures"—as indifferent as they were during the time of the conquistadors.[45] Christianity today "has become willy-nilly the religion of the state and the economic status-quo." It "presumes to save the soul as an eternal piece of private property," and "because it has been so exclusively dedicated to incanting anemic souls to heaven, it has been made the tool of much earthly villainy. It has, for the most part, stood silently by while a predatory economy has ravaged the world, destroyed its natural beauty and health, divided and plundered human communities and households" (114–115). In organized Christianity the physical edifice of the church becomes the only holy place, so the rest of physical creation—including the human body—becomes part of a devalued secular world that one can pollute and plunder at will (103). But for Berry the faulty dichotomies of body/soul and secular/holy, as well as Lynn White Jr.'s environmentalist indictment of Christianity, derive from an inadequate reading of the Bible. If Christians would read the Bible carefully, they would revise their practices, for they would discover what Elihu saw in Job 34:14–15, the panentheistic energy of God suffusing all creation. They would, in Berry's own panentheistic words, "discover that the Creation is not in any sense independent of the Creator, the result of a primal creative act long over and done with, but is the continuous, constant participation of all creatures in the being of God" (97). "God is present in all places to hear prayers," asserts Berry, and his church is not a physical edifice but wherever "two or three are gathered together in my name [Matthew 13:20]" (100–101). Christ preached most often in the great outdoors, Berry observed, and "the great visionary encounters did not take place in temples but in sheep pastures, in the desert, in the wilderness, on mountains, on the shores of rivers and the sea, in the middle of the sea, in prisons" (102). We must understand that humans are "living souls," that the world is a "divine gift," and that work is "a form of prayer."[46]

A Timbered Choir is thus Berry's secular extension of a biblically endorsed way of perceiving the holiness of all creation. Like Fox's "*divine* pattern that connects," Berry wants his readers to perceive God's panentheistic energy without the dogma and pronouncements of institutionalized Christianity—to perceive the way the early Christians and medieval mystics perceived all creation. Paul Klee once stated in his *Notebooks* that the twentieth-century artist did not render representational reality; he "makes secret vision visible" through style and organization.[47] Berry accomplishes this through his stylistic emphasis on how the act of perception makes visible the connections among the instances of light, darkness, tree, seed, work, and song imagery. Berry revitalizes a way of seeing the holiness of creation without preaching or heavily foregrounding biblical quotation. The simple, unadorned lines create an appealing, accessible freshness, and the ingratiating honesty of tone convinces. The poems of *A Timbered Choir* model a way of revising our perceptions to comprehend the biocentric holiness of creation. The major premise of both Fox and Berry is unassailable: if we learn to perceive all creation as holy, in our everyday habits we would refrain as much as possible from polluting that holy creation. We would then live more harmoniously near choirs of forests far less subject to the logger's cry.

Notes

1. Matthew Fox, *The Coming of the Cosmic Christ* (San Francisco: HarperCollins, 1988), 144.
2. Ibid., 82–128.
3. Jaroslav Pelikan, *Jesus through the Centuries* (New Haven: Yale University Press, 1985).
4. Fox, *Cosmic Christ,* 77–78, 108, 128.
5. Pierre Teilhard de Chardin, *The Heart of Matter* (New York: Harcourt Brace Jovanovich, 1978).
6. Quoted in Fox, *Cosmic Christ,* 50.
7. Ibid., 133–135.
8. Ibid., 109–128.
9. Wendell Berry, *A Timbered Choir: The Sabbath Poems: 1979–1997* (Washington, D.C.: Counterpoint, 1998).
10. Wendell Berry, *Sabbaths* (San Francisco: North Point, 1987); *Sabbaths: 1987–1990* (Ipswich, England: Golganooza, 1992). In the five 1979 notes at the back of the 1987 North Point edition of *Sabbaths* (page 97), the references to poem numbers and lines are not accurate. I have therefore used in my text the following corrected references for the five 1979 notes: IV, line 26; VI, lines 2–4; VI, line 6; VI, lines 8–9; VII, line 14.
11. Berry, *Choir,* 98.

12. Lynn White Jr. "The Historical Roots of Our Ecologic Crisis," *Science* 155 (March 10, 1967): 1203–1207.

13. Ibid., 1204–1205.

14. Wendell Berry, "The Gift of Good Land," in *The Gift of Good Land* (San Francisco: North Point, 1981), 267–281.

15. Ibid., 269–270, 272–273.

16. Berry, *Choir,* 14, 16, 29, 49, 66, 98, 121, 149.

17. Lao Tzu, *The Way and Its Power: A Study of the "Tao Te Ching" and Its Place in Chinese Thought,* ed. and trans. Arthur Waley (New York: Grove, 1958).

18. Fox, *Cosmic Christ,* 50–51, 57, 117–118, 124–126, 194.

19. Matthew Fox, *Original Blessing: A Primer in Creation Spirituality Presented in Four Paths, Twenty-Six Themes, and Two Questions* (Santa Fe: Bear and Company, 1983), 90. I am indebted to J. Scott Bryson for locating this source.

20. Berry, *Choir,* 55.

21. Maurice Merleau-Ponty, *The Prose of the World,* trans. John O'Neill, ed. Claude Lefort (Evanston, Ill.: Northwestern University Press, 1973), 59–64, 74–77.

22. Berry, *Choir,* 26.

23. Wendell Berry, *Openings* (Harcourt, Brace, and World, 1968).

24. Wendell Berry, *Collected Poems: 1957–1982* (San Francisco: North Point, 1984), 85–86.

25. Maurice Merleau-Ponty, *The Visible and the Invisible,* trans. Alphonso Lingis, ed. Claude Lefort (Evanston, Ill.: Northwestern University Press, 1968), 100, 123, 134–137.

26. Wendell Berry, *Recollected Essays* (San Francisco: North Point, 1981), 52.

27. Berry, *Choir,* 77.

28. Ibid., 26.

29. See Matthew Fox, trans. and ed., *Breakthrough: Meister Eckhart's Creation Spirituality in New Translation* (Garden City, N.Y.: Doubleday, 1980), 66; Fox, *Cosmic Christ,* 122.

30. Berry, *Choir,* 94.

31. Ibid., 79.

32. Fox, *Cosmic Christ,* 95.

33. Ibid., 111, 113, 120.

34. Ibid., 57, 111.

35. Berry, *Choir,* p. 10.

36. Mircea Eliade, *Shamanism: Archaic Techniques of Ecstasy,* trans. Willard R. Trask (Princeton: Princeton University Press, 1964), 120, 269–274.

37. Ibid.

38. Merleau-Ponty, *Visible,* 30–31, 77, 113–124, 136.

39. Berry, *Choir,* 43.

40. Ibid., 7, 9–10, 29–30, 117–118, 125, 127, 160, 190–191.

41. Ibid., 20, 25, 127, 131, 159.

42. Merleau-Ponty, *Prose of the World,* 104.

43. Chung-Yuan Chang, *Creativity and Taoism: A Study of Chinese Philosophy, Art, and Poetry* (1963; repr. New York: Harper and Row, 1970), 48–49.

44. Berry, *Choir,* 154–155.

45. Wendell Berry, "Christianity and the Survival of Creation," in *Sex, Economy, Freedom, and Community* (New York: Pantheon, 1993), 94, 100.

46. Ibid., 106, 109, 111.

47. Paul Klee, *Notebooks,* vol. 1, *The Thinking Eye,* trans. Ralph Manheim, ed. Jurg Spiller (New York: George Wittenborn, 1961), 93.

Laird Christensen

The Pragmatic Mysticism of Mary Oliver

Although postmodern theory and ecology may appear to be at odds with one another—one questioning the very notions of reality in which the other is grounded—it is useful to consider how these two ways of understanding the world are complementary.[1] Ecology discourages the belief that any organism exists independent of its ecosystem, whereas postmodern theory challenges the concept of an essential individual identity, redefining the "self" as a constellation of subject positions that reflect a variety of overlapping social and cultural influences. Once we add to this composite identity the cycles of oxygen, water, minerals, and energy necessary to life, a postmodern sense of self can help correct our cultural delusions of detachment from ecological communities. This is urgent work, for only by imagining ourselves existing apart from our sustaining ecosystems have we been able to justify actions that degrade them. An ecological reconstruction of identity is part of a larger response to the crisis of consciousness that has left Western culture disoriented as our traditional explanations of human significance continue to erode beneath a steady stream of scientific and historical revisions. By now most contemporary Western theorists and writers are done mourning the loss of stability that so absorbed our modernist predecessors. Rather than sifting nostalgically through the fragments of outdated narratives, postmodern writers are beginning to flesh out the stories suggested by new forms of knowledge. In particular, ecologically informed authors such as Mary Oliver devise strategies for cultural survival by proposing functional alternatives to narratives that no longer make sense in light of our evolving knowledge. Oliver's poetry replaces the old, pernicious myth of human independence with an ecological tale of inclusion in a community of interrelated presences.

During the last seven decades the West has revised its narrative of organisms and environments a number of times. Charles Elton's 1927 concept of ecological communities introduced the notion of food chains and niches, and this model enabled a theory of ecosystems within which "all relations among organisms can be described in terms of the purely material exchange of energy."[2] Scientists began to measure the currents of energy within ecosystems then to describe the transfer of energy between trophic levels of producers, consumers, and decomposers.[3] This evolution of thought has radically altered our understanding of relationships and our fundamental notions of self and other, as J. Baird Callicott demonstrates in "The Metaphysical Implications of Ecology": "[E]cological interactions, primarily and especially trophic relationships, constitute a macrocosmic network or pattern through which solar energy, fixed by photosynthesis, is transferred from organism to organism until it is dissipated. Organisms are moments in this network, knots in this web of life. . . . [W]e may say quite literally and unambiguously that organisms are, in their entire structure—from subatomic microcosm to ecosystemic macrocosm—patterns, perturbations, or configurations of energy."[4] When organisms are understood in this context, there is no longer any possibility of an *independent* self, at least in conventional terms.

Systems theorist Joanna Macy proposes that it is more useful to understand the self as "a metaphoric construct of identity and agency, the hypothetical piece of turf on which we construct our strategies for survival."[5] Clearly the distinction between self and other is complicated by ecology, requiring profound adjustments in our worldview. Equally damaging to the traditional Western emphasis on human significance is the collapse of hierarchy in a world where even secondary consumers inevitably fall prey to the decomposers. Especially since the time of Darwin, Western science has played the role of a frantic editor—scribbling and erasing and tearing out entire pages of those stories we have long relied on to explain our identity and purpose on this planet. So, anxious and unable to find ourselves in this unrecognizable, ongoing revision, we turn to writers like Mary Oliver for "the sustaining truths and feelings that conventional religion and modern society seem unable to provide."[6]

Oliver, like many of our best contemporary poets, wants to help us feel at home in a world that looks dramatically different through ecologically informed eyes. We may have lost our mythic birthright when the hierarchy of species collapsed, but Oliver offers abundant compensation by teaching us to embrace our participation in the community of all life. The dynamic dance of energy that Oliver's poetry celebrates—that "white fire of a great mystery"[7]—is the same one that science describes less ecstatically through its laws of thermodynamics. Physics challenges us to imagine that the atomic building blocks of matter are actually tightly interwoven whorls of energy, and if we admit our ignorance about the source or purpose of this energy, we may conclude quite simply that all things manifest a mysterious power. It only remains to figure this power as divine and we have arrived at pantheism. To Mary Oliver humans are no longer merely favored by a divine power, as our Judeo-Christian heritage suggests; we are inextricable constituents of it.

As she attempts to shift the basis of personal value from individual to collective identification, Oliver follows the lead of American romantics such as William Cullen Bryant and Walt Whitman in figuring physical mortality as redemptive regeneration. Traditional distinctions between mortality and immortality quickly break down in Oliver's poems as the material elements of each being are transformed into the elements of other bodies. This is the dynamic process that Oliver finds so redemptive: fish "rise from the water inseparable / from the gannets' wings," and the "rat will learn to fly" in the muscles of an owl.[8] Nor do the knots of energy that we call human cease when strands untangle, for the first law of thermodynamics promises that "energy can be changed from one form to another, but it cannot be created and it cannot be destroyed."[9] Oliver recasts this doctrine in her poem "Skunk Cabbage," where she reveals that

> the secret name
> of every death is life again—a miracle
> wrought surely not of mere turning
> but of dense and scalding reenactment.[10]

Oliver's choice of adjectives emphasizes that this ceaseless transubstantiation is no ethereal dissipation of unwoven energy. Indeed, *scalding* vividly evokes the image of skin—the "border guard" between self and other, in Gary Snyder's words[11]—blistering and giving way, destroying any final pretense of separation. Moreover, the verb *wrought* insists that even in death something is being *made.*

As Jean Alford observes, Oliver redefines human immortality "as a self-denying mortal life in communion with the eternal processes of nature."[12] This continual reintegration of individual into the whole denies any abiding sense of discrete identity, and Oliver's investment in cultivating a collective identity is especially evident in "Bone Poem," from her 1979 collection *Twelve Moons:*

> The litter under the tree
> where the owl eats—shrapnel
>
> Of rat bones, gull debris—
> Sinks into the wet leaves

Where time sits with her slow spoon,
Where *we* becomes singular.[13]

Oliver's description of the owl's bezoar as "shrapnel" evokes the explosion of individuality as all beings are reduced again to fuel, either in the belly of an owl or in the simmering meld of minerals patiently stirred by personified time. The final clause explicitly replaces a limited degree of individuality with a more comprehensive sense of identification, and as the bones begin their "long fall back to the center," Oliver's careful diction reveals how the dissolve of identity quickens as it nears the ultimate denial of hierarchy: "The seepage, the flowing, // The equity" (46). When at the close of the poem Oliver predicts that "The rat will learn to fly, the owl / Will be devoured" (46), she proposes an ecologically revised doctrine of the transmigration of souls. For the soul in Oliver's poetry more closely resembles what was originally designated by the word *spirit*—breath of life—than any lingering essence of a distinct psyche.

We find Oliver's clearest rejection of the Western tradition of exclusively human souls in "Some Questions You Might Ask," which opens her 1990 collection, *House of Light.* The poem begins by asking, "Is the soul solid, like iron? / Or is it tender and breakable, like / the wings of a moth in the beak of an owl?"[14] Although these questions may seem to extend a generous range of possibilities, the implicit question is not whether a soul exists but how durable it is. It is worth noting that the solid extreme of this range is compared to a manufactured substance used to fashion tools of unnatural strength. Similarly, the next simile does more than just establish the fragile extreme of the range. David Barber has correctly observed that animals in Oliver's poetry "have turned totem," and the owl is one of Oliver's most frequently used symbols, representing the suddenness of death;[15] moths, on the other hand, represent human thoughts in a poem such as "Sleeping in the Forest." Thus, Oliver may in fact be asking whether the soul is merely a product of consciousness that vanishes at the moment of death.

"One question leads to another," until near the close of the poem the speaker wonders,

why should I have it, and not the camel?
Come to think of it, what about the maple trees?
What about the blue iris?
What about all the little stones, sitting alone in the moonlight?[16]

The linear descent from a fellow mammal to obviously animate plants to apparently inanimate stones dismantles our traditional hierarchy and demonstrates how our estimation of value might be extended in a world where all matter is composed of the same energy. Even Oliver's depiction of the stones reinforces this project, for the diminutive adjective prepares the reader to sympathize even more with the stones when they are animated by the verb *sitting*. Moreover, the possibility of being "alone in the moonlight" when the adjective *all* emphasizes the plurality of the stones suggests that any sense of isolation is illusory. Every aspect of the earth has a soul, Oliver insists, or none do, as she makes clear in the title essay of her 1999 collection, *Winter Hours:* "I believe in the soul—in mine, and yours, and the bluejay's, and the pilot whale's. I believe each goldfinch flying away over the coarse ragweed has a soul, and the ragweed too, plant by plant, and the tiny stones in the earth below, and the grains of earth as well. Not romantically do I believe this, nor poetically, nor emotionally, nor metaphorically . . . but steadily, lumpishly, absolutely."[17] Clearly, the only definition of a soul broad enough to suit her is the energy manifest in all entities.

Mary Oliver's ecological pantheism will remain merely an attractive theory, however, unless the enactment of her poetry can induce an actual transformation in how readers engage the world. As Ben Howard observes, Oliver is most inspired by "those numinous intersections of the self and the natural world, those meetings in the woods and by the ponds, which engender a sense of reverence and awe."[18] Howard's choice of the word *intersections* suggests a much more immediate relationship between subject and object than we are accustomed to and thus clarifies the mystical nature of Oliver's project. But it also highlights the problem of trying to communicate such experiences. Because these "numinous intersections" are relational rather than objectified, only a poor caricature of the experience can be rendered in the clumsy building blocks of language. But poetry enables language to transcend objectification, Oliver insists, by creating "an arrangement of words in which an experience or an insight [waits] to be felt through, and I mean in an individual and personal way."[19] It is not so much the *words* of a poem that enact such experiences in the reader's mind but rather the constellation of emotions and implications that accrue to those words and flicker through the spaces between them. Language may be inherently imprecise because it depends on artificial objectification, but Oliver has no other means of sharing the news of her intersections with other presences in the ecological community.

Martin Buber carefully distinguishes between the two ways that humans perceive the world and their identity. "There is no I as such," Buber explains, only a sense of I in relation to those things which I am not.[20] Most of those things are perceived as objects, and Buber designates this as the I-It world. It is how we commonly order experience, and it emphasizes differences to distinguish this It from those Its (55). Language is both product and servant of the I-It world. But there is another way of experiencing that which I am not, and that is our unobjectified relation to another *presence.* To experience a You is to open oneself to a reciprocal engagement that does not require interpretation, for Buber explains that "nothing conceptual intervenes between I and You" (62). I-You moments produce the surges of deeply felt, precognitive responses that are poorly translated to specific labels in an I-It world. The feeling high behind one's sternum, for example, when one is overwhelmed by the presence of an intimate companion will simply not fit into the box tagged "love." Moreover, when we relate to a You it remains a presence only so long as we resist objectifying it; once we do, it is transformed into an object. Of course, we rely almost completely on distinctions between objects to make the most basic decisions necessary to survival, and therefore we must spend most of our lives in an I-It world. Indeed, Buber admits that "without It a human being cannot live. But," he adds, "whoever lives only with that is not human" (85).

Despite the fact that language necessarily diminishes presences to objects, Oliver clearly believes that poetry can call attention to the fact that we dwell in a world of presences. Indeed, encouraging such intimacy with the world is the central project of her poetry, as she demonstrates most succinctly in "Spring": "There is only one question: / how to love this world."[21] The question is not how to *know* this world as thoroughly as possible, although as a fine naturalist she encourages this kind of familiarity as well. Even the most extensive knowledge, however, merely locks the object of study in a more elaborate cage, whereas love suggests the resistance of objectification. Her careful attention to her subjects is informed by the kind of innocence that Annie Dillard describes as "the spirit's unself-conscious state at any moment of pure devotion to any object."[22] Oliver's devotion leads her from observation of an object to the recognition of intersection with another presence; the trick, of course, is reenacting such an experience in the reader.

As Diane Bonds observes, "Oliver's 'mystical' explorations are always firmly located in the materiality of nature."[23] A typical Oliver poem begins with a narrow perceptual focus that frames an animal, a plant, or a portion of landscape. The speaker's precision of attention leads the reader along a well-worn transcendentalist path from direct observation toward revelation and an enhanced recontextualization. However, because the language of an I-It world cannot hope to capture that mystical moment when object dissolves into presence, Oliver relies on the space between objectified attention and a retrospective reflection to suggest what has transpired. There is a necessary leap, but by leading up to the moment of departure and then revealing where the experience has led the speaker, Oliver leaves open a space for presence to occur. As readers detect a consistency in the direction of these leaps from poem to poem, the current deepens the channel and so invites future streams of imagination to flow that way.

"The Ponds," from *House of Light*, provides a fine example of the epiphanic leap from specific observation to metaphysical speculation, as the speaker considers the various imperfections of lily pads that look so perfect from a distance. Even as Oliver introduces the possibility of perfect lilies in the opening lines, she dangles from the stanza break a prescient threat to this illusion:

> Every year
> the lilies
> are so perfect
> I can hardly believe
>
> their lapped light crowding
> the black,
> mid-summer ponds.[24]

Oliver frequently employs a rhetorical question to announce a shift in tone and focus, and in this case she dismisses the possibility of flawlessness by asking, "But what in this world / is perfect?" (58). Closer investigation of the lilies reveals that "one is clearly lopsided," another "wears an orange blight," and still another "is a slumped purse / full of its own / unstoppable decay" (58). As the precision of observation dismantles the illusion of perfection, the corrections to the picture grow increasingly tragic—from mere asymmetry to disease and finally to the certainty of death.

It is at this point in the poem that direct observation ceases and reflection begins. What is the speaker—or the reader—to adduce from this recognition that an apparently perfect scene of white flowers afloat on a pond is actually a vivid portrait of imperfection and a reminder of mortality? The adverb announcing the transition from observation to reflection affirms a resilient hope:

> Still, what I want in my life
> Is to be willing

To be dazzled—
To cast aside the weight of facts

And maybe even
to float a little
above this difficult world.
I want to believe I am looking

Into the white fire of a great mystery.
I want to believe that imperfections are nothing—
That the light is everything—that it is more than the sum
Of each flawed blossom rising and fading. And I do. (59)

Oliver stretches the lines out as the speaker moves deeper into reflection, leaving behind the "short, pulsing lines" that John Elder suggests keep observation so strictly focused.[25] It is clearly "the weight of facts" that prevents the speaker from floating "above this difficult world," and her desire to dispense with them may seem escapist if read carelessly. But this confession is not a denial of life's difficulties; it is an embrace of an expanded context within which the careful distinctions of the I-It world carry less weight. The "white fire of a great mystery"—that energy that fuels and finishes each of its individual manifestations—does not hide or abolish the imperfections, but it diminishes them by being "more than the sum / of each flawed blossom rising and fading." This vision of wholeness beyond "the weight of facts" is accessible to her through the act of belief, as she underscores in her final clause. The desire and, finally, the ability to believe respond to the earlier confession, "I can hardly believe," but the speaker's repetition of what she *wants* defines belief as a choice. This choice is essential to Oliver's poetic vision.

In a postmodern age we have more freedom than ever to determine how we will interpret our perceptions of the world, so long as our subject positions remain consistent with what we *believe* to be true. Indeed, a postmodern perspective insists that it is grounded in a culturally influenced set of beliefs—not in facts. Of course, over time beliefs have a way of petrifying into something that looks very much like fact, and thus Diana Fuss warns that "we need both to theorize essentialist spaces from which to speak and, simultaneously, to deconstruct these spaces to keep them from solidifying."[26] We must never forget that they are contingent, designed with a specific purpose in mind. As Janet McNew demonstrates, Oliver strategically constructs a subjectivity in her poems that denies any essential "separation from a world of objects"[27]—a clearly postmodern project undertaken to correct the destructive illusion of human independence from ecosystems. This revised subjectivity is perhaps most evident in "Sleeping in the Forest," which opens *Twelve Moons.*

The poem begins by announcing the speaker's belief that she has recovered a lost intimacy with the earth:

> I thought the earth
> remembered me, she
> took me back so tenderly, arranging
> her dark skirts.[28]

The personification of the earth as feminine is not without its problems, as many critics and historians have been quick to point out.[29] But in Oliver's poem it pushes the emotional quality of this event far beyond just another reunion; the implicitly maternal quality of the earth identifies this as the most fundamental of homecomings. It is the lap of the mother that welcomes the speaker.

> I slept
> as never before, a stone
> on a riverbed, nothing
> between me and the white fire of the stars
> but my thoughts, and they floated
> light as moths among the branches
> of the perfect trees.[30]

Oliver's description of the stars mirrors "the white fire of a great mystery" that is the sum of all parts in "The Ponds."[31] Because there is nothing between the speaker and this white fire but her thoughts, Oliver suggests how human cognition tends to obscure our integration in the comprehensive web of energy. Her decision to represent these thoughts as "light as moths" emphasizes their basic insubstantiality, and at the same time the linear proximity of the images of moths and white fire suggests an inevitable subsumption of the self into the mystery—the collapse of individual identity into the consuming and regenerative wholeness.

Furthermore, the analogy of "a stone / on a riverbed" plays off its line break to add an unexpected dimension to the cliché of sleeping like a rock. A stone in a river channel both shapes the current and is shaped by the current, suggesting that a similar process occurs as the universal energy flows through each conduit. The more obvious reading of the phrase is not viable, for although the speaker sleeps "as never before," her sleep is not at all restful:

> All night
> I rose and fell, as if in water, grappling
> with a luminous doom. By morning
> I had vanished at least a dozen times
> into something better.[32]

If the stars above the speaker do indeed represent the dynamic, reintegrative source of all being, then the significance of "luminous doom" on a night where no moon is mentioned becomes clear. The white fire is her destiny, ultimately and immediately. It is especially important to note that the speaker's process of "grappling / with a luminous doom" is directly responsible for the rising and falling that allows her to vanish "into something better." Her "movement is earthward and toward immersion in a forest floor that so engulfs her that she feels 'as if in water,'" McNew observes; indeed, the speaker's transformation is precisely "the opposite of transcendence," leading to "a visionary dissolution of her human identity."[33] This dissolution should not be mistaken for the attainment of a sustained selflessness, though. Rather, the speaker's dismantling of an essentialized self precedes a strategic reconstruction of subjectivity built on an expanded identity. The poem succinctly and powerfully demonstrates the recontextualization that occurs when the speaker casts off her assumed identity, vanishing again and again into "something better" than an unsustainable illusion of individuality.

Strategically constructing a subject position based on ecological interdependence will obviously influence how we see the world and how we engage it. Oliver demonstrates how such a construction can empower us in her poem, "The Swan," from *House of Light.* After an evocative rendering of the swan as

> a slim
> and delicate
>
> ship, filled
> with white flowers,

the trajectory of the speaker's leap from objectification past presence is indicated by her recollection of a remark by William Blake's wife: "I miss my husband's company— / he is so often / in paradise."[34] As the swan approaches—

and continues to approach, even as the poem ends—the exquisite pleasure of anticipation overwhelms the speaker, convincing her that paradise is as available to her as it was to Blake:

Of course! The path to heaven

doesn't lie down in flat miles.
It's in the imagination
With which you perceive
This world,

And the gestures
With which you honor it. (17)

In a postmodern world, where the guiding cosmological narrative has been stripped of the old idea of eternal reward, Oliver seizes on the capacity of the imagination to create a paradise here on earth—if only we can learn to love this dynamic tangle of energy in all its manifestations.

Her insistence that the earth can be a paradise, however, deserving of a love we can best demonstrate through the joy of unmediated engagement, never denies the existence of pain or the necessity of death. In "Poppies," from *New and Selected Poems,* Oliver juxtaposes the bright yellow "roughage" that "shines like a miracle / as it floats above everything" with the "cold, // black, curved blade . . . hooking forward," admitting that "loss is the great lesson."[35] Even though the term *roughage* implies the certain ingestion of these fulgent flowers back into the earth, Oliver uses the brief brilliance of these flowers to propose that

happiness
when it's done right,
is a kind of holiness,
palpable and redemptive. (39–40)

The explicitly religious diction of these lines suggests the possibility of finding salvation in this life, saved from *sin* in its New Testament sense of "a separation or missing of the mark."[36] Oliver's example offers salvation from the belief that we are divided from this world, salvation from despair in the face of mortality. The poem closes in ecstatic defiance—not of death but of despair:

I am washed and washed
in the river
of earthly delight—

and what are you going to do—
what can you do
about it—
deep, blue night?[37]

This baptism recuperates the adjective in "the river / of earthly delight" from the pejorative taint it acquires when opposed to a heavenly alternative. Oliver denies this opposition by revealing heaven to be a particular way of engaging the earth.

As attractive as such an attitude may be, it may appear to overlook the pain and suffering that are a part of life on earth. However, these elements are very much a part of Oliver's vision, for as John Elder notes, "There is no place for sentimental love or simple affirmation in a world like ours."[38] Throughout Oliver's poetry violent death waits as the owl in every tree or as the snapping turtle beneath the calm face of the pond. But Oliver's predators are never evil, no matter how much readers may cringe at the terrible pain of the rabbit crumpling in the beak of an owl. Oliver clarifies her attitude toward such violence in her essay "Owls":

> In the night, when the owl is less than exquisitely swift and perfect, the scream of the rabbit is terrible. But the scream of the owl, which is not of pain and hopelessness and the fear of being plucked out of the world, but of the sheer, rollicking glory of the death-bringer, is more terrible still. When I hear it resounding through the woods, and then the five black pellets of its song dropping like stones into the air, I know I am standing at the edge of the mystery, in which terror is naturally and abundantly part of life. . . . The world where the owl is endlessly hungry and endlessly on the hunt is the world in which I live too. There is only one world.[39]

The closing sentence of this passage recalls Oliver's only question: "How to love this world."[40] So how does one love a world such as this? For Oliver the answer involves recognizing that even an owl is acting out of love. The predator and the prey are driven by the same force, as Oliver demonstrates in "Gannets," where she writes that "nothing in this world moves / but as a positive power," and even those fish that feed the gannets "are only interrupted from their own pursuit / of whatever it is / that fills their bellies."[41] Observing the violence in Oliver's poems, John Elder recognizes that she "is drawn to such moments not simply because of a desire to present the whole picture honestly, but also because in the predator's single-mindedness she recognizes a special purity of concentration and intention."[42] Oliver consistently figures this degree of intentionality as "love": not only is it what the anteater feels for "her children," but "perfect love" is also attributed to the black bear "coming / down the mountain, / breathing and tasting."[43]

Oliver most clearly identifies such "purity of concentration and intention" as an act of love in "Writing Poems," from *House of Light*. Here Oliver uses the conceit of bees emerging pollen-dusted from "the frills of a flower" to describe the way that poets share their engagement with the world.[44] The intensity with which the bees are drawn to the instant beauty of new rhododendron blooms leads the speaker to ask, "Is there anything more important / than hunger and happiness?" (29). Although she admits not knowing "if the bees know that otherwise death / is everywhere," she watches them go about their business "with no small amount of desperation—you might say: love" (29). Oliver's unexpected reinterpretation of desperation reveals *love* to mean giving oneself over completely to the business of living, and throughout her poetry bees exemplify this attitude. In "May," for example, from *American Primitive*, the speaker observes the bees as they dive into moccasin flowers:

> Mute and meek, yet theirs
> the deepest certainty that this existence too—
> this sense of wellbeing, this flourishing
> of the physical body—rides
> near the hub of the miracle that everything
> is a part of, is as good
> as a poem or a prayer, can also make
> luminous any dark place on earth.[45]

Oliver's choice of imagery here recalls Whitman's own emphasis on the holiness of physical forms in "Song of Myself," where he proclaims that "there is no object so soft but it makes a hub for the wheel'd universe."[46] The power embodied in the bees' devoted intention to flourish is clearly a holy act for Oliver, and by comparing it to "a poem or a prayer" she identifies precisely how this power functions among humans. Although poems enact new possibilities of how we might make sense of our experiences, prayers more confidently shape our patterns of interpretation through the agency of belief. Both poems and prayers, then, illuminate the dark places by readjusting our orderings of perception. Thus Oliver, like Wordsworth, reminds us of our power to half-create the lives we experience. We can choose to dwell in paradise if we are willing to reconstruct the way we see ourselves and our world, for as we have seen in "The Swan," heaven is always accessible through

> the imagination
> with which you perceive this world,
>
> and the gestures
> with which you honor it.[47]

But as members of a culture that has cushioned itself so effectively from the struggle to survive, how are we to enact such a love, such purity of intention? Oliver shows that by opening ourselves to the presence of others, we may follow our threads of connection back toward the fundamental integration that is our larger self. She demonstrates this process in her account of a meeting with two deer in "Five A.M. in the Pinewoods," which she identifies as "a poem about the world / that is ours, or could be."[48] In structure and theme the poem closely resembles "A Blessing," written by Oliver's mentor, James Wright (to whose memory she dedicated *American Primitive*). Wright's title would fit equally well atop Oliver's poem, for both describe incidents in which the speakers are able to transcend the illusion of separation by opening themselves to the animal presence. In Wright's poem it is a pair of ponies that "come gladly out of the willows" to the speaker.[49] "I would like to hold the slenderer one in my arms," he writes, "For she has walked over to me / And nuzzled my left hand" (135). Oliver's poem features a pair of deer that the speaker has observed

> walking
> like two mute
> and beautiful women toward
> the deeper woods.[50]

She waits for them in the dark before dawn, and when they approach her "one of them—I swear it!—// would have come to my arms" if not warned away by the other (32–33).

The closest and most significant parallel between the poems is found in their conclusions. Warmed by the intimacy he feels while caressing the pony's ear, which is "as delicate as the skin over a girl's wrist," Wright's speaker suddenly realizes that "if I stepped out of my body I would break / Into blossom."[51] This burst of reflection on a vivid moment of intersection with another presence evokes both the opportunity and the fear that accompany such pure engagement. Breaking into blossom may have marvelous connotations, but one must relinquish the comforting belief in a closed identity to achieve this. The speaker's self-conscious reflection suggests that he has caught himself in time, although the abbreviated length of the final line does encourage the possibility that he has let himself go and that his absence has cut short the poem. The closing lines of Oliver's poem offer a more controlled—but hardly less ecstatic—version of the same sense of pure engagement. The deer have already vanished, so the speaker's observation has given over to reflection by the time she confesses thinking: "so this is how you swim inward, / so this is how you flow outward, / so this is how you pray."[52] The motion inward is depicted as more strenuous because it demands an opening of the self, a willing permeability to other presences. Once this relationship has been established, however, the flow outward is as easy as exhalation. Oliver's identification of this encounter as a prayer suggests how opening oneself to presences shapes the way we see and experience the world, enabling our admission into the paradise of complete inclusion.

Being fully present in a world of presences is the most spiritual of acts to Oliver. It is also an utterly practical act because of our urgent need to develop sustainable ways of imagining the human role on the earth. Ecology provides a model that allows us to expand our circles of identity, so perhaps at last we may assume accountability for our actions. Poems like Oliver's are rituals to help us enact this expansion. "We need those orderings of thought," she explains, "proclaiming our sameness."[53] The importance of this evolution of consciousness cannot easily be overstated. But Oliver's poetic vision offers more than just a path to ecological inclusion. It gives us permission to choose happiness in our lives. For even in the most miserable of lives, Oliver promises,

> there is still
> somewhere deep within you
> a beast shouting that the earth
> is exactly what it wanted.[54]

Of course, neither relinquishing the security of belief in an enduring, distinct identity nor embracing the promise of individual mortality is easy. Indeed, to creatures whose attitudes have been shaped by a long succession of stories deeply invested in emphasizing our essential distinction from a material earth, loving it can seem positively unnatural. But Oliver's answer to the only question is to show that when we defeat a way of seeing that leaves us frightened in our separation, we can begin to live more fully. Thus we find the speaker of "Starfish" challenging herself to engage even those aspects of the earth that repulse her. In the end, as the speaker's fear begins to fade, Oliver invites us to join her,

> reaching
> into the darkness, learning
> little by little to love
> our only world.[55]

Notes

1. SueEllen Campbell considers some intersections of ecology and poststructuralist literary theory in "The Land and Language of Desire: Where Deep Ecology and Post-Structuralism Meet," in *Western American Literature* 24, no. 3 (November 1989): 199–211.

2. Donald Worster, *Nature's Economy: The Roots of Ecology* (Garden City, N.Y.: Anchor Books, 1979), 297, 302.

3. Ibid., 303–307.

4. J. Baird Callicott, "The Metaphysical Implications of Ecology," in *Companion to "A Sand County Almanac": Interpretive and Critical Essays, ed. J Baird Callicott* (Madison: University of Wisconsin Press, 1987), 109.

5. Joanna Macy, "The Greening of the Self," in *Dharma Gaia: A Harvest of Essays in Buddhism and Ecology,* ed. Allen Hunt Badiner (Berkeley: Parallax Press, 1990), 53.

6. Anthony Mansousos, "Mary Oliver," in *Dictionary of Literary Biography: American Poets since World War II,* ed. Donald J. Greiner (Detroit: Gale Research, 1980), 114.

7. Mary Oliver, *New and Selected Poems* (Boston: Beacon Press, 1992), 93.

8. Ibid., 29, 195.

9. Penelope and Charles ReVelle, *The Environment: Issues and Choices for Society,* 3rd ed. (Boston: Jones and Bartlett Publishers, 1988), 728.

10. Mary Oliver, *American Primitive* (Boston: Atlantic Monthly Press, 1983), 44.

11. Gary Snyder, *Turtle Island* (New York: New Dimensions, 1974), 84.

12. Jean Alford, "The Poetry of Mary Oliver: Modern Renewal through Mortal Acceptance," in *Pembroke Magazine* 20 (1988): 286.

13. Mary Oliver, *Twelve Moons* (Boston: Little, Brown, 1979), 46.

14. Mary Oliver, *House of Light* (Boston: Beacon Press, 1990), 1.

15. David Barber, review of *House of Light,* by Mary Oliver, *Kenyon Review* 13, no. 1 (winter 1991): 235.

16. Oliver, *House of Light,* 1.

17. Mary Oliver, *Winter Hours* (Boston: Houghton Mifflin, 1999), 107–108.

18. Ben Howard, "World and Spirit, Body and Soul," in *Poetry* 158, no. 6 (September 1991): 343.

19. Mary Oliver, *Blue Pastures* (New York: Harcourt Brace, 1995), 108.

20. Martin Buber, *I and Thou,* trans. Walter Kaufman (New York: Scribner's, 1970), 54.

21. Oliver, *House of Light,* 6.

22. Annie Dillard, *Pilgrim at Tinker Creek* (New York: Harper's Magazine Press, 1974), 82.

23. Diane S. Bonds, "The Language of Nature in the Poetry of Mary Oliver," in *Women's Studies: An Interdisciplinary Journal* 21, no. 1 (1992): 7.

24. Oliver, *House of Light,* 58.

25. John Elder, *Imagining the Earth: Poetry and the Vision of Nature,* 2nd ed. (Athens: University of Georgia Press, 1996), 221.

26. Diana Fuss, *Essentially Speaking: Feminism, Nature, and Difference* (New York: Routledge, 1989), 118.

27. Janet McNew, "Mary Oliver and the Tradition of Romantic Nature Poetry," in *Contemporary Literature* 30, no. 1 (spring 1989): 72.

28. Oliver, *Twelve Moons,* 3.

29. The discussion effectively begins with Annette Kolodny's *The Lay of the Land: Fantasy and Experience of the American Frontiers, 1630–1860* (Chapel Hill: University of North Carolina Press, 1984). It is continued in a more explicit context of environmental philosophy in Patrick Murphy's *Literature, Nature, and Other: Ecofeminist Critiques* (Albany: SUNY Press, 1995). Louise Westling provides the broadest literary and historical context in the opening chapter of *The Green Breast of the New World: Landscape, Gender, and American Fiction* (Athens: University of Georgia Press, 1996).

30. Oliver, *Twelve Moons,* 3.

31. Oliver, *House of Light,* 59.

32. Oliver, *Twelve Moons,* 3.

33. McNew, 62.

34. Oliver, *House of Light,* 16–17.

35. Oliver, *New and Selected Poems,* 39–40.

36. Elder, 224.

37. Oliver, *New and Selected Poems,* 40.

38. Elder, 220.

39. Oliver, *Blue Pastures*, 20.

40. Oliver, *House of Light*, 6.

41. Oliver, *New and Selected Poems*, 28.

42. Elder, 220.

43. Oliver, *House of Light*, 1, 7.

44. Ibid., 29.

45. Oliver, *American Primitive*, 53.

46. Walt Whitman, *Leaves of Grass*, ed. Sculley Bradley and Harold Blodgett (New York: Norton, 1973), 86.

47. Oliver, *House of Light*, 17.

48. Ibid., 32.

49. James Wright, *Collected Poems* (Middletown, Conn.: Wesleyan University Press, 1971), 135.

50. Oliver, *House of Light*, 32.

51. Wright, *Collected Poems*, 135.

52. Oliver, *House of Light*, 33.

53. Mary Oliver, "The Place of Poetry: Symposium Responses," *Georgia Review* 35, no. 4 (winter 1981): 733.

54. Mary Oliver, *Dream Work* (New York: Atlantic Monthly Press, 1986), 7.

55. Ibid., 37.

Jeffrey Thomson

"Everything Blooming Bows Down in the Rain"

Nature and the Work of Mourning in the Contemporary Elegy

The elegy traditionally moves from grief to reconciliation, from loss to consolation. The poet, writing an elegy, and the reader, vicariously participating in that act, receive a kind of solace—a replacement figure—in the form of a linguistic structure that substitutes for the dead, and nature is the traditional ground from which that replacement figure is drawn. When Milton turns Lycidas into "the Genius of the shore," or when Whitman articulates a vision of that "great star" drooping in the West in "When Lilacs Last in the Dooryard Bloom'd," they are engaging in the "work of mourning." Each learns to "*represent absence* . . . by the means of a substitutive figure." So argues Peter Sacks in *The English Elegy.*[1] In both of the previous examples the poet returns the beloved dead to nature, and this new, "natural" position allows the dead in return to offer the poet and reader solace for their deaths. The replacement figure overcomes death as the poet places him or her along the shore or in the sky watching over the world, delivering it from its attendant grief.

In the twentieth century, an age of skepticism and science, such consolation rang perilously false. Most twentieth-century elegies resist consolation; they turn away from nature and its possibilities for solace. Consider Elizabeth Bishop's "One Art," her elegy for Lota Soares, her longtime companion and lover. Bishop suggests, at the end of the poem's recitation of absence and loss, that the forfeiture of nature—"two realms I owned, two rivers, a continent"—isn't a disaster. The loss of a beloved environment, her home in the cliff city, Persepolis, Brazil, the surrounding rivers and beneficent rainforest, is derided as inconsequential. It is the human loss that tears through the surface of the poem, forcing Bishop (unsuccessfully one might argue) to reassert her self-control over her grief:

> Even losing you (the joking voice, a gesture
> I love) I shan't have lied. It's evident

> The art of losing isn't too hard to master
> Though it may look like *(Write it!)* like disaster.[2]

There is no consolation here, even as Bishop looks for something to abet her loss. Bishop tries to assert poetic control over her loss, yet it explodes out of the poem as if in a choking sob. The stuttering repetition of the final simile surrounding the strident parenthetical command (or rebuke—it can be read either way) suggests the depth of the human grief and the difficulty of covering it over so simply. As Jahan Ramazani writes in *The Poetry of Mourning:*

> At its best, the modern elegy offers not a guide to "successful mourning" but a spur to rethinking the vexed experience of grief in the modern world. We should turn to it expecting not so much solace as fractured speech, not so much answers as memorable puzzlings. Anything simpler or easier would betray the moral doubts, metaphysical skepticisms, and emotional tangles that beset the modern experience of mourning and self-conscious efforts to render it.[3]

Bishop's efforts to contain and control her grief fail because, in modern terms, they must; we wouldn't believe her otherwise. As in many contemporary elegies, Bishop's use of nature becomes a backdrop for the more serious human suffering. Nature exists not as participant or attendant muse to support the poet in mourning. It is shoved aside, a mere pittance in the face of true grief.[4]

The problem with these views of the elegy is that, although they accurately depict the situation presented by many poets, they close the door to others. Once one limits the elegy to these two patterns, one is presented with a false dialectic—either one must elevate nature (and the dead) above the living, putting them in a position to offer consolation to the grieving world, or one must refuse solace, refuse any comfort (and comfort from nature specifically) in the face of terrible, human loss. In this model there is no way to balance an all-too-powerful grief and a sense of natural salvation. I will argue that there is a third possibility—one that does not deny the potency of grief but still offers consolation, one that depends on a sense of correspondence with nature and the natural cycle rather than the veneration of it. Before we get to this third option, however, there is one critical hurdle that must be overcome.

As a matter of course in this new century, we distrust the traditional reunion with nature as a means of solace. The belief in the efficacy of the "replacement figure" has dwindled. Part of the difficulty in poetically connecting nature to grief lies in our unquestioning acceptance of the concept of the pathetic fallacy. Nature exists separately from us, the argument goes; we can know it only distantly and inconsequentially, and it certainly does not join us in our grief. To suggest otherwise is to risk foolishness and a kind of adolescent bathos.

Even when modern poets make use of the pathetic fallacy, argues Sidney Burris in the *Princeton Encyclopedia of Poetry and Poetics,* they do so ironically to emphasize "*the loss of communication between the individual and the natural world;* and in its implied envy of an older world where such communication once existed, it resurrects yet another remnant of its ancient origin, pastoral nostalgia."[5] This argument assumes that there is a separation between human beings and nature; it suggests as teleology that nature and culture simply do not (or at least no longer) mix. It seems that there is a basic, *functional* problem with this supposition. There is a primary and necessary division (post-Edenic?) that is assumed to lie between nature and human nature, one that cannot be taken for granted. In an aesthetic sense poetry works by arguing metaphorically—one thing *is* another; thus, poems demand a suppleness in the relationship between the poet and the world at large. It may not be true, to paraphrase Emerson, that nature wears the colors of the spirit, but it is certainly true that many contemporary poets (pathetic fallacy be damned) wear the colors of nature. Their observations of the natural world find those objects that most fit the emotional pattern of the poem and present them to the reader for immediate recognition—good poets do this intuitively; they find the connections that hide beneath our day-to-day consciousness and present them to the reader as something akin to memory.

Thus we arrive at the third option—a form of elegy that grieves deeply and fully and finds a commensurate consolation in nature but not in the form of a figured replacement. Poets such as Jane Kenyon and Mary Oliver make powerful use of nature and present the natural world as a participant in suffering, going so far as to unite the personal and the natural within metaphors of loss and sorrow. However, there is no sense in their work that nature replaces grief or even alleviates it in some way. In the recognition of the patterns and movement of nature their elegies turn away from the unsatisfied protests of most late elegists. For these poets nature is not simply the drapery of emotion; it is the very structure of emotional power.

For Kenyon and Oliver the work of mourning is a successful participation in nature. They connect death and loss to natural systems and images, providing a stance from which to engage in emotion and death. A poem like Kenyon's "Heavy Summer Rain" is a tender suggestion of nature's sympathy with grief. The poem begins: "The grasses in the field have toppled, / and in places it seems that a large, now / absent, animal must have passed in the night."[6] Immediately, Kenyon presents the natural world. This elegy doesn't start with death but rather with fecundity and disarray. The grasses are plastered down by the weight of the night's rain, and, in the midst of this pastoral scene, there lies a looming sense of loss—the "large . . . animal" that "must have passed in the night." Her play on *passed*—the word connotes both passing by and passing on, movement through and death—and the assertive *must* suggests that the poem's natural world is already complicit with the loss that will follow.

The poem turns quickly, however: "The hay will right itself if the day // turns dry. I miss you steadily, painfully" (42). The regeneration of the field belies the loss of the "you" of the poem, presumably Kenyon's father, who was diagnosed with cancer and is evoked earlier in the collection *Let Evening Come.* The grass will rise given sunlight; the absent dead will not, no matter what they are given. No longer will she hear

> your blustering entrances
> or exits, doors swinging wildly
> on their hinges, or your huge unconscious
> sighs when you read something sad,
> like Henry Adams's letters from Japan,
> where he traveled after Clover died. (42)

Here we are given the measure of the loss, that figure who stormed joyfully through houses, smacking doors open and, equally, found deep, emotional connections through language and reading. A kind of elegy within an elegy, Kenyon presents but doesn't deify the dead here. He is remembered in a rosy afterglow but certainly presented as something human.

The last stanza returns to the natural world, seemingly aware of the grief and sorrow that now dominate the poem. But this is no gesture of replacement—no angelic star hovering over the western sky or totemic spirit of the shore safeguarding sailors.

> Everything blooming bows down in the rain:
> white irises, red peonies; and the poppies
> with their black and secret centers
> lie shattered on the lawn. (42)

Nature in this poem, although suggesting a kind of homage to the dead—"everything bows down"—evokes the dark secret of human grief. The fact of cancer—our "black and secret center"—is that our own cells destroy us. Our natural bodies are complicit with our deaths. The black center of our lives, Kenyon argues, is what we carry with us every day. It is the heart of the flower shattered across the lawn; it is the absence in the field where something living has passed; it is the cancer that turns bodies inside out with pain.

Contrary to the traditions of elegy, Kenyon doesn't try to devalue this new awareness of the natural parity of grief by elevating it to an untouchable, natural grace. Neither does she refuse its undeniable presence. Instead, Kenyon's elegy turns the work of mourning outward to nature and addresses its complicity in both our grief and solace. Nature is why we die—our organic bodies turn against themselves or fail, simply shut off, overworked or damaged beyond repair—but also why we live. Life, the bloom of it, is what bows down in the dark rain, but it is the very fact of darkness that lets the light exist. So, as Kenyon suggests in another poem from the same collection, "If it is darkness / we are having let it be extravagant."[7] Death may blow down the grasses in the field; it may take your father's life and then your own, but such trials are the only way to know the light.

What one finds in Kenyon's elegies is neither that peculiar elevation of the dead in an attempt to replace the lost figure with a naturalistic pantheon nor the refusal of solace; she elegizes by meshing with the loss, by descending into it and finding its equivalent in the surrounding natural world. Nature in her poems is neither the backdrop for her deeper human grief nor her possible redemption. It is a partner in ruin, her equivalent foundation.

The elegiac mode in Mary Oliver's *American Primitive* is even more refined.[8] Human grief, distinct and personal, rarely enters into her equations at all. Nature and the natural world define both the path and function of the work of mourning. The tone of the collection is reverential—the poems become sacraments of the dark animal life within the human being and vice versa. Her elegies are barely elegies at all. From the bear-like "paws" and "happy tongue" gathering blackberries in "August," to the mushrooms that rise up like zombies from the soaked earth willing the people to follow them back beneath "the shining fields of rain," *American Primitive* celebrates the communal essence of the world (3–4). The human and the natural are far from separate in her work; their gestures blend and synchronize and finally seem to be nothing more than variations on a theme. Nature's death-into-life-into-death function finds its place in the human world, and the human domain of art and song is echoed in the dazzle and splash of humpbacks and white blossoms. It would seem that the very idea of elegy is entirely absent here. Almost, but not quite.

In poems like "University Hospital, Boston," the elegiac asserts itself. The poem describes a visit to a hospital "built before the Civil War," where a friend of the speaker (perhaps her father, as with Kenyon) lies slowly dying. The ghosts of the countless dead, victims of the century's many wars, linger in the rooms and hallways while the speaker and the dying man hold hands beneath the trees, pretending he is getting better. "I look into your eyes," she writes,

> which are sometimes green and sometimes gray,
> and sometimes full of humor, but often not,
> and tell myself you are better,
> because my life without you would be
> a place of parched and broken trees.[9]

The tension between this metaphor of the trees and the rest of the collection is striking. Rarely in Oliver's work is nature damaged or barren in this way. The loss of this poem's subject, she suggests, would break down the natural cycle, would deprive the speaker of the sense of luminous beauty that fills the rest of the collection. Until this poem death has been a kind of gossamer absence or a tender joining. Here, specific human grief enters and demands recognition. Nature cannot heal this, Oliver seems to say.

This tension kindles the elegiac motion of the collection. From this moment forward a much more palpable sense of loss and emotional clarity informs the poems. It is this human loss (although defined in very natural terms) that creates the need for elegy. Earlier poems, such as "Mushrooms" and the quasi elegy for the buffalo, "Ghosts," suggest a cycle of life-death-rebirth and do not acknowledge the terror of death and the loneliness of life. They are celebratory and full of rejuvenating power, but "University Hospital, Boston" demands a different kind of understanding. The emotional concentration of death, as well as the palpable history of it in the hospital, functions as a distinct counter to the gentle, natural cycle presented in earlier poems:

> Yesterday someone was here with a gasping face.
> Now, the bed is made all new,
> the machines have been rolled away. The silence
> continues, deep and neutral,
> as I stand there, loving you. (43)

This peculiar combination of modifiers, "deep and neutral," argues for both the seriousness of the human situation and the absence of empathy one finds in the world. This is our fate, she seems to say, to die anonymous and alone, gasping like fish for air. And the only thing we can do in the face of this stark and lonesome truth is to love.

This is what the hospital teaches, but what does the world teach? Strangely enough, it is the same lesson. Through "In Blackwater Woods," one of the last poems of the collection, Oliver combines the twin gestures of loss and rebirth and evokes the true work of her mourning. "Look," she says,

> the trees
> are turning
> their own bodies
> into pillars
>
> of light,
> are giving off the rich
> fragrance of cinnamon
> and fulfillment. (82)

In a fall season, the dying time of year, the trees exult in their own self-immolation as the human control of nature begins to disappear:

> every pond,
> no matter what its
> name is, is
>
> nameless now. (82)

The natural world is slipping away from the human; such linguistic absence is a "salvation, / whose meaning / none of us will ever know" (82). There is nothing to replace the vanishing world, no names to be given that will keep it by our side. The promise of solace is gone. But there is something to be learned—the comfort of this contemporary elegy—a trinity of meanings:

> To live in this world
> you must be able
> to do three things:
> to love what is mortal;
> to hold it

against your own bones knowing
your own life depends on it;
and when the time comes to let it go,
to let it go. (82)

The first two commandments are human ones; they suggest the patterns of elegy we have seen before: the love of the mortal and the refusal of solace. The third commandment is nature's, and it is the most important. To love and hold are human traits, but letting go, that is the heroic task. It is the difficult province of nature, and the work of mourning in Oliver's work is to master "letting go" through an intimate and personal connection with the natural world.

What the elegies of Jane Kenyon and Mary Oliver present is a third possibility for grief—one devoted not to a surrogate nature benevolently smiling on the human race nor to an implacable grief that resists healing and succor. Their elegies demand attention not because they try to avoid sorrow but because they recognize in sorrow part of the pattern of the natural world. This elegiac work offers a new flavor to the tradition, as Oliver says, "a taste / composed of everything lost, in which everything / lost is found" (57). In these elegies grief exists not to torment or so that rapture can transpire; loss exists so gain can follow.

Notes

1. Peter M. Sacks, *The English Elegy: Studies in the Genre from Spenser to Yeats* (Baltimore: Johns Hopkins University Press, 1985), 8, 11 (emphasis in original).

2. Elizabeth Bishop, *The Collected Poems of Elizabeth Bishop* (New York: Farrar, Straus, and Giroux, 1969), 178.

3. Jahan Ramazani, *The Poetry of Mourning: The Modern Elegy from Hardy to Heaney* (Chicago: University of Chicago Press, 1994), ix-x.

4. Elizabeth Bishop writes in a letter to Anny Baumann that one of the things she "didn't get into the villanelle that I feel I have also lost, and that I really regret most of all, is that I don't think I'll ever be able to go back to that beautiful island in Maine any more—this is too complicated to go into, but it really breaks my heart." In one sense lost nature exists only outside of the poem—it's impossible for her to even fit it in. *One Art: Letters Selected and Edited*, ed. Robert Giroux (New York: Noonday Press, 1994), 602.

5. Sidney Burris, "Pathetic Fallacy," in *The New Princeton Encyclopedia of Poetry and Poetics,* ed. Alex Preminger and T. V. F. Brogan (Princeton: Princeton University Press, 1993), 889 (italics mine).

6. Jane Kenyon, *Let Evening Come* (St. Paul, Minn.: Graywolf, 1990), 42.

7. Ibid., 13.

8. Mary Oliver, *American Primitive* (Boston: Little, Brown, 1983).

9. Ibid., 43.

Emily Hegarty

Genocide and Extinction in Linda Hogan's Ecopoetry

Linda Hogan, a Chickasaw poet and novelist, is one of the leading articulators of the theme of genocide, an "all-pervasive feature" of Native American poetry.[1] Hogan is also one of the most vital ecopoets writing today. This essay explores the ways in which Hogan connects the Native American experience of genocide with the contemporary threat of extinction posed by the destruction of the global environment.

Genocide is a fair word to use about the Native American experience in the United States. Estimates of the Native American population before European contact range from one million to forty-five million people. The 1890 U.S. census recorded the Native American population as only 250,000. Even doubling that figure to 500,000 to adjust for underreporting and using the lowest precontact figure of one million results in a halving of the Native American population under colonization. By 1990, Native Americans made up about 1 percent of the total American population and experienced poverty and its associated health problems at a rate more than twice the national average. Native Americans die of treatable diseases such as alcoholism, tuberculosis, and diabetes at a rate hundreds of times greater than the general population. During the 1970s the Indian Health Service sterilized many Native Americans without their informed consent. Estimates of the number sterilized range from 25 percent to 42 percent of Native American women and about 10 percent of Native American men.[2]

Hogan addresses these genocidal conditions throughout her work. Her 1995 novel *Solar Storms* opens with a "giveaway" ceremony to mark a woman's grief over a lost child. The ritual becomes symbolic of "all the children lost to us, taken away."[3] Native American "grief over the lost children" is part of the litany of international human-rights atrocities in Hogan's poem "Workday."[4] In another poem, "Folksong," Hogan compares Native American trail songs and Latvian *dainas* and suggests that the "folksongs" of exploited ethnic groups are in reality coded war songs, a way of disguising anger from the oppressor.[5] Hogan's internationalism reflects the holistic worldview of much Native American writing, in which the sufferings of all people are seen as related experiences. We see a similar synthesis of global oppressions in Creek poet Joy Harjo's homage to Audre Lorde in "Anchorage":

> who would believe
> the fantastic and terrible story of all of our survival
> those who were never meant
> to survive?[6]

Hogan pushes such comparisons further. She compares folk songs to birdsongs, suggesting that "the sweet songs of sparrows" are actually "blood feuds" in the birds' territorial disputes.[7] In this, "Folksong" emphasizes two concerns central to Hogan's work. The comparison of humans and birds indicates, as we shall see, the importance of connections across species boundaries.

The concept of the "blood feud" brings us to the question of the uses Hogan makes of racial memory. Hogan's poem "The Truth Is" describes the psychological turmoil of having a mixed racial heritage in a country with a history of genocide. In this frankly autobiographical poem ("Linda, girl, I keep telling you"),[8] Hogan writes of failed attempts to view mixed ethnic identity as a fruitful blend of differences, figured as "a tree, grafted branches / bearing two kinds of fruit": "It's not that way." Instead, the poet is preoccupied by concerns "about who loved who / and who killed who." She seeks "amnesty" rather than peace or forgiveness and not so much for the actual historical crimes as for remembering them.[9] The awareness of racial history becomes a terrible psychological burden. Doing justice to that awareness becomes an ethical problem for a writer committed, as Hogan is, to portraying all beings—even the oppressor and oppressed—as holistically interconnected. In this sense "The Truth Is" is reminiscent of Choctaw poet Jim Barnes's "A Season of Loss," also written in the first person, in which presumably assimilated and/or mixed-race Native Americans lament their disconnection from nature: "Our blood was now too thin to know / . . . our skin too pale." Their attempts to connect to nature are "frail" because their "fathers' blood pulsed slow," and they are left "[o]nly human."[10] The denigrating tone of *only* is complicated by the use of *human* as a category transcending racial difference. Like Hogan's, Barnes's poem belies its self-indictment of failure. Barnes's poetic invocation of nature implies that a connection remains, and Hogan's dramatized internal discourse suggests an interracial conversation containing the "truth" of the title.

The conundrum of "who loved who / and who killed who" is a particular concern of Hogan's. Much of her work focuses on various threats to Native

American reproduction. Her historical novel *Mean Spirit* is a narrative of the corruption, greed, and violence stirred by the discovery of oil on lands allotted to Osage people in Oklahoma. The resulting land rush comes in the form of white men seeking oil-rich Osage wives. Alongside the novel's evocation of government-sponsored exploitation is a poignant portrait of a community whose personal relations both within and between races have been tainted by suspicious motives: love or money? This theme of the problematics of Native American intermarriage has been at issue in American literature since John Rolfe married Pocahontas. In "The Truth Is" Hogan tellingly describes her left hand as a "Chickasaw hand," which "rests on the bone of the pelvis," while reassuring us (and herself?) that the white hand in her right pocket is "mine / and not some thief's."[11] Throughout her work we see Hogan worrying at the concept of preserving Native American genetic reproduction from those who would steal it, even though her holistic vision excludes any kind of separatism. At the end of *Mean Spirit* the protagonists of the Graycloud family have been driven from their home, which burns behind them. Many of their family members have been murdered. But their triumph lies in having preserved their lives. Because they "carried generations along with them," their genetic line has survived.[12]

Hogan's concern for genetic continuance has a specifically environmental component. One consequence of the current environmental crisis is that chemical poisons and radiation have compromised human reproductive health. The Conservation Foundation cites "industrial pollutants as contributors to rising infertility, clusters of birth defects, 'hot spots' of miscarriages, and the unusually early onset of menopause among some women."[13] It is now estimated that every human being under forty years old has some exposure, often beginning in the womb, to toxic chemicals that include hormonally active compounds.[14]

Although these are alarming figures for everyone, environmental racism exacerbates Native American concerns. Native American reservation lands, primarily Navajo, contain half of the known uranium deposits in the United States but well over half of the uranium mines. Since the 1960s, improperly disposed radioactive wastes from these mines have seriously contaminated Navajo and Lakota lands and water supplies. The contamination is increased by nearby nuclear missile sites and alleged nuclear waste dumping by the U.S. military, often on land held to be sacred. A radioactive accident on the Navajo reservation in New Mexico in 1978 caused greater contamination than Three Mile Island. The cancer rate for Navajo teenagers is seventeen times the national average. In Nevada there have been at least one thousand atomic explosions on Shoshone lands. Nor is all the contamination in the western deserts. In upstate New York a leaking Superfund site on reservation land has resulted in a 200 percent greater concentration of PCBs in the breast milk of Mohawk and Akwesasne women than in the general population.[15] In a 1985 interview Hogan said that "most Indian people are living the crisis of American life, the toxins of chemical waste, the pain of what is repressed in white Americans."[16]

Hogan describes this tainted landscape in her poem "The Other Side" as a wasteland of darkness, broken tree limbs, and dying cows. Telling puns condemn what few things grow: trees are "radiating" new leaves, and eggs grow "radiant" in nests. The title of the poem refers to "the other side of creation," which we can only assume is the atomic "sudden light" of destruction.[17] The blight of "The Other Side" is allegorized in "The Alchemists," which depicts the discovery of radioactive mercury as the "fool's gold" of deluded pseudoscientists. This scene of scientific folly is juxtaposed with the voice of a hospitalized father comparing the description of a surgical procedure to a poem. Hogan's voice rejects this comparison because if the surgeon's diagnostic speech "had worked / we would kneel down before it / and live forever."[18] For Hogan the doctor is just another alchemist, and the cancers of radiation poisoning are iatrogenic diseases. "The Alchemists" can be read alongside Adrienne Rich's 1974 poem "Power," which also compares medical and nuclear science. Rich laments the blindness of Marie Curie—both her literal blindness from radiation sickness and the emotional blindness that let her die "denying her wounds."[19] Like Rich, Hogan is determined to speak over the denial that allows physical and cultural destruction to go unchecked.

It is telling that "The Alchemists" appears in a collection titled *The Book of Medicines*. "The Alchemists" rejects the comparison of medical discourse and poetry because, for Hogan, it is poetry that is truly healing. In English's imperfect translation of Native American concepts, the term *medicine* refers to a practice that operates both physically and spiritually. One of the primary practices of healing medicine is the use of healing chants, which are poetic in that they are an arrangement of words with a supramundane meaning but are not strictly poems in the sense that they are not, or not only, art. They are formulae intended and expected to have an actual effect in the physical and spiritual worlds. The relationship between such efficacious and religious language practices as medicine chants and the Western concept of poetry is one of the main disputes in Native American literary studies. The issue is further complicated by troubling problems of translation and by the relation between oral tradition and contemporary theories of textuality.

Hogan has described poetry as "a form of divine utterance that moves us to action, that is action itself." She believes that "language contains the potential to restore us to a unity with earth and the rest of the universe."[20] Her novel *Mean Spirit* features a heroic gospel writer, Michael Horse, who adds a new gospel to the Bible, writing "for those who would come later, for the next generations and the next, as if the act of writing was itself part of divination and prophecy, an act of deliverance."[21] In "The Alchemists," and in her poetic practice generally, Hogan presents the holistic Native American view of language as affecting the world. This view of language as efficacious is shared at least implicitly by most ecopoets, who consider their work to have extraliterary connections to environmental movements. Many also consider ecopoetry a spiritual practice.

A particular spiritual aspect of Hogan's work is her use of poetry to lend a voice to her ancestors. In "All Winter," for example, she alludes to historical genocide when she remembers "how the white snow / swallowed those who came before me" but insists that the dead "sing from the earth. / This is what happened to the voices."[22] In "It Must Be" she describes herself as almost possessed by the ancestor spirits who live within her: "all the old women / who live in the young house of this body."[23] The poem directs its anger at the pathologists, doctors, and psychiatrists who view her haunted condition as a disease rather than as a spiritual condition. The speaker is ambivalent about the ancestors, who are as distressing as they are comforting, and the ambiguity of the title points to the confusion between diagnosis and fatedness. In this sense "It Must Be" echoes "The Alchemists" in its use of Native American spirituality to condemn medical discourses.

One of Hogan's most powerful ancestral poems is "Tear," which describes a genetic memory of the Chickasaws' forced removal to Oklahoma. The sorrowful march is described in detail, although the speaker admits not having been born then, being "only a restlessness inside a woman's body." At the end of the poem, she explains that her ancestors survived the march for her sake, and for the sake of her unborn children. Furthermore, both past and future generations are with her in the present: "The world behind them did not close. / The world before them is still open."[24] Here the technique of repetition common in Native American poetry and often associated with traditional chanting also suggests the replication of generations following generations in an unbroken line, using the medicine of poetry to weave together the generations ripped apart by genocidal history.

Some of Hogan's most environmental work unites the voices of past generations with the voices of the earth. "To Light" listens to the voices of "the great seas" that

have journeyed through the graveyards
of our loved ones,
turning in their graves
to carry the stories of life to air."[25]

"The Direction of Light" continues this theme of intergenerational connection, with each generation growing out of the bodies of the previous one: "Children grow inch by inch / like trees in a graveyard." Hogan implies that language, too, grows out of past speech: "let this word / overthrow the first."[26] In "The Other Voices" the voices of pine needles and night crawlers are indistinguishable from her own—"they are mine / and they are not mine"—but their testimony will not be silenced: "even police can't stop earth telling."[27] The speaking earth is a quintessentially environmental and Native American gesture. One example besides Hogan is Harjo's poem "For Alva Benson, and for Those Who Have Learned to Speak," in which generations of women hear and "speak for the ground" when they give birth.[28] By disclaiming any singular ownership of voice, Hogan, like Harjo, gains the consensus authority of a community of voices. The resulting chorus effect lends great power to her poetry.

Outside of Native American traditional knowledge, the speaking earth has been promoted by Gary Snyder as the ecopoetic concept of biomass. Biomass is an ecological concept that refers to biological information stored at the cellular level in both human and nonhuman nature. According to Snyder, taking biomass into account means "there is more information of a higher order of sophistication and complexity stored in a few square yards of forest than there is in all the libraries of mankind." This information is of a "different order": "It is the information of the universe we live in. It is the information that has been flowing for millions of years."[29] In an article on the ecopoetry of Snyder and Denise Levertov, Dorothy Nielson suggests that biomass is an environmental revision of the poetic conventions of lyric voice. Snyder's essay on biomass specifically cites Native American thought as an influence on his own. It is through concepts like biomass that Snyder and other ecopoets attempt to avoid the hazards of representation entailed in speaking for nature in their work. However, because for Snyder biomass tends to vocalize in the archetypal and "prehistoric" symbols of traditional Native American culture, the hazards of representation are reintroduced within the complex colonial context of speaking for indigenous peoples.[30] Leslie Marmon Silko and other Native American writers have upbraided Snyder and others on precisely these grounds.[31] In contrast to these conundrums, the Native American model of holistic interpenetration, in which the earth's voice, the spirit's voice, and the human's voice are always already interwoven, avoids representational hazards and focuses instead on being heard through the din of the dominant culture's materialist and hierarchical pronouncements.

Native American poetry's emphasis on ancestors leads to a concern with the passage of evolutionary time, a concern shared by much ecopoetry. For example, in his poem "Spreading Wings on Wind," Acoma Pueblo poet Simon Ortiz describes the western landscape as seen from an airplane's window. The sight of craters gives rise to a comparison between prehistoric meteors that crashed to the earth, causing mass extinction, and the arrival of Europeans in the West: "one day there was a big jolt, / flame, and then silence."[32] In Yaqui poet Anita Endrezze's "The Language of Fossils" Endrezze worries that her language will be extinct, merely a fossil curiosity for the future.[33] Hogan likewise inserts her own life into the monumental processes of evolution. Her poem "Partings" echoes Ortiz's planetary scale in comparing the separation between mother and daughter to the rupture of the continental divide or of the ancient break between the earth and its asteroid moon.[34] In "What's Living?" she describes her relationship with her daughter as so primal that it returns them to their prehistoric roots of "feathers and scales." The poem ends in an Ourobouros image of the snaky mother swallowing herself and her children in an endless cycle of rebirth.[35] "Crossings" compares two miscarriages and marks the common physical features of a whale fetus and a human fetus, emphasizing a common evolutionary ancestral connection.[36] Except for the poems celebrating the appearance of the next generation, most of these evolutionary tropes conjure images of extinction and death.

Describing Native Americans as "vanishing" or facing extinction is a classic trope in American literature. In Walt Whitman's "Yonnondio," "the aborigines" are "flitting by like clouds of ghosts, they pass and are gone in the twilight." Likewise, Whitman hints, "the cities, farms, factories" will also "fade" and be "utterly lost."[37] Such texts can be read as complicit in the national erasure of the continent's genocide because they substitute for the violence of colonization the seemingly scientific and impersonal process of evolution and extinction. Michael Hatt argues that the imagery of the "vanishing" Native American in American art is "an implicit consolidation of white power" in that the focus of such texts on extinction bespeaks "white history, white progress, white geographical expansion."[38] Even in invoking some frightening future (white) extinction, as Whitman does, such texts can work to portray white American identity as under siege and in need of protection not from the corporate polluters who really threaten it but from a demonized racial other.

Ecopoetry has made wide use of a variation of the "vanishing Indian" motif in the figure of the "ecological Indian." The "ecological Indian" is a contemporary version of the Noble Savage stereotype, which emphasizes the supposed inherent environmentalism of Native American peoples, thereby connecting Native Americans in an essentialist fashion to nature and connecting the genocide of Native Americans to the destruction of nature deplored by environmentalism. A typical example of the ecological Indian figure is found in Mary Oliver's poem "Tecumseh," in which she drinks from a polluted river in homage to the dead Shawnee chief and imagines that if he were to come again, we (white readers) would know him by his anger. Here the identification with Tecumseh is meant to suggest the death wish implicit in contemporary American society's acceptance of a polluted environment:

> Sometimes
>
> I would like to paint my body red and go out into
> the glittering snow
> to die.[39]

Native American writing eschews the "vanishing Indian" and "ecological Indian" stereotypes in favor of addressing the root causes of genocide, which are, given the holism of Native American thought, generally overlapping. Harjo, for instance, in the poem "Backwards," eerily envisions standing on a moon that is being butchered by a "whiteman" who throws the meat/moon/world to the dogs.[40] More important than condemning the evils of the past, however, is limning the evils of the present. In this sense Hogan's focus on the extinction of animals both marks her environmentalism and resists any kind of universalizing death wish. Hogan is a wildlife conservation activist and obviously sees the preservation of wildlife as part of the same project as preserving human life. Her most recent novel, *Power,* concerns the intertwined fates of the Native people of Florida and the endangered Florida panther.[41] In this intertwining sense her animal extinction poems foreshadow human extinction, but there is no hierarchy of value regarding who should be preserved—all humans and all animals are holistically interconnected.

In "Bees in Transit: Osage County" Hogan compares Osage women murdered for their oil-rich land to doomed bees that have escaped from hives being transported by truck. Both populations, having lost the protection of their hive or community, are bewildered, confused, and face "[d]esertion's sorrow" and "death cold." That the bees were being transported even suggests the sad history of forced Indian removals. The speaker feels their "compound eyes" looking at her and wishes she could either return them to their homes or deny their connection to her.[42] Another complex human/animal connection is found in "Mountain Lion," wherein the speaker recognizes in the endangered mountain lion's fear of humans her own fear of those who do not share her holistic worldview. Hogan interrogates the definitions of *wild* and, by implication, *civilized:*

> I was the wild thing
> she had learned to fear.
> Her power lived
> in a dream of my leaving.
> It was the same way
> I have looked so many times at others.

The speaker has no more hope of finding a world free of deadly "single vision" than the mountain lion has of finding a world free of humans. They share "the road / ghosts travel / . . . in the land of the terrible other." Ultimately, they turn away from the despair they recognize in each other.[43]

The analogy between Native Americans and endangered animals is repeated in "The Fallen," in which the speaker watches an asteroid fall and finds a pregnant wolf dead of starvation in a steel trap in an "eroded field." She contrasts the Native American and Western views of the wolf as symbol. For Native Americans the astronomical figure of the "Great Wolf" was the "mother of all women," but in Western cosmology the wolf "was the devil, falling / down an empty / shrinking universe." The wolf as Lucifer is connected to the guilt ("failings") of those who would kill the earth and each other. The speaker tries to throw the demonic asteroid back into the sky, but it drops back to the earth: "Sky would not take back / what it had done." Western astronomy, like the rest of the Western worldview, has become the dominant paradigm and even rules the sky, which looks down on "the swollen belly / and dried up nipples of a hungry world." Especially in wordplay on *failing* and *falling* Hogan implicitly criticizes the Christian cosmology that demonizes the earth and the material world. "The Fallen" concludes: "That night, / I saw the trapper's shadow / and it had four legs."[44] As in "Mountain Lion," the boundaries between human and animal and between hunter and hunted are unclear. The dangerous vision of "the trapper's shadow" links the fates of the speaker and the wolf. The emphasis on the visual properties of sight and shadow remind us of the dangerous "single vision" of "Mountain Lion." In her essay "Deify the Wolf" Hogan writes that "wolves carry much of the human shadow. . . . More than any other animal, they mirror back to us the predators we pretend not to be."[45]

The status of the Great Wolf as a maternal deity is significant to Hogan's environmentalism. The role of Native American maternal deities is not confined to biological reproduction. Instead these deities, such as Spider Grandmother and Thought Woman, govern all types of creation, even the destruction necessary for new creations. In many instances these deities bring forth life not biologically but through chanting and singing, methods that make their appearances especially resonant in poetry. Paula Gunn Allen emphasizes that the maternal role is in this sense one of great ritual power, not of mute biological fecundity.[46] In this sense, then, the pregnancy of the dead wolf suggests not only the deaths of future generations but also the destruction of the Native American world and cosmology. The poem is a likely allusion to an incident in South Dakota in which starving Nakota people were reduced to eating the poisoned animal carcasses used to bait wolf traps and died of strychnine poisoning.[47]

Hogan's critique has obvious commonalities with the environmental critique of Judeo-Christian traditions about the earth.[48] The title suggests a lost Eden, further critiquing the Western cosmology that could conceive of a paradise that must always already be lost, only to impose that punitive narrative on colonized territories. In this respect "The Fallen" might be compared to William Stafford's "Traveling through the Dark," wherein the speaker finds a dead but pregnant doe by the side of the road. Stafford also juxtaposes the pregnant carcass with images of Western expansion, specifically a slightly demonic automobile emitting glowing red exhaust. In pushing the doe's warm carcass off the highway, Stafford's speaker is concerned to prevent the traffic accidents that "might make more dead" and deliberates "for us all" about the value and quality of an orphaned fawn's life. There is no redemption in this famously ambivalent poem, and Stafford also critiques Western philosophy through his description of thought itself as a type of accident-prone "swerving."[49] Stafford and Hogan share an emphasis on the connections between the deaths of animals and of humans, as well as a sense that carelessness about the former bodes ill for the fate of humans on an earth that has become a shambles.

Hogan's sense of the power of this connection is apparent in "The Ritual Life of Animals," wherein humans internalize the predatory life of animals: "Something inside gets down on its haunches." This "world of animal law" is also "the house of pelvic truth."[50] It is not only the cruel history of genocide that has threatened genetic continuance but also the ongoing death-culture of contemporary American society. In many ways generational and genetic continuance and the transmission of cultural knowledge are Hogan's methodology, as well as her artistic motivation. Her writing is an effort to counteract the effects of physical and cultural genocide and an attempt to reproduce for future generations Native American culture and the viable environment with which it is entwined.

Notes

1. Paula Gunn Allen. *The Sacred Hoop: Recovering the Feminine in American Indian Tradition*, 2nd ed. (Boston: Beacon Press, 1992), 155–156.

2. Since the sterilizations ended, Native American reproductive health has improved, and Native Americans served by the federal Indian Health Service in 1993 had a birthrate 65 percent greater than the general population. The maternal mortality rate has dropped 86 percent since the 1970s, and the infant mortality rate has dropped 61 percent in the same period, although it is still 30 percent higher than the general population's. As of 1998 the Native American population had increased 14 percent since 1990, as compared to 8 percent for the general population during the same period, and the rate of increase is expected to continue through 2020 because of the young median age of Native Americans. Some analysts feel that the population increase is not entirely because of increased births but also because of differences in the methods used by the Census Bureau and an increased propensity for individuals to identify themselves as Native American. None of these population statistics include changes resulting from the federal recognition of "new" tribes, nor do they include populations of First Nation peoples in Canada. Overall, Native Americans continue to constitute only 1 percent of the U.S. population. These statistics and those in the text represent my own synthesis of several sources. See Allen, *Sacred Hoop*, 189. See also essays in *The State of Native America: Genocide, Colonization, and Resistance*, ed. M. Annette Jaimes (Boston: South End Press, 1992). Census information was taken from U.S. Department of Commerce, Census Bureau, "American Indian Heritage Month: November 1–30," press release, October 26, 1998 <http://www.census.gov/Press-Release/cb98ff13.html> (accessed February 24, 2001); and U.S. Department of Commerce, Census Bureau, *We the First Americans*, September 1993 <http://www.census.gov/apsd/wepeople/we-5.pdf> (accessed February 24, 2001); and U.S. Department of Health and Human Services, Indian Health Service, *Trends in Indian Health 1997* <http://www.ihs.gov/PublicInfo/Publications/trends97/tds97pt1.pdf> (accessed February 23, 2001). On the scandalously underreported topic of Indian Health Service

sterilizations see Charles R. England, "A Look at the Indian Health Service Policy of Sterilization, 1972–1976," *Red Ink* 3 (spring 1994). Available: *The People's Paths* <http://www.yvwiiusdinvnohii.net/articles/ihslook.htm> (accessed March 3, 2001).

3. Linda Hogan, *Solar Storms* (New York: Scribner, 1995), 17.

4. Linda Hogan, "Workday," in *Savings* (Minneapolis: Coffee House Press, 1988), 43.

5. Linda Hogan, *Seeing through the Sun* (Amherst: University of Massachusetts Press, 1985), 8.

6. Joy Harjo, *She Had Some Horses* (New York: Thunder's Mouth Press, 1983), 15.

7. Hogan, *Seeing through the Sun,* 8.

8. In an autobiographical sketch Linda Hogan writes: "My father is Chickasaw and my mother is white, from an immigrant Nebraska family. This created a natural tension that surfaces in my work and strengthens it." See the interview with Hogan in Laura Coltelli, *Winged Words: American Indian Writers Speak* (Lincoln: University of Nebraska Press, 1990), 71.

9. Linda Hogan, "The Truth Is," in *Seeing,* 4–5.

10. Jim Barnes, "A Season of Loss," in *Harper's Anthology of Twentieth Century Native American Poetry,* ed. Duane Niatum (San Francisco: Harper San Francisco, 1988), 61.

11. Hogan, "The Truth Is," 4.

12. Linda Hogan, *Mean Spirit* (New York: Atheneum, 1990; repr., New York: Ivy/Ballantine, 1992), 375 (page citations are to the reprint edition).

13. Lin Nelson, "The Place of Women in Polluted Places," in *Reweaving the World: The Emergence of Ecofeminism,* ed. Irene Diamond and Gloria Feman Orenstein (San Francisco: Sierra Club, 1990), 177.

14. John Peterson Myers, "Exposure Is Ubiquitous," *Our Stolen Future,* February 17, 2001 <http://www.osf-facts.org/NewScience/ubiquitous/ubiquitous.htm> (accessed February 23, 2001). The Web site continually updates the information presented in the original book *Our Stolen Future.* See Theo Colburn, Dianne Dumanoski, and John Peterson Myers, *Our Stolen Future: Are We Threatening Our Fertility, Intelligence, and Survival?* (New York: Dutton, 1996).

15. These statistics represent a synthesis of information from several sources. See Ward Churchill and Winona LaDuke, "Native North America: The Political Economy of Radioactive Colonization," in Jaimes, 241–266; Mindy Pennybacker, "The First Environmentalists," review of *All Our Relations: Native Struggles for Land and Life,* by Winona LaDuke, and three other books, *Nation,* February 7, 2000, 29. Available: Infotrac, A59680016 (March 3, 2001); Judith Todd, "On Common Ground: Native American and Feminist Spirituality Approaches in the Struggle to Save Mother Earth," in *The Politics of Women's Spirituality: Essays on the Rise of Spiritual Power within the Feminist*

Movement, ed. Charlene Spretnak (New York: Anchor-Doubleday, 1982), 430–445. Environmental menaces on Native American lands are so commonplace as to defy any comprehensive cataloging here.

16. Quoted in Coltelli, 75.

17. Linda Hogan, "The Other Side," in *Seeing,* 27.

18. Linda Hogan, *The Book of Medicines* (Minneapolis: Coffee House Press, 1991), 55–56.

19. Adrienne Rich, *The Fact of a Doorframe: Poems Selected and New, 1950–1984* (New York: Norton, 1984), 225.

20. Linda Hogan, "Who Puts Together," in *Studies in American Indian Literature: Critical Essays and Course Designs,* ed. Paula Gunn Allen (New York: MLA, 1983), 176–177.

21. Hogan, *Mean Spirit,* 341.

22. Linda Hogan, "All Winter," in *Savings,* 6.

23. Linda Hogan, "It Must Be," in *Savings,* 22.

24. Linda Hogan, "Tear," in *Book of Medicines,* 59–60.

25. Linda Hogan, "To Light," in *Seeing,* 35.

26. Linda Hogan, "The Direction of Light," in *Book of Medicines,* 79–80.

27. Linda Hogan, "The Other Voices," in *Savings,* 46.

28. Joy Harjo, "For Alva Benson, and for Those Who Have Learned to Speak," in *She Had Some Horses,* 18–19.

29. Gary Snyder, *Turtle Island* (New York: New Directions, 1974), 108.

30. Dorothy M. Nielson, "Prosopopoeia and the Ethics of Ecological Advocacy in the Poetry of Denise Levertov and Gary Snyder," *Contemporary Literature* 34 (winter 1993): 691–713.

31. See, e.g., Leslie Marmon Silko, "An Old-Time Indian Attack Conducted in Two Parts: Part One: Imitation 'Indian' Poems, Part Two: Gary Snyder's *Turtle Island,*" in *Nothing but the Truth: An Anthology of Native American Literature,* ed. John Purdy and James Ruppert (Upper Saddle River, N.J.: Prentice-Hall, 2001), 166–171; Wendy Rose, "The Great Pretenders: Further Reflections on White Shamanism," in Jaimes, 403–421; and Ward Churchill, *Fantasies of the Master Race: Literature, Cinema, and the Colonization of American Indians* (Monroe, Maine: Common Courage Press, 1992). Snyder is singled out in these critiques because he is the most prominent ecopoet. However, even his Native American critics acknowledge his respect, sensitivity, and poetic gifts. The Native American critique of literary colonialism extends far beyond Snyder.

32. Simon J. Ortiz, "Spreading Wings on Wind," in *Harper's Anthology of Twentieth Century Native American Poetry,* 141–142.

33. Anita Endrezze, "The Language of Fossils," in *Harper's Anthology of Twentieth Century Native American Poetry,* 320–322.

34. Linda Hogan, "Partings," in *Book of Medicines,* 71–72.

35. Linda Hogan, "What's Living?" in *Seeing,* 49.

36. Linda Hogan, "Crossings," in *Book of Medicines,* 28.

37. Walt Whitman, "Yonnondio," in *Leaves of Grass* (New York: Norton, 1973), 524.

38. Michael Hatt, "Ghost Dancing in the Salon: The Red Indian as a Sign of White Identity," *Diogenes* 177 (spring 1997): 93–121. Available: Infotrac, A19713133 (accessed February 24, 2001).

39. Mary Oliver, "Tecumseh," in *New and Selected Poems* (Boston: Beacon Press, 1992).

40. Joy Harjo, "Backwards," in *She Had Some Horses,* 20.

41. Linda Hogan, *Power* (New York: Norton, 1998).

42. Linda Hogan, "Bees in Transit: Osage County," in *Seeing,* 60.

43. Linda Hogan, "Mountain Lion," in *Book of Medicines,* 27.

44. Linda Hogan, "The Fallen," in *Book of Medicines,* 42–43.

45. Linda Hogan, *Dwellings: A Spiritual History of the Living World* (New York: Norton, 1995; repr., New York: Touchstone/Simon and Schuster, 1996), 71 (page citations are to the reprint edition).

46. Allen, *Sacred Hoop,* 14–15, 27–28.

47. Hogan, *Dwellings,* 68.

48. The classic environmentalist critique of Judeo-Christian cosmology is Lynn White Jr., "The Historical Roots of Our Ecologic Crisis," in *The Ecocriticism Reader: Landmarks in Literary Ecology,* ed. Cheryll Glotfelty and Harold Fromm (Athens: University of Georgia Press, 1996), 3–14. Other critiques are available in Diamond and Orenstein's *Reweaving the World.* It is also worth noting that there has been a Judeo-Christian response to this criticism. See, for example, Wendell Berry's essay "Christianity and the Survival of Creation," in *Sex, Economy, Freedom, and Community* (New York: Pantheon, 1992).

49. William Stafford, *The Way It Is: New and Selected Poems* (St. Paul, Minn.: Graywolf, 1998), 77.

50. Hogan, *Book of Medicines,* 45.

Expanding the *Boundaries*

Zhou Xiaojing

"The Redshifting Web"
Arthur Sze's Ecopoetics

In "The Redshifting Web," the title poem of his sixth book of poetry, Arthur Sze writes:

> The gold shimmer at the beginning of summer
> dissolves in a day. A fly mistakes a
> gold spider, the size of a pinhead, at the center
> of a glistening web. A morning mushroom
> knows nothing of twilight and dawn?
> . . . .
>   You may puzzle
> as to why a meson beam oscillates, or why
> galaxies appear to be simultaneously redshifting
> in all directions, but do you stop to sense
> death pulling and pulling from the center
> of the earth to the end of the string?[1]

These lines are characteristic of Sze's poems, in which familiar images of nature are mingled with those of metaphysics and quantum physics. By titling his sixth volume of poetry *The Redshifting Web,* Sze articulates a worldview that underlies his poetics. The term *redshift* describes the astronomical phenomenon that occurs when stars are moving away from us and the light emitted from them shifts toward the red end of the spectrum. In fact scientists have discovered that most galaxies appear to be "redshifted"; that is, nearly all galaxies are moving away from us and from one another. This indicates that the universe is not static; it is expanding. The distances among galaxies are increasing all the time.[2] Sze uses the term *redshift* to suggest his sense of the constant motion, change, and transformation of things in the universe and in our everyday experience. At the same time, all things in the universe and their constant changes, including those in the human world, are intricately connected, interacting with one another and mutually influencing each other's transformation. This concept of the world, based on the quantum principle, parallels the basic philosophy of Daoism and the Native American view of the universe.

Sze is familiar with all three frames of reference—natural sciences, Chinese culture, and Native American culture—and he absorbs them in his poetics, which might be called "ecopoetics."[3]

The term *ecopoetics* foregrounds the interconnectedness of all things in Sze's poetry, which embodies ecological concepts. This intricate relation of multiplicity and oneness is more than a theme in Sze's work; it shapes his aesthetics, particularly the structure of his poems. In this respect Sze's work is similar to what Leonard M. Scigaj calls "ecopoetry." In his book *Sustainable Poetry: Four American Ecopoets,* Scigaj contends that fostering a "sense of inhabitation and connectedness with planetary processes occurs in both the aesthetic and phenomenological dimensions of ecopoetry."[4] Not only have ecopoets broken away from the view of a subject-vs.-object relationship between human beings and nature, Scigaj notes, but they have also departed from the Western logocentric poetic tradition, which is limited by its dependence on the logic of linguistic systems for uttering experience and representing phenomena. Furthermore, Scigaj observes, "Ecopoets present nature in their poems as a separate and equal other in dialogues meant to include the referential world and offer exemplary models of biocentric perception and behavior" (11). Sze's poetry shares many characteristics with ecopoetry as Scigaj has defined it; however, nature in his poems is not "a separate and equal other," and the modes of perception or activities he represents are multicentric rather than "biocentric." The multiplicity in Sze's poetry entails cross-cultural experiences and multicultural activities that are part of the heterogeneous phenomena in the universe.

Take, for example, the title poem of Sze's fifth book of poetry, *Archipelago,* which interweaves East Asian and Pueblo Native American cultures into the fabric of its text saturated with nature. But these cultures are mobilized into actual experiences and events that are merged and set in motion with the natural world. According to Sze, the book was inspired by the Rock Garden at Ryoanji Temple in Kyoto, famous for its fifteen stones set in a sea of raked gravel. When he visited the garden in 1990, Sze was struck by the fact that as he walked back and forth along the walkway, he could not see all fifteen stones at the same time. "The stones are positioned into clusters and at such angles that the totality can never be seen at once."[5] The configuration of the stones resembles that of an archipelago, consisting of a cluster of apparently separate islands, which are in fact part of the same submarine land mass and of the earth's crust. Sze realized that he "could develop a book" by creating "a series of poems where each poem resembled a rock in a garden. Each poem or cluster of poems would have its unique configuration, but they would all be 'islands' and would fit into a larger whole. . . . The archipelago is thus 'the one and the many.'"[6] This concept is reflected in the content and structure of *Archipelago,* as its title poem illustrates.[7]

"Archipelago" consists of nine sections, each of which can be read as a separate poem, without any sequential narrative or rhetorical connections from one poem to another. Yet all the sections are linked in a way by two simultaneous but independent temporalities: the poet's persona walking in the Rock Garden at Ryoanji Temple and Pueblo women dancing in New Mexico. These two activities, particularly the Pueblo dance, also have the function of creating a sense of time passing, hence a sense of movement within the poem's synchronic structure of collage juxtaposition. Just as these two activities are represented as concurrent, so are the speaker's memories, reflections, and a range of phenomena:

> I walk along the length of a stone-and-gravel garden
> and feel without looking how the fifteen stones
> appear and disappear. I had not expected the space
> to be defined by a wall made of clay boiled in oil
> nor to see above a series of green cryptomeria
> pungent in spring. I stop and feel an April snow
> begin to fall on the stones and raked gravel and see
> how distance turns into abstraction desire and ordinary
> things: from the air, corn and soybean fields are
> a series of horizontal and vertical stripes of pure color:
> viridian, yellow ocher, raw sienna, sap green. I
> remember in Istanbul at the entrance to the Blue Mosque
> two parallel, extended lines of shoes humming at
> the threshold of paradise. . . .
> In the distance, I feel drumming
> and chanting and see a line of Pueblo women dancing
> with black-on-black jars on their heads; they lift
> the jars high then start to throw them to the ground.[8]

The gesture of Pueblo women smashing the objects with which they are dancing has a metaphorical meaning and effect that Sze attempts to materialize in his poem. According to Sze, this ceremonial dance is a real-life incident. It occurred in the San Ildefonso Pueblo, New Mexico, after alcohol-related violence broke out (one man was stabbed) following a wedding in a church. "The women of the pueblo felt so bad that they created black-on-black pots and invited the public to a ceremony where they raised the pots to the crowd and then threw them on the ground."[9] Sze explains that the "throw," which often occurs at the end of a dance, is meant to "connect the dancers to the public and the world at large."[10] In "Archipelago" Sze attempts to make connections between his poem and the reader, and between his art and the world, by constantly breaking the form and style in order to connect to the reader and the world.

The second section of the poem is a good example of this kind of break, or rather "throw." There is no narrative, no reflection, not even a single complete sentence in this section. Rather, the section is made up of fragmentary and heterogeneous images, which help produce multiple temporalities. At the same time, Sze's use of collage juxtaposition enables him to create space and a sense of distance that paradoxically suggest an underlying connection among these seemingly separate phenomena:

> Rope at ankle level,
> a walkway sprinkled with water
> under red and orange maples along a white-plastered wall;
>
> moss covering the irregular ground
> under propped-up weeping cherry trees;
>
> in a corral
> a woman is about to whisper and pat the roan's neck;
>
> an amber chasm inside a cello;
> . . . .
> a woman wearing a multicolored dress of silk-screened
> naked women
> about to peel an egg;
> three stones leading into a pond.[11]

Sze represents these varied, fractional images in such a way that they all seem to be caught in a moment of time, thus suggesting a simultaneity that enhances the invisible connections among them. At the same time, the collage juxtaposition and arrangement of single and multiple lines have the effect of giving equal importance to each phenomenon. Thus, human beings and their activities are only part of all things in motion in the universe, and the poet's presence does not claim centrality but, rather, recedes into the background.

Indeed, the poet's thoughts and feelings are merged with the surrounding world throughout the poem.

In addition to collage juxtaposition, Sze employs modes of simultaneity to achieve the effect of connecting the "I" to others and to blend the metaphysical with the material world. For instance, he uses the images of Pueblo ceremonial drumming, chanting, and dancing as a rhythmic device to punctuate the speaker's meditation and to indicate, as well as generate, changes in both the inner and outer worlds. In section 5 of "Archipelago," Sze interweaves the scene and movement of a Pueblo ceremonial dance with the speaker's experience and imagination, thus creating a simultaneity that links two spiritual journeys undertaken separately yet concomitantly, one communal, the other personal. Although the Pueblo ceremonial dance is taking place in its own location and at its own pace, it intersects the speaker's different spatial-temporal experience, stimulating his imagination and transforming his perception:

> Men dressed in cottonwood leaves dance
> in the curving motion of a green rattlesnake.
> I am walking along a sandstone trail
> and stop in a field of shards: here is a teal zigzag
> and there is a blood-red deer's breath arrow.
> Women dancers offer melons to the six directions
> then throw them to the ground. A wave
> rocks through the crow as the melons are smashed open.
> I know I have walked along a path lit
> By candles inside open-mesh cast-iron carp.
> . . . .
> As a cornmeal path becomes a path to the gods
> Then a cornmeal path again, I see the line
> of women dancing with black-on-black jars on their heads.
> They raise the jars with macaw and lightning patterns
> to the six directions then form a circle
> and throw them down on the center-marking stones. (79)

The speaker's spiritual experience is accompanied by the Pueblo women dancers' gesture of offering "melons to the six directions" and of smashing the melons and the jars to make connections to the crowd and the world. The "six directions" refer to Pueblos' view of the world, which is made up of "above, below, north, west, south and east"; hence, "In the pueblo, one can be in the center of a three-dimensional world."[12] And in making offering to the six directions, the Pueblo dancers are making contact with the "other worlds" of gods and spirits, as well as the human world.[13] The closing lines of this section foreground Sze's philosophy of "the one and the many," which underlies his ecopoetics in terms of the *Archipelago* configuration. As the dancers throw the jars down "on the center-marking stones," the center of their activity resonates with many others where there is "a silence in the shape of a rake," "a shaggymane [is] pushing up through asphalt," and "a mutilated body was found behind the adobe church."[14] These centers and others are like the islands of an archipelago.

In accordance with this ecological concept, the Pueblo dance, although central to the structure and aesthetic of the poem, is represented as one of the multifarious phenomena in the universe. As the Pueblo ceremonial dance opens into a social dance in section 8, the dance becomes one of the multitudinous images and activities taking place in Asia and America, in the human world and in nature:

> Mating above the cattails, red dragonflies—
>
> sipping litchi tea, eating fried scallion pancakes—
>
> bamboo slivers under the fingernails—
>
> playing ping-pong by candlelight in a greenhouse—
>
> digging up and rotating soil in the flower beds—
> pulling and pulling at her throat until it bleeds—
> . . . .
> archipelago:
> an expanse of water with many scattered islands—
>
> a python coiling around sixteen white oblong eggs—
> waking in the dark to pungent hyacinths—
>
> blooming the pure white curve of blooming—
>
> dancers are throwing
> licorice, sunflower seeds, pot scrubbers, aprons, plastic bowls. (83)

By using lines rather than stanzas as distinct units, Sze, again, gives equal weight to each phenomenon. The fragmentary images, in fact, contain all the basic elements from the previous sections, suggesting a link among these disparate things. Just as the Pueblo dancers throw objects to open the ceremony to the spectators, Sze intends to connect his poem to the reader and the world by making "a 'throw' of images out to the reader at the end of the poem, but also at the end of the book."[15] His way of ending a poem or a book with images enacts his aesthetics that resists closure and the privileging of the mind over nature.

The ninth and final section of the poem begins with the objects that the dancers throw at the crowd in the previous section. But these objects immediately give way to numerous images of motion and change and to thoughts and sounds:

> the shadow of a hummingbird—
>
> crab apple blossoms scattering in the street—
>
> . . . .
>
> black, *blak, blaec*—
>
> following the thread
> of recollection through a lifetime—
>
> the passions becoming the chiming sounds of jade—
>
> blue corn growing in the field of sand—
>
> the *chug chug, ka ka* of a cactus wren—. . . .[16]

Sze's metaphorical "throw" of images at the reader here incorporates a series of empty spaces that enhance the significance of each phenomenon taking place in its own time-space. Sze again creates a poignant sense of coexistence and connection among all things through collage juxtaposition of multiple temporalities. The fragmented syntax also helps produce "a resonance and erasure of time."[17] Sze evokes the resonance of time through images such as "the shadow of a hummingbird" and the collating of three versions of the same word: *black* followed by the Middle English spelling *blak* and Old English *blaec,* which have exactly the same pronunciation as *black.* The connections among these words resonate with "the thread / of recollection through a lifetime," suggesting a time line that is erased by other images in other space-time. Perhaps, by leaving empty spaces and by erasing a unifying time line, Sze invites the reader to fill in his or her own memories. At the same time, a multi-centered world emerges from the collage of disjunctive images. Hence, abandoning a unified, absolute, and linear concept of time is crucial for Sze's development of an ecopoetics of which synchronic structure is a salient feature in his composition.

Although this structure resists a hierarchical order, it also entails more possibilities for Sze to open the poetic form to include diversity in the world. As the speaker says in "Viewing Photographs from China," included in an earlier volume, *Dazzled:*

> And instead of insisting that
> the world have an essence, we
> juxtapose, as in a collage,
> facts, ideas, images.[18]

Collage composition also resists presenting the world through a logically organized sequence that tends to eliminate connections among radically disparate things. For Sze an ecological, or Daoist, view of the world demands a new mode of making poetry. In another early poem, "The Leaves of a Dream Are the Leaves of an Onion," Sze makes unlikely connections among all things in the universe, articulating an ecological view that provides the ground for his bold experiment with poetic form in his later volumes. In section 2 of this poem Sze insists on connecting the human world, including scientific discovery and development of technology, to the world of nature:

> A Galapagos turtle has nothing to do
> with the world of the neutrino.
> The ecology of the Galapagos Islands
> has nothing to do with a pair of scissors.
> The cactus by the window has nothing to do
> with the invention of the wheel.
> The invention of the telescope
> has nothing to do with a red jaguar.
> No. The invention of the scissors
> has everything to do with the invention of the telescope.
> A map of the world has everything to do
> with the cactus by the window.
> The world of the quark has everything to do

with a jaguar circling in the night.
The man who sacrifices himself and throws a Molotov
cocktail at a tank has everything to do
with a sunflower that bends to the light.[19]

Here Sze is arguing for an ecological view of the world, but he breaks away from the rhetorical tradition of logical argument, depending instead on juxtaposing images, rather than reasoning through images, to make his point.

It is precisely in rejecting a dichotomous relationship between culture and nature that Sze's ecopoetics differs from that of traditional pastoral poetry. In her discussion of the relation between the natural world and the objectivist poets' pastoral poetry, Judith Schwartz observes, "Pastoral poetry and Objectivist poetry both explore the potentially destructive contact between human artifice and an idealized nature."[20] Although human destruction of nature occasionally appears in Sze's poems, his view of the relation between culture and nature neither emphasizes the former's potential destruction of the latter nor idealizes nature. In fact this binary view of culture and nature runs counter to Sze's ecological view of all elements in the universe. Rather, Sze is concerned with exploring alternative modes for understanding the world and the self in which human beings and nature are part of its "redshifting web." "The world is more than you surmise," says the speaker in "The Leaves of a Dream Are the Leaves of an Onion." For the speaker, as for Sze, "No single method can describe the world; / therein is the pleasure / of chaos, of leap of the mind." Although "The pattern of interference in a hologram" can replicate images of natural objects, it "misses the sense of chaos, distorts / in its singular view."[21]

In resisting a single view of the world and everything in it, Sze not only develops a poetics of synchronic structure and serial representation, but he also incorporates vocabulary and concepts of physical science into his poetry. Take for example these lines from "Every Where and Every When":

Is it true an anti-matter particle
never travels as slow as the speed of light,

and, colliding with matter, explodes?
The mind shifts as the world shifts.

I look out the window, watch Antares glow.
The world shifts as the mind shifts;

or this belief, at least, increases
the pleasure of it all—the smell of espresso

in the street, picking blueberries,
white-glazed, blue-black,

sieved gold from a river, this moment
when we spin and shine.[22]

Sze's mixing of scientific vocabulary with everyday language enables him to break away from the dichotomized paradigm for representing the relations between culture and nature, between the city and the country, and between the corrupted urban society and the simple rural land in pastoral and objectivist poetry.[23]

While exploring alternative modes for representing the interconnectedness of all things, Sze develops what might be called an ecological aesthetics. Peter Harries-Jones, in his essay "Aesthetics and Ecology: A Nonfictional View," observes, "Today ecological aesthetics has moved . . . towards the idea that the beauty of living lies in active participation. The new existential unit is that of self plus nature as a single field of relations and processes."[24] Of the several perspectives of ecological aesthetics that Harries-Jones discusses, three share some similarities with Sze's. One of them is Arnold Berleant's "participatory ecological aesthetics," which is developed from the recognition that "[o]ur bodies respond and reestablish us as we move through space and time in active engagement with changing conditions" (434). At the same time, Harries-Jones adds, "the paradigms and categories of space, time, and movement which are necessary for any active perception of environment are embedded in cultural practices" (434). Berleant's aesthetics thus challenges the privileging of vision over other sensual experiences and reveals the mutually constituent relationship between human beings and their environment. Similarly, in Sze's poems sound and smell are as important as sight; both the vision and action of the speaker alter with the motions in the environment. All these are in constant processes, changing with different time-space. "The mind shifts as the world shifts," says Sze's persona, but that "The world shifts as the mind shifts" may be a "belief" that enhances the pleasure of experience.

The second perspective of ecological aesthetics Harries-Jones discusses is developed by Arne Naess, who combines "insights drawn from natural science about relations in an electromagnetic or quantum field . . . from psychology of perceptual gestalts, and extends there to ethical and spiritual perspectives about unity in nature" (435). Like Naess, Sze incorporates insights drawn from natural science, philosophy, and spiritual beliefs into his development of an ecological aesthetics, but he differs from Naess in embracing chaos rather than seeking "unity in nature." Sze's ecological aesthetics also departs from that of Berleant and Naess in its multicultural perspectives. In this respect Sze's aesthetics shares more similarity with that of Fritjof Capra. According to Harries-Jones, Capra believes that a new aesthetics developed after the discovery in quantum physics that "destroyed the concept of an independent world" and changed our role in nature from an "observer" to a "participator."[25] Furthermore, "Capra evokes the Eastern worldview and the mystical traditions of Hinduism, Buddhism and Taoism to demonstrate parallels between their views about the interconnectedness and interdependence of natural phenomena and the views of modern physics. Both describe a universe where all things and events are ultimately related."[26] These kinds of parallels between modern physics and Eastern and Native American worldviews are precisely the epistemological basis for Sze's ecological aesthetics.

Another serial poem, "The Silk Road," illustrates well this aspect of his aesthetics and reveals another dimension of Sze's ecopoetics, which has absorbed elements from physiology, Daoism, and other aspects of Chinese culture.[27] The title of the poem alludes to the historical route of cross-cultural interactions, but the poem "is ultimately a journey into the deepest self to recognize death and use it as a point of transformation."[28] But rather than trying to reach "the deepest self" in the "poet-I" through contemplation, Sze seeks to confront it through multiple selves of more than one person in different cultures and time-space. Eventually, this search for the deepest self in the quest to understand the meaning of death becomes an exploration of the fact that death and life are to be understood as one, coexisting in all things at various moments.

As Scigaj says of ecopoets who "are much more concerned with affirming the integrity of the lived body of quotidian, prereflective experience as the base of all thinking,"[29] Sze begins "The Silk Road" with the bodily experience of a diabetic:

> The blood in your arteries is contaminated with sugar.
> You may hate the adrenal reduction of the mind to
> the mind of a dog, but *sic, run* may be forms of sugar.
> You may whet for the smell of rain on a clear summer night.
> You may whet for the sugar in red maple leaves.
> . . . .

> but discard dream structure for a deeper asymmetry,
> You thirst in your mind for an insulin, death:
>
> death in the yellow saguaro flower opening at midnight,
> death in a canyon wren's song at sunrise,
>
> death in red carp swimming in a clear pool of water,
> death in an April moonrise. Now the figure-of-eight knot, . . .[30]

Rather than privileging the mind over nature, Sze shows that the mind depends on material substances for its basic functions. To explore something deeper than dream—death—the diabetic yearns "for an insulin" that will enable him or her to understand the paradox of death in the fullest moment of life. Yet the meaning of death is like "the figure-of-eight knot." A sideways figure of eight is the mathematical sign for the infinite. Sze combines this sign with the image of a knot to convey a Daoist view of infinite mystery of life and death beyond any single definition through logical reasoning.

Sze explores metaphysical questions of death not only in relation to physiology and imagination but also in terms of multiple temporalities. This plurality in space-time enables him to explore death in different forms and from varied perspectives. In section 2 Sze indicates that nuclear tests have created new forms of dying and disorientation unlike that of the diabetic: "A turtle pushes onto the sand of Bikini Island, / and, disoriented by radiation, pushes further and further / inland to die."[31] The mortal effect of nuclear radiation on life in nature is also affecting human lives in different ways: "This sand was black and silver shining in the megalight. / Now the radiation is in my hands and in your face" (15). But how is one to understand the immanence of death when it is manifested or hidden in so many different forms?

> To argue that you must know the characteristic
>
> that makes all birds birds before you can identity
> a bird—and here you must discard antinomies—
>
> postpones *auk* to that indeterminate time in the fallout
> of the future when you shall have knowledge of the form *Death.* (15)

Here Sze alludes to Plato's concept of "form" as an independently existing pure essence of being, while questioning its assumption of universal, totalizing knowledge. He subverts a Western philosophical tradition based on monolithic universalism and a unified, absolute concept of time by juxtaposing the Platonic notion about knowledge with the Daoist notion of reality and time: "A merchant from Xi'an brought ceremonial caps to Kuqa, / but the Kuqa people shaved their heads and tattooed their bodies" (15).[32]

> There are apricots beginning to drop from branches to the earth;
> there are apricots not yet beginning to drop from branches;
> there are apricots not yet not yet beginning to drop.[33]

"The Silk Road" and Sze's other poems incorporate these concepts of multiple values, realities shaped not simply by different space-time but also by memory and imagination.

Arthur Sze develops an ecopoetics with insights derived from natural sciences, philosophies, imagination, and everyday experience. His poetry itself is like a redshifting web, connecting vastly dissimilar things and opening to those beyond our immediate surroundings:

> I find a rufous hummingbird on the floor
> of a greenhouse, sense a redshifting
> along the radial string of a web.
> . . . .
>   staring through a skylight
>   at a lunar eclipse;
> a great blue heron,
> wings flapping,
> landing on the rail of a float house;
>   near and far:
>   a continuous warp;
> . . . .
>   hiding a world in a world:
>   1054, a supernova.[34]

There are worlds without boundaries in this poem, in which Sze expands a moment of perception by dislodging it from a single space-time and situating it in juxtaposition to a wide range of phenomena in the universe, where past, present, and future collapse into one and multiple simultaneities. This and other poems illustrate that Sze's ecological poetics of "the one and the many" resists homogeneity and breaks down binaries such as culture vs. nature, East vs. West, and margins vs. centers. Such an ecological concept of the world, then, offers much more than a new mode of poetics. As our globalized economic, cultural systems are expanding, an ecological concept of the world enables us to reconceptualize the past and to reimagine the future by providing us with a necessary alternative to binary, hierarchical systems of thought. In this sense Arthur Sze's ecopoetics embodies a politics that seeks to transform and renew.

Notes

1. Arthur Sze, *The Redshifting Web: Poems 1970–1998* (Port Townsend, Wash.: Copper Canyon Press, 1998): 227.

2. See Stephen Hawking, *A Brief History of Time from the Big Bang to Black Holes* (New York: Bantam, 1990): 38–39.

3. Arthur Sze, a Chinese American, used to be a science major. While studying physics at MIT, he decided that writing poetry was much more challenging. He then took intensive courses in Chinese literature at the University of California at Berkeley, where he also studied poetry with Josephine Miles. His translations of classical Chinese poetry appeared in two volumes: *The Willow Wind* (Berkeley: privately printed, 1972) and *Two Ravens* (Gudalupita: Tooth of Time, 1976). He had a special relationship with Native American culture in the West, for he was married to a Hopi weaver for seventeen years and had a son with her. Also, he is professor of creative writing at the Institute of American Indian Arts at Santa Fe, New Mexico, where he has been teaching for more than fourteen years.

4. Leonard M. Scigaj, *Sustainable Poetry: Four American Ecopoets* (Lexington: University Press of Kentucky, 1999), 10.

5. Arthur Sze, letter to the author, December 22, 1996.

6. Ibid.

7. A longer and slightly different reading of this poem appears in my article "Intercultural Strategies in Asian American Poetry," in Ruth Hsu et al., eds., *Re-placing America: Conversations and Contestations* (Honolulu: University of Hawaii Press, 2000): 92–108.

8. Arthur Sze, *Archipelago* (Port Townsend, Wash.: Copper Canyon Press, 1995), 75.

9. See "Arthur Sze," interview, in Eileen Tabios, *Black Lightning: Poetry-in-Progress* (New York: Asian American Writers' Workshop, 1998), 8.

10. Sze, letter to the author, April 23, 1997.

11. Sze, *Archipelago*, 76.

12. Tabios, "Arthur Sze," 8.

13. The Pueblo concept of the six directions corresponds to the traditional Chinese view of the world, which also consists of six directions: east, south, west, north, plus heaven and the netherworld. See *I-Ching*, or *The Book of Changes*.

14. Sze, *Archipelago*, 76, 80.

15. Sze, letter, April 23, 1997.

16. Sze, *Archipelago*, 84.

17. Tabios, "Arthur Sze," 13.

18. Arthur Sze, *Dazzled* (Point Reyes Station: Floating Island, 1982), 13.

19. Arthur Sze, *River River* (Providence: Lost Roads, 1987), 14.

20. Judith Schwartz, "'The World Is the Greatest Thing in the World': The Objectivists' 'Immanent' Pastoral," in Patrick D. Murphy, ed., *Literature of Nature: An International Sourcebook* (Chicago: Fitzroy Dearborn, 1998), 33.

21. Sze, *River River*, 15, 18.

22. Ibid., 24.

23. See Schwartz, 33–35.

24. Peter Harries-Jones, "Aesthetics and Ecology: A Nonfictional View," in Murphy, 434.

25. Ibid., 437. See also Fritjof Capra, *The Turning Point: Science, Society, and the Rising Culture* (New York: Simon and Schuster, 1982): 47–49.

26. Harries-Jones, 438.

27. According to Sze, the poem was inspired by the Chinese composer Tan Dun's combination of Beijing opera singing with unusual Chinese instruments "to create provocative tonal effects." See Arthur Sze, notes on "The Silk Road," in *Patterns/Contexts/Time: A Symposium on Contemporary Poetry*, ed. Phillip Foss and Charles Bernstein (Santa Fe: TYUONYI, 1990), 224. Sze developed a performance piece with the collaboration of Joan La Barbara (New Music soprano), Shi-Zhen Chen (Chinese opera vocalist), Christopher Shulties (leader of the New Mexico Percussion Ensemble), Yao An (*zheng*/Chinese zither player), and Tan Dun, who scored for himself (Chinese pottery pipe) and Chinese fiddle. This performance premiered at the Center for Contemporary Arts, Santa Fe, on April 1 and 2, 1989. Sze's reading of "The Silk Road" was part of this performance. For Sze's description of it see his notes on "The Silk Road."

28. Sze, letter to the author, January 12, 1997.

29. Scigaj, 11.

30. Sze, *Archipelago*, 11.

31. Ibid., 12.

32. The merchant from Xi'an, capital of the Tang Dynasty, situated at one end of the Silk Road, represents one reality, which coexists with another of a different culture in another location: Kuqa, a site of remote wilderness on the actual silk road. The fact that

the ceremonial caps of people in Xi'an become useless for people of Kuqa suggests that there is another reality beyond one's knowledge limited by geography or circumstances. These lines actually allude to a passage in a text attributed to Zhuangzi. See *Chuang Tsu: Inner Chapters,* trans. Gia-Fu Feng and Jane English (New York: Vintage Books, 1974), 15.

33. Sze, *Archipelago,* 14. These lines allude to Zhuangzi's concept of time, which subverts the linearity of time in a unified form of past, present, and future: "There is a beginning. There is a not yet beginning to be a beginning. There is a not yet beginning to be a not yet beginning to be a beginning." See *Complete Works of Chuang-Tzu,* trans. Burton Watson (New York: Columbia University Press, 1968), 19.

34. Sze, *The Redshifting Web,* 233–234.

Beverly Curran

In Her Element
Daphne Marlatt, the Lesbian Body, and the Environment

> catch
> in the mesh of a net we refuse to see, the accretion of all our actions, how they interact, how they inter/read (intelligence), receive, the reading the sea, a vanishing marsh, a dying river, the mesh we are netted in, makes of *us.*
>
> —Daphne Marlatt, *Steveston*

> All my poetics are, is connections.
>
> —Daphne Marlatt, "Given This Body"

Over the past three decades the writing of Canadian poet Daphne Marlatt has revealed a deep interest in the local and in the poet's finding her place in it. Marlatt has described her ongoing writing project as a process of translation, of translating text into context in an awareness of "the extensiveness of that cloth of connectedness we are woven into."[1] For Marlatt such a translation's priority is not faithful accuracy but rather a foregrounding of the difference and slippage of meaning that occur between authorial intention and the play of words in the act of writing, and in reading. Marlatt has suggested that writing can be more intercommunicative by "reading what we are in the mi(d)st of, reading the world," through an articulation of an individual's porous self and collaborative relationships with others and the environment.[2] Such a praxis has implications that extend beyond writing to propose a different view of how we live in and with the world around us.

Marlatt's interest in place and "the notion of here, what being here means" is evident in her early writing from the 1960s.[3] Along with other Vancouver poets such as George Bowering and Frank Davey, Marlatt was inspired and influenced by William Carlos Williams, Robert Creeley, and Charles Olson, especially by their "sense of place, of 'locus' as Olson would have put it, a sense of the crucial relations among themselves, their community, and their language."[4] In *Vancouver Poems,* her long poem unearthing the "buried" history of Vancouver, she explores the remnants of cultural memory still clinging to "this present / city, as a residue we / Cannot, rid our selves of."[5] Excavations of collective memory continue in *Steveston,* her long poem about a Japanese fishermen's community. The poem weaves documentary interview fragments of individual life stories into a discernible social design of dispossession and exploitation of human and natural resources.[6] By including others' speech in her poems, Marlatt creates in her writing a collaboration of voices, with her authorial self interacting with others as she reads from where she stands "in this body at this moment in this place marked by, bearing traces of, the places, moments and people lived with, in and through to this point."[7]

In the 1980s, as Marlatt's writing rereads *Steveston* through a feminist lens, the nets of commercial exploitation that entrap the lives of salmon and marginalized fishermen and cannery workers are extended to explicitly include women. Critics have noticed links between Marlatt's *Steveston* and Williams's *Paterson,*[8] and Marlatt has acknowledged connections with Olson's *Maximus Poems;* but as Brenda Carr has pointed out, *Steveston* also reveals affinities with H. D.'s *Trilogy* and a feminist long-poem tradition.[9] Marlatt will begin to consciously work out of this tradition, "salvaging" poems she had written about Steveston and rereading them as "shoreline poems . . . written on that edge where a feminist consciousness floods the structures of patriarchal thought."[10] Informed by feminist critical thought and a lesbian consciousness, Marlatt's interest in the energy of place develops into a relational lesbian poetic that is still profoundly ecological. Her writing attempts to tell a story of the present that resonates with past and future, and the interdependency of all living beings, to participate in "a certain luminosity of being (as Virginia Woolf would put it)" that undoes "oppositions in a multivalent desire for relationship, whether with women or men, children, cats, trees, the particular slant of light in a street or a breaking wave."[11] Writing against callous exploitation, Marlatt asserts the erotic rhythms of the earth and somatic sensory connections. She immerses herself in the medium of language, listening to the words that come and letting silence, too, find a place in her text. Drifting where the words take her, Marlatt lets her thoughts be taken by surprise, lets her writing be relocated. In this essay I will consider the porous drift of Marlatt's poetic, which listens as much as it speaks, and how it shapes the writer's sense of place as an interactive field of worlds and words, of touch and tongue, where any body can feel at home in its element.

Marlatt's poetics of place has its beginnings in her own life story. Born in Australia, she spent her early childhood in Malaysia before immigrating with her family to Canada when she was nine. In the transition from a privileged colonial childhood to suburban North Vancouver, where her "foreign" lexicon was a liability, Marlatt was suddenly aware of herself as many selves and the place she occupied as multidimensional. The poet recalls how her "immigrant imagination" began to grasp the mutable nature of the world and language when she moved to Canada: "When you are told, for instance, that what you call earth is really dirt, or what you have always called the woods (with English streams) is in fact the bush (with its creeks), you experience the first split between name and thing, signifier and signified, and you take that first step into a linguistic world that lies adjacent to but is not the same as the world of things."[12]

In her novel *Ana Historic* Marlatt invents "a historical leak, a hole in the sieve of fact" to imagine lesbian lives left out of historical records and to enter their stories. She creates Mrs. Richards and her lover, Birdie Stewart, and writes them into the local history of Victorian British Columbia. In doing so she seeks to connect the private act of imagination with "the public act of performing a recognizable self"[13] on the stage of history. In *Steveston,* more than a decade earlier, Marlatt employed a collaboration of voices to make space for Asian immigrant workers marginalized by race and language; in *Ana Historic* she weaves lives marginalized by sexuality into the history of that place, establishing a context that holds both past and present lives as it holds both legends of the sacred salmon and salmon rivers polluted with dioxins: the context is "huge, a living tissue we live together with/in."[14] Marlatt conflates lesbian consciousness and ecological concerns in her re-vision of the world as a shared narrative that challenges the dominant power structures that have rendered workers exploited, lesbians invisible, and the environment subject to destruction in the name of economic dominance. "The cave speaks, the desert sings and the unexamined world which was merely background for his exploits suddenly becomes so live, so resonant with alternative givens, there is no longer any sure footing in the old order of things."[15] Her writing uncovers the hidden and lets a multiplicity of voices connect as speaking subjects, not as a unified whole but as threads that extend the limits of what constitutes community.

In *Steveston* this network of connection was formally signaled in the collaboration between Marlatt and photographer Robert Minden. The long poem and black-and-white photographs reveal a tension between the mutability of poetry and the moment "taken" by the camera: "The poems have verbal vestiges of their subjects embedded in them (their own words) but they do not shimmer with this sense of actual presence and are not located in time as a photograph is."[16] Minden's photographs focus on the faces and human activity of the Japanese fishing community of Steveston, a small town at the mouth of the Fraser River, just outside Vancouver, British Columbia. Marlatt's poems share the photographer's interest in that largely male population of workers, in the context of "how they inhabited that place, their relationship to the place itself, not just as a human community, but as an ecological site, the whole 'river-ing' ecology, going out to sea and back."[17] For Marlatt the fishing community embodies a different order, based on the primacy of the environment, that resists the notion of the individual "at the centre of his world as dominant figure controlling by will &/or authority," a position the poet perceives as the basis for capitalist exploitation of the land and of each other, a position destructive because it "ignores the reverberation of any action within the web (e.g. how our pollution comes back to us)."[18] Marlatt's use of the first-person plural admits her own membership in the culture of consumerism and her complicity in the damaging of the environment, but it also seeks out her reader in an act of collaborative resistance. Her poetic act of reading the cultural other is simultaneously an act of being read as part of a collective environmental text, what "the sea, a vanishing marsh, a dying river, / the mesh we are netted in, makes of us."[19]

In spite of her interest in the community of Steveston, it was the river that seduced the poet. In *Steveston* the prose poems flow with the river, acknowledging worlds beyond words, beyond human stories, and situating lives within an ecosystem, "the largest sense of what we're involved in as living beings."[20] In a 1997 interview Marlatt recalls an early visit to Steveston and her initial encounter with a system not built on a human scale: "First of all, you're standing on an island that's below sea level so it's an incredibly liminal place between water and earth. But especially if you're standing there in the Spring, with the freshet pouring down the Fraser, you get an incredible sense of the power of that water moving out to the sea."[21] The medium of *Steveston* is water: the river and the delta, where the salt of the sea and the freshet mingle, where "water swills, / endlessly out of itself to the mouth / ringed with residue," and the ocean, where men search for fish.[22] In the *Steveston* poems Marlatt tries to write the flow of the river in extended lines. Her attempts are simultaneously searches to find a home in the immediacy of language and in the moment of writing, as well as extensions of that home beyond temporal constraints and the limits of the printed page. Like the river, "the poem . . . is constantly trying to arrive in the now, bringing all of the past it has passed with it."[23] Against and with the flow of the line, "mouths," "rings," and "residue" voice a different version of time, evoking the somatic "memory" that perpetuates the cycle of spawning salmon that swim upstream to birth and, dying, drift downstream to the sea again. Marlatt's poetic interconnects words and place in rings of relationships among human beings, their languages, and their surroundings.

The small fishing community of Steveston, built on the banks of the Fraser River, is subject to seasonal flooding. At times the lines of *Steveston* overflow as well, as the poem, like the river, strains "at its container, uncontainable."[24] In *Steveston*'s "Pour, pour" the title spills into the body of the poem; it bursts open a parentheses leaving one agape. From its repetitive opening line the poem grows and gains force; lines run on until they look like paragraphs, gathering voices and languages ("This river is / *alive,* he says"; and "goku goku," the Japanese onomatopoeic term for drinking in great gulps), and names: "Roberts Bank past Albion Dyke, then Woodward Reach opposite Woodward Landing (where the ferry ran)," residual fragments that enter a human history into the flow of the river. All of these are caught up in the movement of the river/poem: "this river is rivering." Amid this pouring, tumultuous flow are words sealed inside parentheses, drifting like flotsam in the current of the poem: (renew), (hence renewable), (unable), (bunkhouse), (source), (need as cash), (is he? accountable?), (money). The poem is a polluted river cluttered with the debris of commerce, "swollen with filth, with sewage, milldirt," disrupting the homing desire of the fish who "seek their source, which is, their proper place to die."[25] Marlatt explores contradictory currents in her awareness of the organic growth of the poem. Although she is fascinated by how the poem catches "all kinds of things as it's rolling along . . . : what entered the poem through the movement of the sentence, just that jumping from word to word, from phrase to phrase," she is also aware that the homing instinct of the salmon is inhibited by the clutter, "knots of, black chunks of history," introduced into the river flow.[26] Critical but still playing with the commercial connotations of words like *renew* and *accountable,* Marlatt is able to translate them through association into a lexicon of ecological "accountability," her network of connections compounding interest in the accumulation of different meanings.

In *Steveston* the "multiplicity simply there: the physical matter of the place (what matters)"[27] shows Marlatt's resistance to the lines of reasoning and airtight logic that render so much invisible or irrelevant. Thus, "[r]educed to the status of things, We orient / Always toward the head, & the eyes (yes) of knowing, & knowing us, or what / we do" (23). It is this tendency, suggests Gemma Corradi Fiumara, in *The Other Side of Language,* that has helped write an ecological history that has consisted "of an uninterrupted series of acts of domination which have been performed by means of a symbolic superiority . . . a linguistic power that in the long run becomes an end in itself and that ultimately stiffens and becomes inertial, thus impeding an equilibrium of survival and coexistence."[28] In lieu of masters (or mistresses) of the universe Marlatt proposes a "network of salvagers" that sustains context in life and writing by paying attention "to systems of meanings that matter," that is, ecosystems.[29]

Even in writing poetry Marlatt is aware of and immersed in the medium that collaborates in writing the poem. She explains:

> Once we get into the water, which is a foreign element to us, we're very aware of the difficulty of moving thru that element. That's like poetry. You are aware that you are moving in an element in a medium, & that there is a constant resistance to your going forward. And that, in fact, any moving forward you make is thanks to that element that you're moving in. So that language . . . writes the story as much as you do.[30]

In writing, then, Marlatt is acknowledging the gifts that come as a surprise to the writer and take the poem in new directions. She finds the imagination more useful than intellectual rigor in the project of transforming her relationship to the literal place she finds her "selves" in. The associative network that links language, somatic and textual bodies, and the environment is "a form of thought that is not rational but erotic because it works by attraction."[31] Using etymology to trace the root and growth of words, and similes of sound and sense to draw words together and create shifts in meaning, Marlatt lets language call up connections as lovers do, through touch and provocation. As Pamela Banting has said, this use of attraction is a "translating forward" to form new alliances.[32] For Marlatt change and slippage, not permanence, are the principles of place: "*changing* ground changing channel . . . the fish come and go, as the river does—land & water's *recreation* of form outlasts this species' need to fix it, own it—because we are subject to death."[33]

In writing the poems of *Steveston* Marlatt felt the river as a distinctively female presence, a "creature, swelling up & birthing, huge, past all their plans and plants, / its urgency to meet the sea where men go, when they are able, like the / fish."[34] The language of pregnancy and birth has ecological resonance for Marlatt, who considers her own pregnancy one of her "first in-body experiences of a kind of limited ecological consciousness,"[35] raising her awareness of "the nameless interbeing we were born with,"[36] the experience of being interwoven with another. As Marlatt points out, "Even in nursing there's still such an amazing phenomenon because the infant's nursing actually heals the mother's womb, so the interbeing is still happening even though it's two separate bodies and two separate skins."[37]

Almost a decade after *Steveston* Marlatt was coming out as a lesbian in her life and in her writing, and the "interbeing we were born with," which had been played out in the (amniotic) sea of the womb between child and mother, was being reconfigured in the lesbian relationship. As she attempted "to illuminate poetics with feminist theory"[38] and to write a lesbian erotic in *Touch to My Tongue,* she found both her theory and poetry haunted by the rhythms of the river/poem *Steveston.*

> What struck me when I started working on "Touch to My Tongue" was that the rhythms in those poems very closely echo the rhythms of the poems in *Steveston,* and here it's a lesbian erotic. And I knew it had something to do with the movement of the river. I mean, I didn't think of it in terms of a lesbian erotic when I was writing *Steveston;* I just knew there was something very female about it.[39]

"Touch to My Tongue" and "musing with mothertongue" are both concerned with the connections between the body, the body of language, and the imaginary: "putting the living body of language together means putting the world together, the world we live in: an act of composition, an act of birthing, us, uttered and outered there in it."[40]

Therefore, the erotic and the ecological attract each other in Marlatt's lesbian poetics. The "raw power" of the erotic is "a current surging through my body surging beyond the limits of self-containment, beyond the limits of syntax and logic and of the daily order that keep me organizing time into small manageable chunks tailored to the work at hand. . . . Like water or fire, it seeks to go beyond limits, above all the limits of self as distinct from other."[41] Love of place and love of women fuse in Marlatt's writing. She locates both "in the body because the body doesn't speak in systems of power, its 'speaking,' an upheaval, breaks through the codes that repress it."[42] This excess, this flood of feeling, makes an intimate connection between loving bodies immersed in the imagining of a context that includes bodies with or without words. As Lorraine Weir describes it, Marlatt's "ecology of language" is about our bodies being inhabited by language and how "when a response comes which is not silence but the discovery of *place* in an/other, [it] makes possible community which is con/text."[43] This dynamic, both ecological and erotic in *Steveston,* becomes an explicitly lesbian poetic in Marlatt's later writing as she makes intertextual connections between women and the texts they read, without losing any of its ecological consciousness in "our connectedness to what surrounds us, the matter, the matrix of our shared lives, our ecosphere, the multidimensional 'ground' we stand on and with."[44]

In her foreword to *Salvage* Marlatt discusses the "aquatic" process of rereading the poems from *Steveston* and rewriting them by "working with the subliminal currents in the movements of language whose direction as 'direction' only became apparent as i went with the drift, no matter how much flotsam seemed at first to be littering the page."[45] "Litter.wreckage.salvage," for example, rewrites *Steveston*'s "Imperial Cannery, 1913" with a different consciousness of women's roles and ecological responsibility. "Imperial Cannery, 1913" begins with a young girl "standing inside the door" of the cannery, so confident of her own erotic power, and the security of her future as a married woman, that she imagines herself free. Although conscious of her sexuality and its power, the girl is unaware of the social controls orchestrating her "destiny"; although she feels she is "in her element," her dream is of rings of dependency: "sails, her father's or a friend's son, at the Imperial which owns their boat, their net, their debt."[46] Even in this prefeminist poem Marlatt is juxtaposing the image of the hopeful girl leaning into the future, "into the threshold, waiting for work and marriage" (15), with an image of her mother inside the cannery "working, with the smallest one standing by her skirt in grubby dress" (15), caught like the fish on the cutting board she works.

In "Litter.wreckage.salvage" the days of a "cannery boomtown: 'salmon capital of the world' "[47] are over, along with the teeming schools of fish that fed the industry. The poem does not start with the image of the young girl but "below water level, behind," to recall a community left behind: "Steveston: / your women invisible, your men all gone." The women do not linger in doorways in a languor of anticipation, but "swim / in long slow gleams between blinds, day incessant with its / little hooks, its schemes inconsequential finally." The dreams built on the flow of progress, a young girl's ineluctable movement toward marriage has ebbed: "What matters, mattered / once has seeped away." Instead of the confidence in a (falsely) secure future, the voice of the young woman in this poem is full of fear "of the marketplace, of going outdoors . . . of leaving home. 'the phobia of every day.' she trembles like a leaf" as she recognizes her value in patriarchal society as a commodity, just like the salmon. Leakage and loss have depleted the big picture of its certainty and reduced it to her "tidal pool" in which

> the small things of her concern still swim alive alive-oh-
> The salmon homing in this season, spring, the sewer out-
> falls upstream, oil slick, the deadly freight of acid rain—
> she reads the list of casualties in the ongoing war outside
> her door.[48]

This seepage in fact is a gift, which, like the "excess, spillage and loss of signifiers and signified in translation," has relocated meaning. Instead of looking inside the door of the cannery, and finding her future waiting for her in the repetition of a fate depicted by her mother on the cannery floor, the woman in "Litter.wreckage.salvage" looks outside *her* door and recognizes her connections with an ailing earth. Nature is not idealized here, but in an "attempt to form a meeting ground on the very fractured margins" she inhabits, this woman imagines the possibility of being a part of all that surrounds her: "i want to imagine being in my element, she said."[49] Drawn into this, too, is the (woman) reader, who is invited to "imagine her in her element," not to be taken in its restrictive sense as home (is her, closed in). No longer stranded by the ebb of an old destiny script, any woman can let her line drift and find her "in her element in other words," words that alter "his definition of her."

To open ourselves to answers other than those anticipated; to listen with our bodies and drift beyond cognition to the feeling of home in the skin, with "the body being in its place"; to "open our minds, and take in everything around it without getting caught up within analysis" is Marlatt's ongoing writing project.[50] The body, the present, the body in the present, is a shifting place with a feeling of home where the sensual lives like otters "who live here with all the pleasure of beings who belong . . . sliding into the water, their dark coats slicked back," like lovers "undoing nipples, lips with tongue talk."[51] To find that liminal home requires unraveling the "linear version of our lives . . . this plot we're in, wrapped up like a knife fork & spoon,"[52] and listening for the spiritual resonance of a place, "the interaction between the eternal & what's timebound, & what's particularly local."[53]

In rethinking writing as immersive, collaborative, and imaginative, Marlatt offers "the expression of erotic power as a transforming energy we revel in each time we move our lovers, our readers and ourselves to that ecstatic surging beyond limits."[54] Recognizing difference and common ground—"her story & our history"[55]—the writer and her reader are balanced "between i and we—and neither capitalized nor capitalizing on the other."[56] In the "threads of our collective life, is where we find the weave of each life" (4), where the imagination transports us *here,* to this liminal place where, drifting, we find our element in an "immersion as / complete as the pouring of water into water" (4).

Notes

1. Daphne Marlatt, "Self-Representation and Fictionalysis," *Tessera* 8 (1990): 15.

2. Daphne Marlatt, "Writing Our Way through the Labyrinth," in *Readings from the Labyrinth* (Edmonton: NeWest Press, 1998), 34.

3. Daphne Marlatt, *Ghost Works* (Edmonton: NeWest Press, 1993), vii.

4. Caroline Bayard, *The New Poetics in Canada and Quebec: From Concretism to Post-Modernism* (Toronto: University of Toronto Press, 1989), 104.

5. Daphne Marlatt, *Vancouver Poems* (Toronto: Coach House Press, 1972), n.p.

6. The fragments come from interviews collected as part of an oral history project initiated by the Provincial Archives of British Columbia. Many of the interviews were conducted in Japanese and translated. They have been published as *Steveston Recollected: A Japanese-Canadian History,* ed. Daphne Marlatt (Victoria: Provincial Archives of British Columbia, 1975).

7. Daphne Marlatt, "Accountability and Audience," in *Readings from the Labyrinth,* 206.

8. See Chris Hall's "Two Poems of Place: Williams' *Paterson* and Marlatt's *Steveston,*" in *Canadian Review of American Studies* 15 (1984): 141–157.

9. Brenda J. Carr, "Daphne Marlatt's Salmon Texts: Swimming / Jumping the Margins / Barriers" (Ph.D. diss., University of Western Ontario, 1989), 129. Carr notes that Marlatt reviewed *Trilogy* for *Open Letter* and explored the work extensively in correspondence with writer Penn Kemp in 1975.

10. Daphne Marlatt, foreword to *Salvage* (Red Deer: Red Deer College Press, 1993), n.p.

11. Daphne Marlatt, *Readings from the Labyrinth,* 66.

12. Daphne Marlatt, "Entering In: The Immigrant Imagination," in *Readings from the Labyrinth,* 23.

13. Marlatt, "Accountability and Audience," 206.

14. Marlatt, "Fictionalysis," 15–16.

15. Daphne Marlatt, "Old Scripts and New Narrative Strategies," in *Readings from the Labyrinth,* 65.

16. Daphne Marlatt, "On Distance and Identity: Ten Years Later," in Daphne Marlatt and Robert Minden, *Steveston* (Edmonton: Longspoon Press, 1984), 93.

17. Daphne Marlatt, interview by author, Victoria, B.C., August 18, 1999.

18. From Marlatt's Steveston journals, cited in Carr, 141.

19. Daphne Marlatt, "Intelligence (as if by radio?)," in *Steveston,* 70.

20. Daphne Marlatt, interview by author, August 27, 1997.

21. Ibid.

22. Daphne Marlatt, "Imagine a Town," in *Steveston,* 14.

23. Marlatt, "On Distance and Identity," 93.

24. Daphne Marlatt, "Pour, pour" in *Steveston,* 17.

25. Ibid.

26. Marlatt, interview, 1999.

27. Daphne Marlatt, "Steveston as You Find It," in *Steveston,* 23.

28. Gemma Corradi Fiumara, *The Other Side of Language: A Philosophy of Listening,* trans. Charles Lambert (London: Routledge, 1990), 39.

29. SueEllen Campbell, "The Land of Language and Desire: Where Deep Ecology and Post-Structuralism Meet," in *The Ecocriticism Reader: Landmarks in Literary Ecology,* ed. Cheryll Glotfelty and Harold Fromm (Athens: University of Georgia Press, 1966), 134.

30. Daphne Marlatt, "Given This Body: An Interview with Daphne Marlatt," interview by George Bowering, *Open Letter* 4, no. 3 (1979): 62.

31. Daphne Marlatt, "musing with mothertongue," in *Touch to My Tongue* (Edmonton: Longspoon Press, 1984), 45.

32. Pamela Banting, "The Reorganization of the Body: Daphne Marlatt's 'musing with mothertongue,'" in *ReImagining Women: Representations of Women in Culture,* ed. Shirley Neuman and Glennis Stephenson (Toronto: University of Toronto Press, 1993), 221.

33. From Marlatt's Steveston journals, cited in Carr, 140–141.

34. Marlatt, "Pour, pour," 17.

35. Daphne Marlatt, letter to the author, March 14, 1998.

36. Daphne Marlatt, *Taken* (Concord: House of Anansi Press, 1996), 21.

37. Daphne Marlatt, interview by author, August 28, 1997.

38. Marlatt, "musing with mothertongue," 49. *Touch to My Tongue* consists of "Touch to My Tongue," a collection of poems, and "musing with mothertongue," a creative theoretical "essay-ing."

39. Marlatt, interview, 1999.

40. Marlatt, "musing with mothertongue," 49.

41. Marlatt, "Fictionalysis," 123.

42. Marlatt, *Labyrinth,* 15–16.

43. Lorraine Weir "Daphne Marlatt's 'Ecology of Language,'" *Line* 13 (1989): 62.

44. Marlatt, *Readings from the Labyrinth,* 147.

45. Marlatt, foreword to *Salvage,* n.p.

46. Daphne Marlatt, "Imperial Cannery, 1913," in *Steveston,* 15.

47. Daphne Marlatt, "Steveston, B.C.," in *Steveston,* 85.

48. Ibid.

49. From Marlatt's introduction to *Telling It,* cited in Smaro Kamboureli, *On the Edge of Genre: The Contemporary Canadian Long Poem* (Toronto: University of Toronto Press, 1991), 158.

50. Marlatt, interview, 1997.

51. Marlatt, *Taken,* 15.

52. Daphne Marlatt, "How Hug a Stone," in *Ghost Works* (Edmonton: NeWest Press, 1993), 131.

53. Marlatt, "Given This Body," 58.

54. Marlatt, *Readings from the Labyrinth,* 49.

55. Poet Phyllis Webb's description of Marlatt's "How Hug a Stone," quoted in *Readings from the Labyrinth,* 3.

56. Marlatt, *Readings from the Labyrinth,* 137.

Roy Osamu Kamada

Postcolonial Romanticisms
Derek Walcott and the Melancholic Narrative of Landscape

In *Arctic Dreams* Barry Lopez describes his journey aboard a cargo ship taking supplies to an arctic mine. While leaning over the calm waters of Melville Bay, he reflects on the icebergs surrounding his ship, comparing their implacable austerity to the gothic magnificence of European cathedrals; he cites the building of cathedrals as a wild leap of spirit, an impassioned attempt to illustrate how "the cathedrals, by the very way they snared the sun's energy, were an expression of God and of the human connection with God as well."[1] He says that the beauty of the icebergs struck terror in him but that the very attempt to apprehend the sublime, cathedral or iceberg, was indicative of love, of "a humble and impassioned embrace of something outside the self."[2] For Lopez, appealing to a universalized experience of awe, this revelation is powerful but simple and uncluttered by historical or cultural baggage. Describing a seascape that lacks history, he is able to imagine his own relationship to that environment in fairly simple terms: the self reaches out to an *Other* in an embracing gesture of longing. Similarly, two centuries earlier, Wordsworth sought out a "simpler" world where "the passions of men are incorporated with the beautiful and permanent forms of nature."[3] He declares the natural world a place where

> the ever-living universe
> And independent spirit of pure youth
> Were with me at that season, and delight
> Was in all places spread around my steps.[4]

Lopez, along with a cadre of other writers, such as Terry Tempest Williams, Annie Dillard, Wendell Berry, to name just a few, has been at the creative forefront of a developing trend in literature that considers the many implications of the relationship between the human and nonhuman worlds. In literary criticism this trend has been met with an increasing number of critical studies devoted to the themes and problems of environmentally oriented literary studies. Anthologies of critical essays have been published that engage the wide variety of methodologies employed by ecocriticism; landmark texts have appeared by Lawrence Buell, Jonathan Bate, and Leonard Scigaj; and issues of *PMLA*, *New Literary History*, and the *Chronicle of Higher Education* have devoted a large number of pages to ecocritical concerns. As William Slaymaker observed in a recent *PMLA* article, "'ecocrit' and 'ecolit' have arrived."[5] Slaymaker has also observed that despite the growth in environmentally oriented literary studies, the "tide" of ecocriticism has "had only minor ripple effects" in the black Atlantic communities.[6] He notes that this has been, in part, because of the "lack of nature writing traditions" (1100) in the diasporic African communities. Slaymaker also notes that "ecocrit and ecolit appear to many academic and literary observers positioned around the margins of the black Atlantic as another whiteout of black concerns, by going green" (1101).

Dominic Head expresses a similar concern about the intersections of ecocriticism and cultural studies in his reading of J. M. Coetzee.[7] Head does suggest that there are potential connections and parallels between postcolonialism and ecologism, yet he warns against the recentering and privileging of the object (in the case of ecologism, the planet or the "natural" world). Thus although Lopez (or Wordsworth) might undertake a romantic quest to transcend the solipsistic bounds of self, and although that quest might be remarked on by the ecocritic as indicative of a larger, nonhuman, ecologically oriented ideology, that quest and critique are at risk of simply reversing the human/nonhuman, subject/object hierarchy. Such literary and critical maneuvers risk recentering the Enlightenment subject that postmodernity has worked so hard to decenter, or at the very least, replacing the Derridean center with "Nature" instead of the Enlightenment subject. And although Slaymaker might argue the absence of nature writing traditions in the black Atlantic communities, the romantic quest to transcend the solipsistic bounds of self in its experience in the "natural" world is made powerfully complex in the work of postcolonial writers such as Derek Walcott.

Walcott, like Lopez or Wordsworth, shares concerns and themes that the ecocritic might consider ecologically oriented; however, Walcott is not just writing about the human encounter with a natural world to which he may or may not completely belong. His concerns are also historical. Walcott, also writing about a sublime landscape, is unable to detach that landscape from its history of colonialism and all the attendant consequences of that history. For although Lopez does discuss the human history of the Arctic along with its neocolonialist consequences elsewhere in his book, he remains a detached observer, able to sunder his appreciation for the landscape from his knowledge of history. Walcott has no such luxury. The landscape he writes about is necessarily politicized; his own subjectivity is intimately implicated in both the natural beauty and the traumatic history of the place; he must directly acknowledge the history of St. Lucia and the Caribbean, the history of diaspora, of slavery, of the capitalist commodification of the landscape, and the devastating consequences this history has on the individual.

This essay examines the ways that Walcott, in his poem *The Schooner Flight,* explores landscape even as he explores the problematics of a postcolonial subjectivity. In this poem, which prefigures his obsession with *The Odyssey,* Walcott yokes together the identity of his poet/speaker, Shabine, with descriptions of the landscape to create a notion of self that, like the landscape he describes, is capable of containing multiple and conflicting terms.[8] Refusing more simplistic, nativist, and ultimately essentialist models of identity, Walcott creates a character whose very nature is a dynamic model of postcolonial identity, a model that finds its mirror in Walcott's presentation of the problematic relationship between a sublime landscape and a history of dispossession and trauma. Rather than close off the ontological possibilities for either the landscape or the postcolonial subject, Walcott offers us a melancholic narrative of identity and landscape where the traumas of the past remain legible in a liminal yet continually present fashion. The ghosts of history are kept present in landscape and subject; they are not consigned to the oblivion of "that which is past." Instead, trauma and history are subjected to what I am calling a kind of "healthy" process of melancholic identification where trauma is not "gotten over," but neither does it disable the formation of subjectivity. Walcott suggests just such a liminal legibility in his personified description of History: "History" is

> a parchment Creole, with warts
> like an old sea bottle, crawling like a crab
> through the holes of shadow cast by the net
> of a grille balcony."[9]

Walcott figuratively suggests that history, here characterized in an almost gothic fashion, is in a continual state of emergence, constantly crawling out of the dark of the past, making itself known and remembered. Through an aesthetics informed equally by political and formal concerns, he maintains the imperatives of memory even as he immerses himself in the sublimity of the landscape.

Robert Young observes that "since Sartre, Fanon and Memmi, postcolonial criticism has constructed two antithetical groups, the colonizer and colonized, self and Other . . . a Manichean division that threatens to reproduce the static, essentialist categories it seeks to undo."[10] Young argues that we need "organic metaphors of identity or society" to counter the tendency toward fragmentation and dispersion that arises from the construction of these two groups. He "suggests a different model from that of a straightforward power relation of colonizer over colonized." The model that Young suggests is that of "the structure of pidgin—crudely the vocabulary of one language superimposed on the grammar of another" (5). According to this model, cultural contact, here represented synecdochically by the languages of two cultures layered on one another, is implicated in an interactive and dynamic process. Walcott seeks to enact a similar process of contact, intrusion, interpenetration, and disjunction between terms of identity and metaphors for the landscape. He creates a poem that, like the creolized English in which Shabine speaks, layers the vocabulary of history over the grammar of the landscape. However, we cannot forget that like Young's linguistic model, the representation of postcoloniality needs to take careful account of the modalities of history and power implicit in models of cultural contact.

In his evocation of a sublime landscape that is nonetheless cathected with the traumas of history, Walcott employs a kind of postcolonial romanticism. He seeks a redemption in the landscape even as some romantics did; however, Walcott deploys, at times ironically, this romantic trope of landscape with the interventionist sensibilities of the postcolonial. Referring to the retribution he intends to bring on those who exploit the economic vulnerabilities of the postcolonial state, Shabine declares, "Ministers, businessmen . . . I shall scatter your lives like a handful of sand, / I who have no weapon but poetry and / the lances of palms and the sea's shining shield!" (16). His threat suggests a certain belief in the efficacy of poetry, but also, and most important for my purposes, it suggests that a poetic evocation of the landscape itself will be part and parcel of the technology of his retribution. Walcott, like a number of other contemporary postcolonial writers, evokes the landscapes of the postcolonial state in ways that recall the landscapes imagined by eighteenth-century British romantics: sublime, beautiful, and threatening.[11] However, Walcott's evocation marks a contemporary romanticism inflected with the historical concerns of the postcolonial; it requires that we consider the Caribbean landscape not only as a place of beauty but also as a place where the Middle Passage ended and the horrors of North American slavery began. To stage these imperatives, Walcott figures the landscape and the postcolonial subject as having a kind of melancholic relationship to a history of trauma. To parse this, I will turn briefly to Freud and Anne Cheng's rereading of his 1917 essay "Mourning and Melancholia."

Reversing established notions of mourning and melancholia, Cheng notes that Freud's essay offers a potentially effective lens through which the problematic of race and historical dispossession can be viewed. Cheng interrogates the problematic of mourning: "For Freud, mourning entails, curiously enough, a forgetting. . . . Upon a closer look, the kind of healthy 'letting go' Freud delineates goes beyond mere forgetting to complete eradication. The successful work of mourning does not only forget, it reinstates the death sentence."[12] Such mourning effaces the materialism of a historical event. As Cheng points out, such "'getting over' . . . means, in a sense, never getting over those memories [of the originary traumatic event], so that health and idealization turn out to be nothing more than continual escape, and nothing less than *the denial and pathologization of what one is*" (50, emphasis mine). Such attempts at mourning, at getting over, at inscribing narrative closure to a historical site that confounds articulation risk disarticulating the event and reducing it to a narrative fragment.

For Cheng "melancholia provides a provocative metaphor for how race in America or more specifically how the act of racialization works" (50).[13] Melancholia, for Freud, is essentially an economy of loss, an economy that prevents the melancholic from abandoning the object of loss. Instead, the melancholic incorporates the object of loss into his or her own ego. "In this way an object-loss [is] transformed into an ego loss."[14] Thus, "[t]he wounded subject, finally, is imprisoned within the brooding cell of melancholy . . . unable to abandon the lost object of desire, unable to return to it, and unable to erase the marks of its degradation from his own person."[15] Cheng argues that "minority identity reveals an inscription marking the remembrance of absence,"[16] and it is precisely this remembrance of absence, of the object-loss or trauma of racialization, that informs the postcolonial experience. And although such melancholic identification is not free of problems, it does allow for the opportunity to interrogate the historical materiality of an object of loss or an event of trauma. Thus the minority subject is a kind of "haunted" subject, haunted by a past of trauma and cultural dispersion. But it is the nature of this haunting that is so essential to the confrontation with that past; the postcolonial, like the landscape itself, must be represented as haunted to escape the bind of mourning. This revised Freudian form of melancholic identification allows us to trope loss in a specifically historical fashion that Young's model of hybridized linguistic layering doesn't quite allow for.

For Walcott the landscape of the Caribbean, like Shabine himself, bears the history of loss within it; both are subjects haunted by the melancholic imperatives of history. The character of Shabine seeks, through a process of implication and interrogation of dualities, to transcend the polarized oppositions of colonial/postcolonial, black/white, and self/other. Shabine is a character who on all levels straddles oppositional forces; he is of mixed racial background, simultaneously both black and white but remaining neither; he is a poet and a sailor, a tender sentimentalist and a vicious fighter; he, in the course of the narrative, journeys between life and death with apparent ease; he loves both his wife and his mistress; and, like Odysseus, he is a figure of both everyman and no man ("either I'm nobody, or I'm a nation" [4]); he is simultaneously the representative of a communal sensibility and a concrete individual. Even as Shabine seeks to resolve these oppositions within his own character, so too does Walcott seek to unravel his relationship to the landscape; for even though he understands the historicity of the landscape and the devastations brought on by colonialism, he strives to imagine the sublimity of the landscape while remaining conscious of these devastations. Thus, in Freudian terms he follows the imperatives of mourning while retaining the melancholic affect.

So just as Shabine himself cannot be conveniently identified as black or white, as poet or sailor, as faithful husband or adulterer, so too does the landscape that the poem engages resist any easy figuring. For like Shabine the landscape of the poem is a dynamic site where conflicting terms come together. Although it is a place once considered a "paradise," now the "slums of empire" hold sway; where Shabine might entreat "the fierce salt" of the "Green Islands . . . [to] let my wound be healed" (14), he finds instead visions of the skies aflame and "leprous rocks . . . and the noise of the soldiers' progress through the thick leaves" (15). The landscape in this poem is hardly the image that a tourist board would generate. Furthermore, the very act of imagining the landscape is implicated in the project of colonialism. Earlier in the poem, Shabine, recalling the many names given to stands of trees leaning out toward the sea, allows that these trees have been named and renamed many times. Suggesting a kind of analogous colonial remaking of himself and his people, he says, "we live like our names and you would have / to be colonial . . . / to know the pain of history words contain" (12). Here Shabine suggests that it is the violence of this remaking and renaming produced by the process of colonialism that results in the corrupted landscape and in the corrupted and degraded people: "we, / if we live like the names our masters please, / by careful mimicry might become men" (12). Here Shabine laments the adoption of the names, of the terms of identity imposed on him. Saying, however, "we live like our names," he also confesses his own complicity and passivity in accepting these terms. He implicates himself in this corrupted landscape.

Yet it is also within this same landscape that Walcott's poet/sailor finds a kind of redemption. For when, at the poem's start, Shabine is weary of living under a corrupt government, in a corrupt society ("they had started to poison my soul / with their big house, big car, big time bohbohl" [4]), he leaves the island and goes down the road to enlist on the schooner *Flight.* And saying "I taking a sea bath," as he walks down the road to start his odyssey through the Caribbean and through history, Shabine announces his intention to undergo a cleansing process, a kind of baptism where he might be washed clean of the very corruption he despises. And although ultimately figuring both landscape and character as caught in a collapsing moment of transcendence, a moment made possible only by imagination and sacrifice, Walcott nevertheless seeks redemption and resolution and the establishment of a postcolonial identity capable of containing the multiple histories of trauma and beauty. He seeks to mourn while remaining a melancholic.

The narrative of the poem follows Shabine through "a veritable Odyssey" that, like the Homeric epic, begins in medias res and is ultimately the story of a journey home.[17] Shabine is inscribed linguistically and racially as a figure of two cultures:

> I . . . a rusty head sailor with sea-green eyes
> that they nickname Shabine, the patois for
> any red nigger. . . .
> I'm just a red nigger who love the sea
> I had a sound colonial education,
> I have Dutch, nigger, and English in me. (4)

Here Shabine describes not only his racial duality but also his possession of what Dorothy Hale calls a Du Boisian double consciousness, in which the personal identity of the black man is encoded in two contradictory impulses: for Shabine the love of the sea and the demands of a colonial education.[18] However, despite this dual nature, Shabine is not accepted by either of his cultures, the black or the white. "After the white man, the niggers didn't want me / when the power swing to their side" (8). He also critiques the racist cultures that both generate in their false formulation of oppositional relations. In the "Rapture of the Deep" section of Walcott's poem Shabine narrates his experience as an employee of O'hara, the big-government man who is an emblem of the corrupt postimperial official who, while investigating a scandal he himself is responsible for, appoints "himself as chairman investigating himself" (6). Shabine later generalizes about the corrupt structure of the postimperial government:

> You saw them ministers in *The Express,*
> guardians of the poor—one hand at their back,
> and one set o' police only guarding their house,
> and the Scotch pouring in through the back door. (6)

Similarly, Shabine's vivid, almost cinematic, description of the revolutionaries taking up arms against this postimperial corruption is not free of critique. For although the revolutionaries are earnest, they are also doomed:

> I no longer believed in the revolution.
> . . . Young men without flags
> using shirts, their chests waiting for holes.
> They kept marching into the mountains, and
> their noise ceased as foam sinks into sand,
> They sank in the bright hill like rain, every one
> with his own nimbus, leaving shirts in the street,
> and the echo of power at the end of the street.(9)[19]

Mirroring this situation of mutually implicated corruption and impotence is Walcott's evocation of a lush tropical landscape, itself corrupted by the consequences of history. Shabine remarks that

> this Caribbean so choke with the dead
> . . . [that] I saw them . . . the dead men.
> I saw that the powdery sand was their bones
> ground white from Senegal to San Salvador. (7)

Shabine is made firmly and fully conscious of the corruption around him. Rejected by both of his cultures, unable to access either's essentialized mythic identity, and caught in this double bind illustrated by the degraded landscape mirroring the corruption and impotence of the postcolonial human society, Shabine turns to imagination and language to generate his own self. Haunted by visions of "dead men . . . their bones / ground white from Senegal to San Salvador" and by hallucinations of the "great admirals, / Rodney, Nelson, de Grasse, [and] the hoarse orders / they gave those Shabines [the slaves on their ships]" (11), and convinced that he is heir to no tradition, Walcott's narrator declares his only inheritance and legacy to be his poetry. Speaking to his wife, whom he has abandoned for another woman, Shabine says, "I have kept my own / promise, to leave you the one thing I own / you whom I loved first: my poetry" (13). Shabine develops and asserts his own subjecthood through a poetic and imaginative act. He says, "my common language go be the wind, / my pages the sails of the schooner *Flight.* . . . I had no nation now but the imagination" (5–8).

However, subjecthood is available only at the moment of its utterance, at the moment of the act. Walcott denies, in the section titled "Maria Concepcion & the Book of Dreams," the ability of language to fully decode any traumatic experience, even a dream. "She said: 'I dreamt of whales and a storm,' / but for that dream the book had no answer" (15). Even this seemingly harmless dream, this experience, resists the decoding that a book, that language, might provide. And later, when Shabine wakes "screaming and crying, my flesh / raining with sweat" (16), the "Book of Dreams" is unable to find any meaning in his trauma. Thus, placing priority on the moment of utterance and the transitory and momentary respite from postcolonial trauma, Shabine sings:

> All you see me talking to the wind, so you think I mad.
> . . . All you fate in my hand,
> ministers, businessmen, Shabine have you, friend,
> I shall scatter your lives like a handful of sand,
> I who have no weapon but poetry and
> the lances of palms and the sea's shining shield! (16)

The poetic act, the utterance of an imaginative construct, is not the only thing necessary in this poem for the constitution of subjecthood. Shabine, although a figure of authority and learning in the poem, learns the lesson of self-sacrifice from his captain. Near the end of the poem, as the schooner *Flight* is caught in a great storm, Shabine and the rest of the crew prepare themselves for death and the destruction of their subjecthoods. However, through the Christ-like devotion of their captain as he is bound to the helm, "crucif[ied] to his post" (18) the crew survives. Walcott, invoking the virtue and primal power of self-sacrifice, establishes the second condition necessary for transcending oppositional dualities: one must be willing to be devoured by the very forces of history that one seeks to, at least, momentarily decode.

Once Shabine has survived his adventures and avowed the contingent nature of his subjectivity and willingness to submit that subjectivity to the melancholic memory of historical trauma, he declares, "I am satisfied / if my hand gave voice to one people's grief" (19). He is able, drawing on complex and contradictory terms of identity, to articulate, for a moment, the cry of a postcolonial; he mourns the past while imagining that past in melancholic terms: trauma remains but does not disable. And although Walcott, like Shabine, notes that there are "more islands there, man, / than peas on a tin plate, all different size" (19) and implies the unfinished work of recovery that remains, he successfully articulates, momentarily, a postcolonial subjecthood that admits to the trials and travails of colonialism and then transcends them. The transitory and fleeting nature of this subjectivity is, in the end, a necessary aspect of Walcott's project. For him to posit some lasting transcendence of trauma would be for him to implicate his project in a narrative of mourning, a narrative of "getting over" the past, of denying and pathologizing history. By allowing only a momentary transcendence, and an incomplete one at that, Walcott retains the essential affect of the melancholic: the object of loss, while figured alongside the beautiful and transcendent, remains present.

At the end of the poem, Shabine sets down his poems, abandons his speech, and studies the stars:

> Sometimes is just me, and the soft-scissored foam
> as the deck turn white and the moon open
> a cloud like a door, and the light over me
> is a road in white moonlight taking me home. (20)

Thus although Shabine is able to successfully articulate his subjecthood despite the internal contradictions of the postcolonial, he does in the end set aside his linguistic tools and surrender himself to the world. And although this final moment of the poem is clearly an indication of redemption and transcendence, of Walcott's narrator finding himself, at last, able to imagine a way home, a way to a physical and an emotional place of refuge, this remains a moment that, with the absence of a permanent transcendence, is collapsing and transitory. For although "the moon open / a cloud like a door" and the light over Shabine is a road home, it is only a pathway to a destination; it is not the actual destination, the actual permanent transcendence of earthly and historical concerns. The final lines, despite the lyric rapture suggested, are ultimately, once again, a deferral of Shabine's rest. For even as Odysseus, at the end of Homer's epic, suggests that although he has come home to Ithika, he must, according to Teiresias, "take an oar / and trudge the mainland"[20] until he makes the proper sacrifice to Poseidon, so too does the end of Walcott's poem suggest that Shabine's journey is incomplete. The postcolonial's subjectivity, then, is troped as what Stuart Hall refers to as a "diasporic identity": "cultural identities [that] are the points of identification, the unstable points of identification or suture, which are made, within the discourses of history and culture . . . [n]ot an essence, but a *positioning*."[21] Like the landscape of the Caribbean, Shabine's subjectivity contains multiple and sometimes contradictory constitutive elements; their articulation within the text of the poem is unstable, momentary, and articulated through the retention of a melancholic affect. There are suggestions of a transcendence of historical trauma, both in the subject of Shabine and in the sublimity of the Caribbean; however, these suggestions are only strategic and provisional. The possibility of "getting over" the past, of a "healed" and "only beautiful" subject and landscape, is continually deferred, yet this deferral does not result in some kind of Joycean paralysis. Instead, although a desire for a prelapsarian landscape or subjectivity remains as problematic as ever, Shabine, the prototypical postcolonial melancholic, retains his agency, continually reforms and recasts his subjectivity, and persists in his "vain search for one island that heals with its harbor / and a guiltless horizon, where the almond's shadow / doesn't injure the sand" (19). For Shabine, as for Odysseus, the ideal of home and hearth remains, necessarily unfulfilled but still sought after.

Notes

1. Barry Lopez, *Arctic Dreams: Imagination and Desire in a Northern Landscape* (New York: Bantam Books, 1986), 248.

2. Ibid., 250.

3. William Wordsworth, "Preface to the Lyrical Ballads (1802)," in *Romanticism: An Anthology*, ed. Duncan Wu (Oxford: Blackwell, 1994), 252.

4. William Wordsworth, *The Prelude*, 6:701–705. I do not mean to suggest, by any means, that this is a homogenous conception of landscape for the romantics. John Barrell contrasts the "sense of place" in John Clare's poetry to Wordsworth's sense of place. He characterizes Clare as having an almost mournful sense of Helpston that focused on "one particular landscape [that] might be inseparable from the whole of man's knowledge" (*The Idea of Landscape and the Sense of Place, 1730–1840* [Cambridge: Cambridge University Press, 1972], 182). In contrast Barrell observes how close "Wordsworth [was] to the picturesque travellers whom he despised. . . . [H]e opens up the landscape and explains its mysteries in a way not substantially different from the

way William Gilpin . . . might have reclaimed a similarly rough, secluded landscape for the metropolitan imagination" (183).

5. William Slaymaker, "Ecoing the Other(s): The Call of Global Green and Black African Responses," *PMLA* 116, no. 1 (January 2001): 129.

6. William Slaymaker, "Letter," *PMLA* 114, no. 5 (October 1999): 1100.

7. Dominic Head, "The (Im)possibility of Ecocriticism," *Writing the Environment: Ecocriticism and Literature*, ed. Richard Kerridge and Neil Sammells (London: Zed Books, 1998), 27–39.

8. Walcott would go on to produce *Omeros*, as well as a stage version of *The Odyssey* during the 1990s. In both texts he restages the Homeric quest for "home" in the context of a postcolonial's continual and unfulfillable quest for a prelapsarian bliss—a bliss that would imply the constitution of an almost Cartesian subjectivity set in a sublime landscape. See John Thieme's *Derek Walcott* (Manchester: Manchester University Press, 1999), esp. 151–197. Thieme says, "the traveling Odyssean protagonist . . . increasingly becomes a vehicle for expressing his [Walcott's] sense of the need to escape static, essentialist constructions of personality. . . . [This] Odyssean protagonist is a metonym for [Walcott's] complex beliefs about cultural affiliation. . . . He is a figure who not only crosses lines of longitude and latitude at will, but also engages in a similar movement along a discursive continuum which offers emancipation from . . . Manichean binaries" (152).

9. Derek Walcott, *The Star Apple Kingdom* (New York: Farrar, Straus, and Giroux, 1979), 8–9. Subsequent quotations from this work are referenced parenthetically in the text.

10. Robert Young, *Colonial Desire: Hybridity in Theory, Culture, and Race* (London: Routledge, 1995), 5.

11. My purpose in tracing this particular theme is not to indicate any kind of "debt" that Walcott bears in regard to his colonial cultures but rather to resituate his aesthetics within an already established tradition of opposition to modernization. The use of such "Western" tropes is not, of course, without its critiques. Although the question of imposing a conceptual framework whose origins lie in the very culture that has sponsored the colonial encounter is an important point, the postulation that comparative postcolonial criticism is a false homogenizing practice overlooks the dialectical nature of the postcolonial state. See Graham Huggan's "Philomela's Retold Story: Silence, Music, and the Post-Colonial Text," *Journal of Commonwealth Literature* 25, no. 1 (1990): 12–23. Huggan observes that

> the tendency of some of the more extreme nationalist critics to wish away the existence of a European cultural heritage, however distorting and/or debilitating that heritage may have been, seems not only to divest post-colonial writing of much of

> its oppositional power in exposing and critiquing the material conditions which govern its cultural production, but also to risk corralling nation- or race-based literatures into separate, jealously protected territories which resist intrusion to the extent that they become accessible only to those "exclusive insiders" possessed by virtue of birthright or immediacy of experience of an intimate knowledge of their own "field." (20–21)

Additionally, romanticism itself has been troped as a discourse of opposition to modernization. See Saree Makdisi's *Romantic Imperialism: Universal Empire and the Culture of Modernity* (Cambridge: Cambridge University Press, 1998). Makdisi observes that even as the culture of modernity was beginning to consolidate under the indices of capitalism and imperialism, romanticism emerged as a salient ideological discourse that had the capacity to contest the homogenizing historicization occurring under the rubric of modernization. Romanticism, according to Makdisi, operates as a critique of modernization. He does, however, take to heart Marilyn Butler's observation that "romanticism is inchoate because it is not a single intellectual movement but a complex of responses to certain conditions which Western society has experienced and continues to experience since the middle of the eighteenth century." See Marilyn Butler's *Romantics, Rebels, and Reactionaries: English Literature and Its Background, 1760–1830* (Oxford: Oxford University Press, 1981), 184. Makdisi does remark that as the romantic period in Britain marks "the moment of the emergence of the culture of modernization . . . romantic engagements were dialectically bound up with modernization, and contributed to its development as a cultural dominant" (7). In my larger project I trace the entanglements of romanticism and postcoloniality in a larger scope.

12. Anne Cheng, "The Melancholy of Race," *Kenyon Review* 19, no. 1 (winter 1997): 53.

13. Judith Butler remarks in *Gender Trouble* that "Freud revises this distinction between mourning and melancholia and suggests that the identification process associated with melancholia may be 'the sole condition under which the id can give up its objects'" (Judith Butler, *Gender Trouble: Feminism and the Subversion of Identity* [New York: Routledge, 1990], 19). In other words, the identification with lost loves characteristic of melancholia becomes the precondition for the work of mourning. The two processes, originally conceived as oppositional, are not understood as integrally related aspects of the grieving process.

14. Sigmund Freud, "Mourning and Melancholia," in *The Standard Edition of the Complete Psychological Works of Sigmund Freud,* trans. and ed. James Strachey (London: Hogarth, 1953–1974),14:247.

15. Ian Baucom, *Out of Place: Englishness, Empire, and the Locations of Identity* (Princeton: Princeton University Press, 1999), 184.

16. Cheng, 52.

17. Ned Thomas, "Obsession and Responsibility," in *The Art of Derek Walcott,* ed. Stewart Brown (Bridgend, Mid Glamorgan: Seren Books, 1991), 86.

18. Dorothy J. Hale, "Bakhtin in African American Literary Theory," *ELH* 61 (1994): 451–453.

19. The dynamic imagery describing these failed revolutionaries contrasts the stagnation of the postcolonial bureaucracy. Walcott goes on:

> Propeller-blade fans turn over the Senate;
> the judges, they say, still sweat in carmine, . . .
> In the 12:30 movies the projectors best
> not break down, or you go see revolution. (9)

Ironically, in the end the only thing that might startle the bureaucrats out of their coma of inaction is the denial of their entertainment, their "spaghetti West- / ern with Clint Eastwood" (9). He suggests that a corrupt bureaucracy will react only to a threat to its own selfish and trivial interests. Even as the young revolutionaries are doomed to fail, so too are hopes for governmental reform.

20. Homer, *The Odyssey,* trans. Robert Fitzgerald (New York: Anchor Books, 1963), 438.

21. Stuart Hall, "Cultural Identity and Diaspora," *Colonial Discourse and Post-Colonial Theory: A Reader,* ed. Patrick Williams and Laura Chrisman (New York: Columbia University Press, 1994), 395 (Hall's emphasis).

Maggie Gordon

A Woman Writing about Nature

Louise Glück and "the absence of intention"

> I'm not the enemy.
> Only a ruse to ignore
> what you see happening
> right here in this bed. . . .
> . . . .
> . . . I was here first,
> before you were here, before
> you ever planted a garden.
> And I'll be here when only the sun and moon
> are left, and the sea, and the wide field.
>
> —Louise Glück, "Witchgrass"

Louise Glück would perhaps no more consider her work "nature writing" than she would consider herself a "woman poet." In fact, she writes, "If there are such differences [between the writing of women and that of men], it seems to me reasonable to suppose that literature reveals them, and that it will do so more interestingly, more subtly, in the absence of intention."[1] Some years ago a comment by Robert Hass about "nature writing" lent proof in my mind to this theory of Glück's. Responding to a question about his "environmental work" (he had been named Educator of the Year by the North American Association on Environmental Education in 1997) posed during a discussion session after a reading, Hass talked about River of Words, a poetry contest for U.S. elementary-school children he founded during his tenure as poet laureate. Then, considering his poetry, he said, "Of course, *I'm* not a 'nature writer.'" I understood the distinction he was making—he went on to discuss what he referred to as the "thematically driven" work of Barry Lopez, Annie Dillard, and Gary Snyder—yet the remark took me by surprise, knowing how rooted Hass's poetry is in the spirituality of day-to-day living and in an awareness of the interdependence of human and nonhuman nature. Perhaps he was correct to emphasize in his response that he does not seek to confront explicitly environmental issues in literature the way some do. Yet it is evident throughout his poetry, from *Field Guide* in 1973 to *Sun under Wood* in 1996, that Hass's way of being in the world engages ecological principles and that a personal sense of the sacred interconnectivity of all life does inform his work. Perhaps, then, the ecological vision revealed by the poetry is in fact made more richly complex by the kind of "absence of intention" of which Glück writes.

In the same way, it is precisely because Glück does not self-consciously write *about* nature *as* a woman—although she is always a woman writing about nature—that her poetic career illuminates the ecofeminist movement it parallels. Glück's career, from 1968's *Firstborn* to the present, spans approximately the same period as the emergence and development of American ecofeminism and embodies some of the core values of ecofeminist philosophy and theology. In the nearly three decades since Françoise d'Eaubonne coined the term *ecofeminisme* in "*Le Féminisme ou la mort,*" there have been, generally speaking, three paths to ecofeminism: the study of political theory and history; exposure to nature-based religions; and environmentalism.[2] As a social change movement, like the environmentalism and second-wave feminism from which it partly derives, ecofeminism develops out of experience, whether it be academic study, religious practice, or social activism. Similarly, the ecofeminist vision of Glück's poetry—the sense of the interdependence of human and nonhuman nature and the profound awareness of human bodily nature—emerges from the physical and psychological experience of being a woman in the latter half of the twentieth century.

Ecofeminism challenges conventional perceptions of subjectivity and relationality, and although, as Carol J. Adams suggests, we might rightly speak not of ecofeminism but of ecofeminism*s*, Ynestra King's classification of shared concerns provides a useful framework for articulating what it is that is "ecofeminist" about Glück's poetics.[3] King writes that ecofeminist thought in its myriad forms is marked by the following shared beliefs: "one) the oppression of women and the building of 'Western industrial civilization' are interrelated through the belief that women are closer to nature; two) life on earth is heterarchical, 'an interconnected web'; three) a balanced ecosystem of human and nonhuman 'must maintain diversity'; four) species survival necessitates a 'renewed understanding of our relationship to nature, of our own bodily nature and nonhuman nature around us.' "[4] Glück's contemplation of bodily experience fosters such ecofeminist appreciation of the shared materiality of the earth body and the personal, particularly the female, body.

This ecofeminist awakening comes early in her career, as meditations on the exclusively female experiences of adolescent anorexia and maternity reform the poet's understanding of identity and relationship.[5] In her first four collections—*Firstborn, The House on Marshland* (1975), *Descending Figure* (1980), and *The Triumph of Achilles* (1985)—Glück draws the kinds of ecofeminist conclusions King identifies regarding the relationship between human and nonhuman nature and human bodily nature, and such conclusions function as the basis of her poetics. The poet treats maternity in her first volume, *Firstborn,* and adolescent anorexia in her third, *Descending Figure,* as threshold experiences, the discoveries of which foster the speaker's identification with nonhuman nature, prompting a fresh understanding of subjectivity, corporeality, gender, and spirituality. It is this intensified awareness of the heterarchical nature of all life and appreciation for the shared materiality of the personal and earth bodies that leads to the use of a myth-narrative lyric that becomes a hallmark of her career. Like that of so many contemporary feminists and environmentalists, Glück's thought—specifically, her ecopoetics—emerges from a personal experience of being a daughter, a sister, a lover, a wife, and a mother. With the notable exception of *The Wild Iris,* the 1992 collection for which she was awarded the Pulitzer Prize, Glück has rarely taken the actual or assumed relationship between women and nature as the explicit subject of her poetry and is, of course, not a "nature writer" in the conventional sense. Yet an ecofeminist perspective clearly informs her poetry and shapes her poetics throughout her career, which, with 1999's *Vita Nova,* spans eight collections and more than thirty years. That it does so in the "absence of intention" illuminates the ways that for so many women in the late twentieth and early twenty-first centuries the personal has become the ecological and the ecological in turn become political.

Glück's consideration of maternity in her earliest work leads to an appreciation for the heterarchical nature of all life that informs the poet's characteristic use of narrative personae. As Glück emphasizes in her representations of pregnancy in *Firstborn* and *The House on Marshland,* in maternity the reproductive body highlights the natural cycle of birth, life, and death common to all living things. As we see in poems such as "The Wound," pregnancy alienates the speaker from the human community and suggests instead an affinity with reproductive elements of the nonhuman natural world. "Faking scrabble" with neighbors, the speaker is detached from the human world, observing her husband "clutch [his] blank" and dismissing the other couple, "both on Nembutal / the killer pill."[6] Pregnant, she cannot identify with these impotent and incapacitated others but rather sees herself reflected in the nonhuman, first in the wallpaper, "paisley, like a plot / Of embryos" (11–12), then in nature beyond the walls of her confinement, where shrubs and hedges "grow / Downy, bloom and seed" (15–16) and "[r]ipe things sway in the light" (30).[7]

Poems about the speaker's own pregnancy in *Firstborn* are echoed by similar treatments of other experiences of maternity—specifically, those of her own mother (in "For My Mother") and of the Virgin Mary (in "Nativity Poem")—in Glück's next collection, *The House on Marshland.* "For My Mother," for example, has the speaker ostensibly recalling the initial experience of the maternal body: prior to her own birth. Her mother's experience mirrors the maternity presented in *Firstborn,* and the last lines of the poem associate the maternal body with nonhuman nature in an image reminiscent of the "[r]ipe things" of "The Wound," as "Schools of spores circulate / behind the shades, drift through / gauze flutterings of vegetation."[8] In poems such as "The Wound," "The Egg," "For My Mother," and "Nativity Poem," the female bodily experience of pregnancy suggests a kinship with nonhuman nature to a woman feeling alienated from the human community because of her experience.

This sense of kinship extends beyond pregnancy itself, as we see in "The Egg," a poem that, in its three parts, represents the maternal body before, during, and after birth. In the third section, having given birth, the speaker perceives her postpartum body as having been emptied out; she sees fish coming in to the beach:

> . . . Without skins
> Without fins, the bare
> . . . .
> Husks, husks. . . .
> . . . Through gaping mussels.
> Pried flesh.[9]

Here the nonhuman natural world mirrors not only the pregnant, but also the postpartum, body, suggesting that the sense of interconnectivity first experienced during pregnancy lastingly shapes the speaker's perception of her relationship to nonhuman nature.

Just as reflections on maternity suggest an ecofeminist understanding of interconnectivity in these first two collections, in Glück's third volume, *Descending Figure,* poetic consideration of another decidedly female bodily experience, adolescent anorexia, prompts the kind of "renewed understanding of [human] bodily nature" of which King writes. The poet's analysis of her own experience of anorexia reinforces the appreciation for the heterarchical nature of all life prompted by maternity, and the recovered anorexic's deepened understanding of mortality highlights the shared materiality of personal and earth bodies.

Charlene Spretnak writes that it is in light of the association and degradation of women's bodies and the earth body that "[d]epression, fear, [and] self-loathing are common psychological themes for women raised under patriarchy."[10] For the adolescent female raised under patriarchy, such psychological themes often become manifest in anorexia. For many cultural ecofeminists and feminist theologians, to recover from such self-loathing, women must recognize their feelings as an internalization of the patriarchal assertion that the personal (particularly woman's) body and earth body are degraded.[11]

Throughout her work, and especially in poems such as "Witchgrass" and "Jeanne D'Arc" (in which Joan believes her burning at the hand of the Inquisition is the playing out of God's will on her body), Glück is critical of what she perceives as the Church's sanctioning of the persecution of women on the basis of their bodies. In "Witchgrass" she writes:

> as we both know,
> if you worship
> one god, you only need
> one enemy.[12]

Glück embodies the voice of the persecuted other (literally, here, a weed in the garden) in these lines and those quoted in the epigraph above, making overt a central ecofeminist critique: the historical association, and subsequent oppression and domination, of women and nature. "To the issues of sexism, racism, classism, and heterosexism," Adams writes, "ecofeminists add naturism—the oppression of the rest of nature."[13] For the "witchgrass" that itself speaks the eponymous poem, such "-isms" represent merely "another / way to blame / one tribe for everything."[14] Like the personae of "Gretel in Darkness" and "Jeanne D'Arc" (both from *The House on Marshland*), this speaker recognizes sexism as merely one manifestation of a process of demonization not only condoned by, but, according to the poet, in fact a product of, a monotheistic worldview that codifies binary thinking.

Glück's treatment of anorexia in *Descending Figure* and her discussion of it in the essay "Education of the Poet" suggest that in her experience anorexia is not so much an attempt to attain a culturally dictated body image (as it is popularly represented) but rather an internalization of a dominant ideology that perceives the body and soul as discrete and the female body as particularly foul. In "Dedication to Hunger" the poet describes anorexia, the "deviation" of "certain *female* children," as "fear of death, taking as its form / dedication to hunger";[15] in other words, for adolescent girls in particular, according to Glück, anorexia is an attempt to deny mortality by denying one's physicality, as evidenced by the reliance on food for survival. In "Education of the Poet" Glück takes the experience of and recovery from anorexia as metaphor for her poetry and states that ultimately the anorexic's effort "proves not the soul's superiority to but its dependence on the flesh."[16]

For Glück the anorexic's recovery fosters in her an intense awareness of her own corporeality, evidencing as it does that the spirit and the flesh are one. Through examination of the anorexic's refusal to accept her own bodily nature, the poet arrives at a deepened appreciation for the inseparability of soul and body. Recovery from anorexia thus signifies a rejection of Western patriarchal assumptions about the body and an acceptance of physicality. Spretnak discusses a similar awareness of the inextricability of body and soul and affirmation of the relationship between personal and earth bodies in "women who [drift] out of patriarchal religion."[17]

This appreciation of shared materiality between human and nonhuman recurs throughout Glück's work following *Descending Figure.* The association of personal and earth body seen in "Dedication to Hunger," in which the horrified speaker realizes that "a woman's body / *is* a grave,"[18] is echoed in the burial of the family patriarch in 1990's *Ararat.* Glück's four most recent collections—*Ararat, The Wild Iris, Meadowlands* (1996), and *Vita Nova*—are poem cycles, volumes in which theme, recurrent motifs, personae, and imagery, and consistencies of tone, syntax, and vocabulary, bind the poems together in a whole. (In *The Wild Iris,* for instance, the poems are set over the course of a single seasonal cycle of the garden, and in *Meadowlands, The Odyssey* is used to parallel the dissolution of a modern marriage.) Given the importance of *Ararat* in this context, it is significant that its core theme is funeral, a communal ritual in which the body is returned to the earth. In funeral, the shared materiality of personal and earth body is ritually made sacred. In *The Wild Iris,* the volume following *Ararat,* flowers themselves speak of their own death and burial. "Lover of Flowers" (among others) from *Ararat* seems to foreshadow *The Wild Iris,* as Glück writes of a sister obsessed with planting flowers at their mother's house following the death of their father. Their mother pays for the flowers because, Glück writes, "it's her garden, every flower / planted for my father. They both see / the house as his true grave."[19] The importance of funeral recurs most recently in "The Open Grave" (*Vita Nova*), in which the speaker now gives her mother's body to the earth as well. Such ritualized recognition of corporeality as we see in burial—both in funeral and in gardening—makes sacred the material kinship of human and nonhuman nature.

According to Spretnak, women who reject the Western patriarchal division of body and spirit, as does Glück's recovered anorexic speaker, and in fact accept and celebrate corporeality are able to "view culture not as a struggle in opposition to nature but as a potentially harmonious extension of nature, a human construction inclusive of creative tensions and reflective of our embeddedness in the Earthbody and the teachings of nature: diversity, subjectivity, adaptability, interrelatedness. Within such an orientation—let's call it ecological sanity—the bodily affinity of females and males with nature is respected and culturally honored, rather than denied and scorned."[20] Glück's recognition and acceptance of ecofeminist principles regarding heterarchy and physicality foster in the poet an "I-Thou" relationship with human and nonhuman others that informs her poetics, particularly her characteristic use of narrative and mythic personae.

In *The Wild Iris* the human gardener speaks of feeling

> . . . passionately
> attached to the living tree, [her] body
> . . . .
> almost able to feel
> sap frothing and rising.[21]

The first of the volume's many "prayers," "Matins" sets the tone for the collection, in which the poet speaks not only in the "I" voice of conventional lyric but also, alternately, as elements of nonhuman nature (as in "Witchgrass"), a woman gardener praying in poems titled "Matins" and "Vespers," and a voice that seems at times to be responding to the prayers.[22] This is, of course, not Glück's first use of personae; in fact, it becomes a characteristic poetic strategy as early as the middle section of *Firstborn,* titled "The Edge," following the poems of maternity in the volume's first section, "The Egg." The difference in their use in *The Wild Iris,* then, is a matter of degree, not kind, as here she seeks to embody and give voice not to mythological or fictional characters but to plant life and even abstract concepts.

The woman gardener's attachment to the "living tree" evokes the "I-Thou" relationship of which theologian Martin Buber writes: "[I]f will and grace are joined . . . as I contemplate the tree I am drawn into a relation, and the tree ceases to be an It. The power of exclusiveness has seized me."[23] It is in such an "I-Thou" relationship that Glück speaks as (rather than *for*) aspects of the nonhuman natural world in *The Wild Iris.* Establishing this sense of interconnectivity here in this first prayer poem of the collection illuminates the poet's assuming of various "personae" throughout her career and especially in this radically heteroglot volume. A sense of the heterarchical nature of all life suggests that individual identity is itself fluid, yet because the lyric persona depends on at least the illusion of a Cartesian fixed, stable identity—a voice to speak the "I" of the poem—such understanding of ecological subjectivity necessarily shapes Glück's poetics. The ecopoetics shaped through the discoveries of relationality and physicality early in her career are the basis for a poetics in which the poet is constantly shifting among identities, from, for instance, that of a seventeenth-century prioress in "The Cell" in *Firstborn* to that of an entire field of "Daisies" in *The Wild Iris.*

Throughout her career, both in her poetry and in her prose, Glück's prevailing metaphor for her poetry is as a vocation. For Glück it is a vocation that demands a commitment to engage the materials of this world—language, experience—in an effort to make contact. The recognition and acceptance of the relationality of personal and earth bodies authorizes artistic creativity, which for Glück is a manipulation and interaction with organic materials; in the metapoetic *Meadowlands,* for instance, the poetic craft is paralleled by the cooking done by the modern wife and the ancient Penelope's weaving. In "Phenomenal Survivals of Death in Nantucket," from *Firstborn,* the speaker returns from the threshold of human experience with the knowledge of the materiality of the human body, as the ocean and, the metaphor implies, the earth, as well, intermingle with the "material" of the speaker herself:

> Here in Nantucket does the tiny soul
> Confront water. Yet this element is not foreign soil;
> I see the water as extensions of my mind
> . . . .
> Awake I see Nantucket but with this bell
> Of voice I can toll you tokens of regions below visible.[24]

Glück's poetry is set in a New England and eastern coastal landscape throughout her career, and, as we see here, it is a world infused with the numinous, to which the poet offers the reader insight. From the island towns of her earliest work to the Vermont farmland of *The Wild Iris* and *Meadowlands,* and, most recently, the cultural landscape of the Cambridge to which the poet moves after a second divorce, Glück sees herself as not entirely separate and is therefore able to offer the reader access to spiritual, invisible, realms. In light of her developing appreciation for the heterarchical and corporeal nature of earthly existence, the poet perceives the interconnectedness of elements: "soul," "water," "soil," "mind." Having established such a relationship to her materials, the poet transforms what she consciously sees (Nantucket), using poetic constructions (the "voice" that is a "bell") to give form to the abstract. In the above lines we see Glück's characteristic evocation of the mythic within the ordinary, the "toll" and "tokens" of "regions below visible" simultaneously suggesting the journey to hell and a subway ride.

In light of such an apparently ecofeminist ideology at work in her poetics, it is important to note that although she gives voice to many classical gods and goddesses and other mythological figures throughout her work, Glück never explicitly turns to the so-called goddess spirituality often associated with cultural ecofeminism. In fact, she writes critically of Czeslaw Milosz, "The paganism he defends is maternal. Earth centered. Moon centered. Fruitful. Predictable. Cyclical. This is the same fecund earth Hass reveres. Both approve it as the wise man approves woman, radiant in otherness."[25] Glück dismisses this kind of "maternal paganism" in her male contemporaries as equally reductive as the degradation of the female/earth body that she has so often criticized in Judeo-Christian thought and practice.

Although she arrives at apparently ecofeminist conclusions regarding heterarchy, human bodily nature, and the relationship between Western patriarchal ideology and the connected oppression of women and exploitation of nature, Glück's foremost concern is poetic rather than political. That is to say, her work is not driven overtly by themes of feminism and environmentalism. Yet, as we have seen, her poetics emerges from the personal bodily experience of being a woman in the latter half of the twentieth century, and it is in the kind of "absence of intention" of which Glück suggests gender difference may emerge in writing that an ecofeminist vision shapes her poetics and informs her poetry.

Notes

1. Louise Glück, "Education of the Poet," in *Proofs and Theories: Essays on Poetry* (Hopewell, N.J.: Ecco, 1994), 7.

2. Charlene Spretnak, "Ecofeminism: Our Roots and Our Flowering," in *Reweaving the World: The Emergence of Ecofeminism,* ed. Irene Diamond and Gloria Feman Orenstein (San Francisco: Sierra Club Books, 1990), 3–14, esp. 5–6.

3. Carol J. Adams, introduction to *Ecofeminism and the Sacred,* ed. Carol J. Adams (New York: Continuum, 1993), 1.

4. Quoted in Patrick D. Murphy, *Literature, Nature, and Other: Ecofeminist Critiques* (New York: SUNY Press, 1995), 7–8.

5. Eating disorders, including anorexia, are of course not restricted to any particular gender, race, age, or socioeconomic class. Yet because adolescent anorexics experience the "disorder" during a period in which sexual maturation catalyzes a gender-identity crisis, I would suggest *each* experience of anorexia is, in some sense, gendered. The anorexia Glück presents in *Descending Figure* and in the essay "Education of the Poet" specifically pertains to female sexual development and to the adolescent's more sophisticated recognition and interrogation of cultural gender roles and therefore may be considered "exclusively female."

6. Louise Glück, "The Wound," in *The First Four Books of Poems* (Hopewell, N.J.: Ecco, 1995), 20–24.

7. "The Wound" echoes Charlotte Perkins Gilman's "The Yellow Wallpaper," in which the narrator, Jane, suffers postpartum depression and is similarly treated condescendingly and made to "convalesce." Like Glück's speaker, detached from human interaction, Jane sees her own circumstance reflected in the wallpaper. For an insightful discussion of the "domestic carceral" and contemporary rhetoric on pregnancy, see Helena Michie, "Confinements: The Domestic in the Discourses of Upper-Middle-Class Pregnancy," in *Feminisms: An Anthology of Literary Theory and Criticism,* ed. Robyn R. Warhol and Diane Price Herndl, 2nd ed. (New Brunswick, N.J.: Rutgers University Press, 1997), 57–69.

8. Glück, "The Wound," 25–27.

9. Louise Glück, "The Egg," in *First Four Books,* 6–8.

10. Charlene Spretnak, *States of Grace: The Recovery of Meaning in the Postmodern Age* (San Francisco: HarperCollins, 1991), 119.

11. See, especially, Spretnak, *States of Grace;* and Carol P. Christ, *Rebirth of the Goddess: Finding Meaning in Feminist Spirituality* (New York: Routledge, 1997).

12. Louise Glück, "Witchgrass," in *The Wild Iris* (Hopewell, N.J.: Ecco, 1992), 11–14.

13. Adams, introduction, 1.

14. Glück, "Witchgrass," 8–10.

15. Louise Glück, "Dedication to Hunger," in *Descending Figure* (Hopewell, N.J.: Ecco, 1980), 49 (emphasis added).

16. Glück, "Education," 10.

17. Spretnak, *States of Grace,* 136.

18. Glück, "Dedication to Hunger," 52–53.

19. Louise Glück, "Lover of Flowers," in *Ararat* (New York: Ecco, 1990), 15–17.

20. Spretnak, *States of Grace,* 136.

21. Louise Glück, "Matins [2]," in *The Wild Iris,* 9, 12–13. Eight poems in *The Wild Iris* are titled "Matins." I include page numbers for clarity.

22. The titles of the poems of this last speaker (e.g., "Retreating Wind," "Early Darkness," "September Twilight") suggest that it is an embodiment of an abstract concept of

the sacred rather than an anthropomorphic being; and, given the critical tendency to refer to this speaker as "the god," or even "God," it is important to note that not even the gardener uses such terms. Furthermore, it is only the titles assigned the poems, and not the poems themselves, that identify the gardener's poems as "prayers." Ironically, only the flowers use the word *god* (as well as *father* and *master*), and they do so apparently in reference to the human.

23. Quoted in Christ, 114.

24. Louise Glück, "Phenomenal Survivals of Death in Nantucket," in *Firstborn,* 1–3, 11–12.

25. Louise Glück, "Obstinate Humanity," in *Proofs and Theories,* 65–71, esp. 66.

Richard Hunt

How to Love This World

The Transpersonal Wild in Margaret Atwood's Ecological Poetry

Asked how ideas come to her, Margaret Atwood once said, "You put your left hand on the earth and hold your right hand in the air. Sooner or later, you will get an idea."[1] And although one might dismiss this response as rather glib, much of Atwood's poetry does appear to have been generated with her left hand so situated.

Consider, for instance, "Frogless," from *Morning in the Burning House*, which speaks of a future without frogs. Biologists tell us that frogs, a primary indicator of an ecosystem's health, now seem to be vanishing in many parts of the world. But in Atwood's poem far more than just frogs are at risk; we see, for instance, a deformed eel, born with "a dead eye / grown from its cheek." Trees become "sore" from "a hot gauze of snow" that sears their roots. Even the worms are "drunk and burning" from the "pure antifreeze" in the streams. And what of the humans in this place? They "eat sick fish / because there are no others. Then they get born wrong."[2]

"This is home," Atwood reminds us.[3] Yet perhaps we are more fortunate than she; although this is *her* vision of the future, it is not yet necessarily ours. Still, she says, it's coming: "Travel anywhere in a year, five years, / and you'll end up here" (56–57). "Here": a landscape barren of frogs, barren of edible (read "healthy") fish. Some years earlier Atwood had recalled Northrop Frye's observation that the question "Who am I?" is often subservient to the question "Where is here?"[4] The "here" in "Frogless" is severely damaged; it can only lead to an equally severely damaged "I."

The environmental awareness in "Frogless" is not an isolated occurrence in Atwood's work. If it comes as something of a surprise to think of Atwood as a nature writer, perhaps it is because American readers, for the most part, think of her as primarily a novelist; and of her novels only *Surfacing* would likely be included in a course in environmental literature. But throughout her career attentiveness to the natural world has been a recurring and important feature of her poetry. Atwood's interest in the natural world goes back to her childhood: her father, an entomologist, "used to bring home these 'things'" for her to study. "Later on," she says, "I studied chemistry and biology and zoology, and if I hadn't been a writer I'd have gone on with that."[5]

But if it is clear that the natural world often plays a role in Atwood's work, it is often less clear just *what* role it plays. Critics have tended to see Atwood's use of nature primarily as a metaphor for human relationships. Coral Ann Howells, for instance, argues that Atwood's nature serves a Canadian nationalist purpose. The wilderness, she writes, is "a crucial feature of Atwood's construction of Canadian identity."[6] John Wilson Foster considers Atwood's nature poetry in terms of a journey "inwards, an exploration of the self and its relationships."[7] Also arguing for a psychological reading, Gary Ross sees an "unspecified conflict between the poet and landscape" in which "the wilderness world comes to stand for the outside correspondent of some internal state."[8] Finally, although Judith McCombs does look at Atwood as a "nature writer," comparing her work with that of Annie Dillard, among others, she too casts the work in terms of gender, in which "[t]he relation of the *I* to nature shifts from the men's sexual power struggle to the women's identification and alliance."[9]

Although these responses to Atwood's nature poetry differ greatly, each proceeds from a commonly held anthropocentric understanding of the natural world. More, they presuppose in Atwood a similar view. I will argue, however, that Atwood is far from anthropocentric in much of her nature poetry, that she is often highly attentive to environmental issues, and that indeed neither the intensity nor the direction of her environmentalism has yet been fully recognized.

Nature typically plays one of two roles in Atwood's poetry. In the first, which predominates in her earlier work, nature serves primarily as setting or background for poems dealing with other issues. But although even a look at the way nature serves as background can illuminate a writer's understanding of the natural world, I prefer instead to focus on nature's second role, in which the natural world is the subject of a particular poem. As we will see, those poems often address explicitly environmental issues, from the exploitation of resources and animal rights in the earliest work to environmental degradation and species extinction in more recent poems.

The Circle Game, winner of the Governor General's Award in 1967, was the first of Atwood's works to see wide circulation.[10] Although most of the poems feature nature as background, we can still see the beginning of Atwood's uneasiness with the effects of human intervention in nature. "The City Planners," for instance, critiques suburbia, where "the houses in pedantic rows, the planted / sanitary trees, assert / levelness of surface like a rebuke."[11] The rebuke is returned, though, as the too-fixed stare of the wide windows

give[s] momentary access to
the landscape behind or under
the future cracks in the plaster

when the houses, capsized, will slide
obliquely into the clay seas, gradual as glaciers
that right now nobody notices. (27)

In "Pre-Amphibian" the speaker, presumably no longer in the morass of suburbia, finds herself in a swamp "where we transmuted are / part of this warm rotting / of vegetable flesh."[12] The distinction between mediated and unmediated nature is clear, as are Atwood's preferences. She depicts the suburbs in harsh terms: cracked plaster, capsized houses sliding into the sea. The artifice of the contemporary suburb can lead only to oblivion, both for the land itself and for the speaker. In contrast, Atwood depicts humans as "warm fish moving" through that primordial swamp, back to the sea, to which, as she well knows, all life can trace a common ancestry.

With *The Animals in That Country* Atwood continues her critique of our culture's intrusive relationship with nature. The title figure of "Progressive Insanities of a Pioneer" moves further and further toward insanity as he asserts himself on what he perceives to be a hostile farmland. At the poem's center is a telling sequence in which the pioneer complains about the resistance of the land he has sought unsuccessfully to tame:

This is not order
but the absence
of order.

He was wrong, the unanswering
forest implied:

It was
an ordered absence.[13]

The pioneer does not, Atwood implies, understand the land he has been working. The pioneer is "obstinate"; refusing to take the land on its own terms, demanding that it be as his fancy prescribes, he vanishes "down through the stone" (38). Because he does not know how—or is unwilling—to reconcile his own needs with those of the land he seeks to inhabit, the pioneer seems likely to disappear entirely, one more disappointed, displaced visitor in a land to which he never would belong. He dissolves into the land, becomes part of the land, leaving only a "green / vision" behind (39). Atwood leaves the pioneer sunk only knee-deep in the soil; his eventual place remains undetermined. He continues to stand, like so many of us, poised both as a part of and apart from the land and now seems, in effect, to occupy two places at once.

In "The Animals in That Country," Atwood defines those two places in terms of their animal inhabitants: "that country"—in which "the animals / have the faces of people"; and "this country"—in which they "have the faces of / animals."[14] The narrator stands *between* the two countries. Atwood considers the process by which one country has mutated into the other in "Elegy for the Giant Tortoises." The speaker wants to engage in "a meditation / upon the giant tortoises / withering finally on a remote island" (23). But she is unable to concentrate on the disappearing tortoises; she tries to focus, but the site of her meditations—subways and (city) parks—proves too much of a distraction. In the end we see the tortoises

> lumbering up the steps, under the archways
> toward the square glass altars
>
> where the brittle gods are kept,
> the relics of what we have destroyed,
> our holy and obsolete symbols. (23)

The ancient animals may well be holy, but in a world of subways and cities, where ancient species survive only in "square glass altars," that very holiness itself is becoming "obsolete." The poem ends on this note; there is no message of hope nor even a call for reconciliation. The two countries have irrevocably split, and we humans are left in the lesser place.

The title character in Atwood's next book, *The Journals of Susanna Moodie,* speaks from that lesser place.[15] Always a stranger in her wilderness home, in "Disembarking at Quebec" Moodie complains that "The moving water will not show me / my reflection."[16] As a recent immigrant she realizes that she has "entered a large darkness" in the wild and, further, that "It was our own / ignorance we entered. // I have not come out yet" (12). Like the insane pioneer whose situation she so recalls, Moodie never comes to love, nor even to truly inhabit, the land. In "Death of a Young Son by Drowning" she contrasts the image of a child "hung in the river like a heart" with the place of the tragedy, where "the sun kept shining, the new grass / lept to solidity"; she plants her dead son in the ground "like a flag" (31). But a flag is always both an artifice and an abstraction; both her dead son and the land in which he is buried remain artificial. In the book's final poem, "A Bus along St Clair: December," Atwood imagines Moodie as an old woman riding a city bus, circa 1970. She looks about her and realizes that the modern streets she sees cover the wilderness of her youth. She speaks to a fellow passenger:

> Turn, look down:
> there is no city;
> this is the centre of a forest
> your place is empty. (61)

This is but a nostalgic recollection, though; Moodie remains essentially ignorant. She felt no less "empty" when living in the wilderness; she ceases to regard the wilderness as ugly and hostile only when she is far enough removed from it that it can offer her no further threat.

The constraints of the *Moodie* project allow Atwood only so much space for maneuver; however stylized her Moodie becomes, Atwood cannot turn the *historical* Moodie into a contemporary environmentalist. But Atwood uses Moodie's experience as a map to the prevailing cultural attitude toward nature. In her second 1970 publication, *Procedures for Underground,* Atwood expands on the questions she could not have Susanna Moodie consider. She offers a counter to Moodie's prolonged estrangement from the land with "Two Gardens," in which a planted garden contains

> fabric—
> textured zinnias; asters the colours of chintz; thick
> pot-shaped marigolds, the sunflowers brilliant as
> imitations."[17]

Each flower, although brilliant and beautiful, is described in terms of a human-made object. Outside this cultured garden is the second garden, where

> plants that grow
> without sunlight
> . . . have their roots
> in another land. (16–17)

Our vision may linger only on the surface of the cultivated flowers; but the others "are mist," and "if you touch them, your / eyes go through them" (17). The wild plants, Atwood tells us, have a depth to them that those of the domestic garden cannot approach.

Atwood's resistance to control seems particularly strong in her next volume, the aptly titled *Power Politics.* Unlike her previous books, *Power Politics* has no table of contents and thus even in its structure resists being "domesticated" or controlled. In addition, many of the poems are untitled, further resisting control. In one of the untitled poems the speaker recalls the split we saw in "Two Gardens":

> You want to go back
> to where the sky was inside us
> animals ran through us, our hands
> blessed and killed according to our
> wisdom.[18]

But Atwood is no sentimentalist wishing for a return to some proto-Rousseauian benign jungle; we cannot go back to an animal existence, she declares, for

> we have been
> improved, our heads float several inches above our necks
> moored to us by
> rubber tubes. (9)

Although she may be less than generous in this description, she recognizes the inevitability of human progress. Such a recognition, though, does not obscure the dangers inherent in that progress. In a later poem in *Power Politics* she speaks in the voice of nature, which, she implies, is becoming increasingly tired of our continued interference, our manipulations, our blunders:

> I'm through, I won't make
> any more flowers for you
>
> I judge you as the trees do
> by dying. (32–33)

It is a harsh judgment, although perhaps one not entirely unwarranted.

Atwood's next book, *You Are Happy*, consists of four separate poem cycles, two of which focus on elements of the natural world. In "Songs of the Transformed" Atwood speaks in the voices of ten different animals, offering validations for the harsh judgments of *Power Politics*. In "Pig Song" the pig complains that humans have transformed it into nothing more than "a greypink vegetable with slug / eyes, buttock / incarnate."[19] Elsewhere we encounter worms who "know the philosophy of boots" that squash them into the pavement. The worms remind us, though, of their inevitable retribution:

we are waiting
under your feet.
When we say Attack you will hear nothing
at first (35).

In the final poem of the sequence, "Corpse Song," the speaker offers

something
you do not want:
news of the country I am trapped in,
news of your future:
soon you will have no voice. (43)

Thus the sequence that begins with the transformation of a pig into a mere commodity, and moves from there to a reminder that the worms will get you in the end, closes with a corpse telling of a silent future "swollen with words you never said, / swollen with hoarded love" (44). We might read such a sequence as a cause-and-effect scenario, in which rampant commodification of nature leads to both physical and spiritual corruption. "Songs of the Transformed" both calls our attention to our fundamentally dysfunctional relationship with the natural world and implicitly demands that we take action to avoid the dire results of that dysfunction.

The second "nature" cycle in *You Are Happy*, the "Circe / Mud Poems," consists of two dozen untitled poems, each spoken by the mythical Circe about her encounter with Odysseus. In the title's conjunction of character and land Atwood offers an alternative to the relationship depicted in "Songs of the Transformed." We enter through a landscape marked by a "forest / burned and sparse" (46), in which the events of the sequence occur. The landscape plays a crucial role in the entire sequence, but Atwood's speaking persona, whether Circe or landscape, refuses to *describe* the landscape to the reader: "Why should I describe the landscape for you?" she demands. "You live here, don't you? . . . See for yourself" (52). The irony in this, of course, is that Odysseus did not actually *live* on Circe's island at all. He was just visiting. The implication is clear: we, who too often proceed as though we were merely visiting the land, are equally incapable of seeing it for ourselves.

In another of the "Circe / Mud Poems" Circe relates a secondhand tale, one told "by another traveller, just passing through" (61). This traveler tells of two boys who fashion a woman out of mud on an island. They use the mud woman for sexual gratification, "sinking with ecstasy into her soft moist belly" until finally the mud woman is "swept away in a sudden flood." The traveler concludes by saying that "no woman since then has equalled her." Circe then regains the narrative, asking the reader, "Is this what you would like me to be, this mudwoman?" (61). The question is provocative, especially when combined with Atwood's association of Circe and mud. It is as though the land itself were speaking, asking us what it is we want of it. The story of the mud woman also calls attention to the biblical traditions that have so often led us to think we can, like the boys on the island, have our way with the land. But, as Atwood has often warned us, that biblical tradition can work two ways. Although it may appear to permit us to transform the land as we please, those transformations may have dire consequences—a sudden flood may, indeed, occur, leaving us as empty as it left the two boys whose creation was washed away.

Not flood but fire opens *Two-Headed Poems.* In "Burned Space" Atwood looks at the aftereffects of a forest fire. "Before the burn," she writes, "this was a forest. / Now it's something else."[20] Something else: another "transformation." Unlike the one performed on the pig, however, this transformation is not about degradation but regeneration; for amid the fire's "dampened embers" we also see "reddish flowers and glowing seeds" (9–10). In "Marsh, Hawk" Atwood pictures a swamp filled with garbage, which "spreads on the / land like a bruise" (87). The speaker knows that the swamp, however fouled, remains an important link between the human and the nonhuman worlds. We can see only so much, Atwood offers, and it is "from the places / we can't see" that the

> guttural swamp voices
> impenetrable, not human,
> utter their one-note
> syllables, boring and
> significant as oracles and quickly over. (87)

The speaker, although able to hear these voices, is unable to attract their attention, is unable to gain entry to the world of the swamp. We might suspect that such entry would be akin to that of the relentless pioneers of Atwood's earlier poems. But, we quickly learn,

> intrusion is not what we want,
> we want it to open, the marsh rushes
> to bend aside, the water
> accept us." (87)

The matter remains, in the end, unresolved: the speaker wants to merge with the swamp,

> to have it slide
> through us, disappearance
> of the skin, this is what we are looking for
> the way in. (88)

This is clearly not the stuff all those pioneers are made of; at last we begin to see the suggestion of a new role for humans in the natural world.

For Atwood seeks to inspire a change in the way we perceive the relationship among all living things. In "Vultures," from *True Stories,* Atwood writes of creatures whose role is to carve out "a little / territory of murder."[21] The speaker asks the vulture, "frowzy old saint," a single question: "what do you make / of death, which you do not / cause, which you eat daily?" The vulture replies, "I make life, which is a prayer" (73). Atwood does two interesting things in this passage. First, she illustrates the economy of nature that the great scavengers personify. All things lead into one another, she tells us; all are connected—an understanding that might have made Susanna Moodie's life in the bush far happier, that might have saved the pioneer of *The Animals in That Country* from his progressive insanity.

The second point Atwood makes in "Vultures" is perhaps more subtle. She equates not life itself but the *making* of life with prayer. The praying figure is a vulture, a creature that plays its particular role in the cycle of life and death; here Atwood recognizes its actions as holy. It is not so much the particulars of the vulture's actions that are holy but the way it fits into its own environment. Perhaps, Atwood suggests, we would be wise, like the vulture, to know our proper role within the natural world and to treat that role with reverence. It is not necessary, Atwood proclaims, that we understand every feature of the natural world, but we must acknowledge that nature has inherent rights of its own.

Those rights are addressed in another of Atwood's poem cycles. In the eleven "Snake Poems" of *Interlunar* Atwood suggests that the snake, among the most despised of creatures, is "a snarled puzzle," the only animal that does not sing. "The reason for them," Atwood concludes, "is the same / as the reason for the stars, and not human."[22] The snake is thus portrayed in a manner that eludes anthropocentricity, a theme Atwood returns to frequently as she seeks to establish a renovated relationship between the human and the wild in nature.

If there remains little doubt where Atwood stands, we are not yet enlightened as to how we might respond beyond a lingering sense of unease or guilt. But ever the activist, Atwood is not content merely to complain, which returns us to *Morning in the Burned House.* In one of that collection's strongest ecological poems, "The Moment," Atwood tells the descendants of her insane pioneer—those who firmly believe that "hard work and a long voyage" give them some sort of cachet to do as they please with the land—to understand that all their *sturm und drang* on the land has been for naught. Once anyone, any pioneer, says "I own this," the natural world simply recedes: the trees, the birds, the cliffs, the very air retreat. In the poem's concluding lines Atwood moves beyond her individual voice and begins to speak once more in the voice of that receding natural world:

> *You own nothing.*
>
> *We never belonged to you.*
> *You never found us.*
> *It was the other way round.*[23]

In the final line we see Atwood beginning to approach the basis for what Rebecca Raglon has called a "kinder, more ethical relationship with the natural world."[24] The error of someone like Atwood's pioneer, someone like her Susanna Moodie, is to think of the land as something one can own, something on which one can impose one's own human will. By presenting a natural world that belongs only to itself, "The Moment" echoes Aldo Leopold's land ethic, in which "the role of *Homo sapiens* [changes] from conqueror of the land-community to plain member and citizen of it."[25] For such a change to occur, Leopold continues, our "ethical sequence" must move away from the current paradigm, in which "the land-relation is still strictly economic"—that is, one based on *ownership*—into one "dealing with man's relation to land and to the animals and plants which grow upon it" (207). This is the ethical stance we see emerging through ecological poetry, but in itself this ethic offers no modus operandi.

An ethical stance suggested by Australian philosopher Warwick Fox offers one possible way to implement Leopold's enhanced ethical sequence. Fox's proposed "transpersonal ecology," where an individual's "forms of identification . . . tend to promote impartial identification with *all* entities," leads to an "approach to ecology [that] is concerned precisely with *opening* to ecological awareness."[26] Atwood's insane pioneer shows no such awareness; indeed, that lack proves his undoing. Atwood's regard for the endangered tortoises, along with her concern for vanishing frogs, further illustrates the transpersonal ecology underlying her ecological poetry. Whether assuming the voices of animals, as she does in "The Songs of the Transformed," or the collective voice of the natural world, as she does in "The Moment," Atwood initiates Fox's "distinctive approach" to ecological awareness. "The end that such approaches serve," as Fox explains, is to regard "members or aspects of the nonhuman world [as] morally considerable" in their own right.[27] Fox's design is not so much to step outside one's individual self but to extend that individual self to encompass the rest of the natural world. Atwood does precisely that in many of her poems, and as her speaking self expands to encompass all of nature, she also extends the inherent moral rights of humanity to include the whole of the natural world.

Atwood scholars have long assured us that Atwood's "use of landscape is predominately and consistently figurative," but in many cases I have found its function to be quite the opposite.[28] I believe her "use of landscape" is very often transpersonal and represents an effort to subvert the deleterious effects so often associated with self-interest.[29] By employing the expanded vision of self available through a transpersonal reading, Atwood translates that overweening human tendency for self interest—which apologists cite as a "natural" feature of humanity and to which many of the figures in Atwood's poetry (the insane pioneer and Susanna Moodie come instantly to mind) fall victim—into a position that enhances rather than diminishes the natural world. I would argue that such a position, based on an enlightened and expanded self-interest, is the underlying ethical premise we see in Atwood's ecological poetry; it is also a way to achieve the sort of ethical stance Aldo Leopold argued for half a century ago, a stance for which the time has clearly come.

Notes

1. Junichi Miyazawa, "Atwood Is in Japan," e-mail to atwood-l listserv, April 2, 1997.

2. Margaret Atwood, *Morning in the Burned House* (Toronto: McClelland and Stewart, 1995), 56.

3. Ibid., 57.

4. Margaret Atwood, *Survival: A Thematic Guide to Canadian Literature* (Toronto: House of Anansi Press, 1972), 10.

5. Margaret Atwood, *Conversations,* ed. Earl G. Ingersoll (Princeton, N.J.: Ontario Review Press, 1990), 46.

6. Coral Ann Howells, "'It All Depends on Where You Stand in Relation to the Forest': Atwood and the Wilderness from *Surfacing* to *Wilderness Tips,*" in *Various Atwoods: Essays on the Later Poems, Short Fiction, and Novels,* ed. Lorraine M. York (Toronto: House of Anansi Press, 1995), 47–70.

7. John Wilson Foster, "The Poetry of Margaret Atwood," *Canadian Literature* 74 (autumn 1977): 17.

8. Gary Ross, "The Circle Game," *Canadian Literature* 60 (spring 1974): 54.

9. Judith McCombs, "Atwood's Nature Concepts: An Overview," *Waves* 7, no. 1 (1978): 71, 72.

10. Atwood's first book, *Double Persephone* (Toronto: Hawkshead Press, 1961), was published in a limited, hand-set edition of 250. *The Circle Game* was reissued in 1996 by House of Anansi Press.

11. Margaret Atwood, *The Circle Game* (Toronto: House of Anansi Press, 1966), 27.

12. Ibid., 63.

13. Margaret Atwood, *The Animals in That Country* (Boston: Little, Brown, 1968), 37.

14. Ibid., 2–3.

15. Margaret Atwood, *The Journals of Susanna Moodie* (Toronto: Oxford University Press, 1970). Susanna Moodie (1805–1885) was an English immigrant to Upper Canada (Ontario) in 1832. Moodie wrote two books about her life in the wilderness, *Roughing It in the Bush* and *Life in the Clearings,* both of which are still in print. Moodie and her husband lived for seven years in the wilderness before finally settling in the nearby town of Belleville, Ontario, which is now a part of the city of Toronto. In the afterword to *The Journals of Susanna Moodie* Atwood writes that her own poems were "generated by a dream" (62) about Moodie's life but are not a literal retelling of the events in Moodie's books.

16. Atwood, *Journals of Susanna Moodie,* 11.

17. Margaret Atwood, *Procedures for Underground* (Toronto: Oxford University Press, 1970), 16.

18. Margaret Atwood, *Power Politics* (Toronto: House of Anansi Press, 1971), 9.

19. Margaret Atwood, *You Are Happy* (Toronto: Oxford University Press, 1974), 30.

20. Margaret Atwood, *Two-Headed Poems* (1978; repr., New York: Touchstone, 1980), 9 (page citations are to the reprint edition).

21. Margaret Atwood, *True Stories* (Toronto: Oxford University Press, 1981), 72.

22. Margaret Atwood, *Interlunar* (Toronto: Oxford University Press, 1984), 12.

23. Atwood, *Morning in the Burned House,* 109.

24. Rebecca Raglon, "Women and the Great Canadian Wilderness: Reconsidering the Wild," *Women's Studies* 25 (1996): 529.

25. Aldo Leopold, *A Sand County Almanac, and Sketches Here and There* (1949; repr., New York: Oxford University Press, 1987), 204 (page citations are to the reprint edition).

26. Warwick Fox, *Toward a Transpersonal Ecology: Developing New Foundations for Environmentalism* (1990; repr., Albany: SUNY Press, 1995), 265, 198 (page citations are to the reprint edition).

27. Ibid., 213.

28. Ross, 52.

29. My own reading of Fox suggests that his transpersonal self offers an enlightened form of self-interest; if a tree, for instance, is conceived as a part of our (transpersonal) self, we will be less likely to damage or destroy it than would be the case were the tree conceived as external to our sense of self.

Bernard W. Quetchenbach

Primary Concerns
The Development of Current Environmental Identity Poetry

From Contemporary to Current

Contemporary poetry as we know it emerged in the 1950s and 1960s, after a prolonged aesthetic struggle between the "academic" late moderns and the proponents of a new, open-form, personal, and immediate poetics, which, the story goes, eventually prevailed. As a result, the poetics advanced by Robert Lowell, Robert Bly, Allen Ginsberg, and others of their generation became the established idiom of American poetry for several decades. In many ways it is still the dominant idiom. However, in the mid- to late-1970s significant changes occurred in the way poets conceived of the relationship among themselves, their subject matter, and their audience. These changes, the result of both the rise of multiculturalism in American art and education and contemporary poets' frustration with the limitations of the immediate, personal character of contemporary poetics, hold significant promise for the poetry of environmental concern, offering complex new ways of looking at nature and expanding the developing body of "ecopoetry," and of environmental literature in general, to embrace writers and readers across the sociopolitical spectrum.

During the late 1970s and early 1980s I was a student in the creative writing program at SUNY-Brockport. The central anthology in use at the college was A. Poulin Jr.'s *Contemporary American Poetry,* then in its second and third editions and now in its sixth. The anthology was chosen for the obvious reason that Poulin was a professor at the college but also because it contained an intelligent selection of most of the poets that the faculty thought important. The collection's publication history and durability reflect the perceptiveness and care of its editor, and the poets represented are well served. But a brief survey of the contents of the fifth (1991) edition shows just how homogeneous even a relatively recent version of the book is in socioeconomic and demographic terms. Despite significant differences in ideas, poetic styles, and lifestyles, the great majority of the poets are white and attended highly regarded colleges and universities; many went on to become literature or creative writing professors. Of the fifty-six poets included, only twelve are female, and only five are people of color. Jewish and gay and lesbian poets are represented, but Native American, Asian American, and Hispanic poets are not. My professors and I never would have thought of an anthology including the likes of Bly and Ginsberg as conservative. In an essay of his own Poulin declares his allegiance to the "radical tradition," which he considered to be the main source of American poetry.[1] But by post-1970s standards the impression of a rather closed society of elite figures is inescapable. Even the exceptions are predictable, consisting of well-established voices such as Rita Dove and Gwendolyn Brooks.

Poulin's collection contrasts sharply with such multicultural anthologies as *An Ear to the Ground*, edited by Marie Harris and Kathleen Aguero, that reflect the development of what I will call "current" poetics. Neither *Contemporary American Poetry* nor *An Ear to the Ground* is particularly dedicated to ecological themes, but ecopoetry does appear in both. Although Poulin's anthology includes romantic nature poems by writers such as Galway Kinnell and James Wright, environmental concerns appear in Harris and Aguero's book cast in a more challenging and sweeping sociopolitical context. Harris and Aguero assert that their anthology's multicultural framework brings to light "artists whose historical and literary presence has been ignored or denied altogether."[2] As the founders of contemporary poetry did before them, Harris and Aguero place themselves in opposition to "the university" with its emphasis on "male, white bourgeois culture" (xx). By figuring poetry as "land" Harris and Aguero phrase their goal in environmental, or at least geographical, terms: "Our maps are out of date and lead us over and over the same terrain. We hope to begin to chart not new territory, but a land that has too long gone unmapped" (xix).

At first glance the current poets seem simply to represent a younger generation of contemporary poets, and this has come to be the assumption in considerations of what *contemporary* means in American poetry. Clearly, there has not been an obvious break in style and poetic philosophy, as there was in the rejection of the 1950s academic verse that gave rise to the contemporary generation. This is not to say that there has been no ongoing sense of conflict in poetry since the 1950s. In introducing Adrienne Rich's edition of the *Best American Poetry 1996*, David Lehman notes that "American poetry sometimes seems to be split down the middle."[3] American poetry has never really resolved the dialectic of "academics" or "insiders" versus "outsiders," although, ironically, the outsider poets of the 1950s are now cast as insiders. Poet and editor Andrei Codrescu recognizes this irony, noting that the "drunken village of poet-professors" of the 1950s was replaced in the mid-1970s by "the professor-poet."[4] Eliot Weinberger observes that the dialectic remains, even though its terms may have changed, and, "even more confusing, the ruling party tends to adopt, years later, the opposition platform."[5] There has been considerable discussion of renewing poetic form and technique, but despite the l=a=n=g=u=a=g=e poets and New Formalists, the personal lyric in free verse is still the dominant mode. In fact, mainstream literary magazines often include such pillars of contemporary poetics as Robert Bly and W. S. Merwin in company with young poets just out of MFA programs. Despite the renewal of "anthology wars," signaled by such works as *An Ear to the Ground*, the reexamination of audience and subject has come into American poetry as a kind of undercurrent. One could probably read several issues of the major university journals before detecting it.

The distinction that I seek to establish between contemporary poetry and current poetry is primarily a matter of assumptions concerning the relationship among writer, subject, and audience. Current poetry shares contemporary poetry's personal focus. But there is an important difference. In a typical contemporary poem the speaker is usually indistinguishable from the poet her- or himself, whereas the current poets tend to see themselves as spokespersons for or examples of particular social, ethnic, class, racial, or gender-defined communities. The poetry may still be personal, but it is shown to originate in the shared experience that determines and constitutes a poem's subject matter. For example, Jimmy Santiago Baca's poem "Ese Chicano" draws on his own prison experience, but the title and second-person narration place the autobiographical content in a socially defined context: "You wear dark glasses / like your Indio ancestors / wore black war paint."[6] The blending of languages in Hispanic and to a lesser extent in current Native American and Asian American poetry serves to further identify the poetry's "primary audience" as people who share a common blending not only of language but of whole cultural milieux. The resulting poetry is individual, but it assumes a commonality that goes beyond what contemporary poetics could offer. In doing so it restructures the relationship among poet, subject, and audience. The audience for such poetry need not be defined according to aesthetic or technical preferences. Instead, the reader is drawn to the work by a faith that the poet may be saying something important. Current poetry, like poetry in general, demands a kind of attention that other literature does not. But a reader motivated by the possibility of finding something other than technique may be more willing to expend the kind of energy needed to come to grips with poetry. Moreover, a poetry that redefines the relationship among writer, subject, and audience might attract general readers who, having no stake in the literary discussion of what constitutes a good poem, have recently opted for other genres that speak more directly to them and their concerns.

Just as contemporary poetics both derived from and rebelled against the modernism it followed, so current poetry has ties to the earlier contemporaries. The idea of "primary audience" itself is a child of the Black Arts Movement of the 1960s and the feminist poetry of Adrienne Rich and others in the 1970s. As has been the case with these two movements, the influence current poets have had is not limited to their primary audiences. The audience for a current poem can be seen as a series of concentric circles rippling from the defined primary audience through increasingly broader audiences sharing essential characteristics with the primary audience and, ultimately, to the larger sphere of the reading public in general. In this outer circle the poems serve the purpose of consciousness raising. And the necessary overlapping of outer circles reveals affinities among apparently disparate writers and audiences. Even the primary audience itself is likely to be multifaceted and complex. In Paula Gunn Allen's poetry, for example, the poet addresses Native American, feminist, and environmental "interest groups" and illustrates common threads running through all three.

The implications of the development of current identity poetics for environmental poetry are significant and far-reaching. The "ecopoet," like the prose nature writer, is a kind of missionary, motivated by a fierce devotion to a subject matter that is endangered and absolutely crucial to the poet's well being and, as even the largest circle of the general public is increasingly aware, to the world at large. Because it seeks to establish a community of readers whose common experience is assumed to be prior to and essential to the poetry, current identity poetics is well suited to reveal connections between individuals and communities. The kind of sociospiritual link between individual and society envisioned by contemporary theorist-practitioners like Robert Bly is brought to life in the work of poets like Baca and Allen, for whom the connection between personal psyche and culture is the source of a richly layered sense of spiritual, intellectual, and practical reality.

It may appear that the development of current identity poetics constitutes an intensification of the individualism of contemporary poetry because the background of the poet is central to the engendering and experience of the poem. But it is not so much the writer's identity that is important as it is the reader's identity, or the subject of identity itself. For one thing, identity is not always a matter of ethnic origin. In cases in which the primary audience is defined by something other than heritage—such as in the work of Vietnam veterans, gays and lesbians, feminists, and environmentalists—the writer's intended audience is not obvious from the poet's name or photograph. Moreover, readers drawn by a writer's heritage are sometimes disappointed when the writer strays from the expected subject matter. In a current interview in *The Missouri Review* Li-young Lee remarks that "early on an Asian told me he was really offended by my book. I asked him why and he said he went through the table of contents and didn't find any references to anything Asian."[7] Lee's impatience is understandable, as any writer is likely to object to "people thinking in classifications" (89), especially if those classifications have to be so obvious as to be apparent simply from perusing a book's table of contents. But this example illustrates that the writer's identity may ultimately be less important than a reader's expectations regarding subject matter and its relevance.

Perhaps the most significant assumption of current poets is that subject matter is a key to establishing a connection between writer and reader. This contradicts a long-held principle of American aesthetics—that it is artistic attention that enlivens neutral subject matter, that the source of a poem's value is not so much what the poet says as how the poet says it. But it is undeniable that subject-based writing has made significant inroads even in the literary quarterlies and university presses. And perhaps the frustration that so many poets express with the extensive but self-contained world of poetry and its aficionados is a reflection that there are alternatives, that contemporary poets like Adrienne Rich and Gary Snyder, who "sold out" to politically defined audiences, may actually have helped open doors that lead to a larger poetry with concerns that are simply more important than the domestic content that has long dominated contemporary poetry. In editing her 1996 edition of *The Best American Poetry,* Rich found many poems in major literary reviews "personal to the point of suffocation." She concludes that "[a] great many poems rang hollow and monotonous to me; at best they seemed ingenious literary devices, at worst 'publish or perish' items for a vita or an MFA dissertation—academic commodities."[8] She believes, however, that there is also a current poetry that does have substance, and for this, according to series editor Lehman, she employs the ecological metaphor of a living river, "a pulsing, racing convergence of tributaries—regional, ethnic, racial, social, sexual."[9]

Varieties of Ecological Awareness in Contemporary and Current Poetry

Rich's "tributaries" appear in several forms of environmental awareness evident in recent poetry. Contemporary and current poets show renewed interest in pastoralism and regionalism. Mary Oliver in New England, Gary Snyder and, later, Vi Gale in the Northwest, Maggie Anderson in Appalachia, and Wendell Berry in Kentucky are just a few examples. Poets such as W. S. Merwin and Richard Shelton have become public spokespersons for their bioregions and have given their places prominence in their work. Snyder lists the Pacific and Sierra forests in the acknowledgments of *No Nature,* his 1992 selected poems.[10] Furthermore, Antler is identified by Harris and Aguero as a "Great Lakes Bioregion poet," following Snyder in moving from traditional regionalism to bioregionalism.[11] The regional impulse is perhaps most prominent in the West, where a literary examination of the idea of "westernness" is under way in both prose and poetry. In the Northwest especially, as Lars Nordström has established, regionalism and environmentalism have converged in the work of Snyder, Gale, William Stafford, and others.[12]

The ethnic and racial tributaries have also produced poets with ecological sensibilities. Most obviously, Native American poets have spearheaded ecological awareness in current American poetry. But environmental themes are not unknown in the works of other groups either. In his essay "The Black Aesthetic" Timothy Seibles describes Bob Kaufman's 1965 collection *Solitudes Crowded with Loneliness* as including "a number of pastoral poems which featured a speaker at peace with, even delighted by, certain intervals of life." Seibles quotes "Cocoa Morning," in which Kaufman combines the pastoral impulse with the urban sound of jazz, "Dreaming of wild beats, softer still / Yet free of violent city noise."[13] That this impulse is still alive in poetry by African Americans is evidenced by Primus St. John's poems in the October 1999 issue of *Calapooya Literary Review.* In "Listening to the Curandera" the speaker longs to "be birdlike in my feelings / for things on the earth / that are really dancers."[14] In another poem, "Lemon Verbena," the speaker's sexuality is compared to that of a bugling elk plunging down a Northwestern "ridge / Above a river."[15] And in "*¿Que Pasa?*" St. John again figures emotional responses in natural imagery, echoing the ecopoet's faith in nature as a source and test of authenticity:

> I'm in there, somewhere
> Like a new moon
> And my stillness is a hunger
> Cunning as a wild animal—.[16]

Among the young African American poets whose work is collected in Clarence Major's *The Garden Thrives,* Leonard D. Moore's "From the Field" blends appreciation for the natural order with knowledge of the hard history of African American farm labor. The poem demonstrates sympathy for the rejection of that history by the young, who "won't do field work anymore," but concludes that "Rich soil linked us / like blessings that speak to us / without a sound."[17] In "Earth Screaming," also selected by Major, Esther Iverem evinces an environmentalist's sense of empathy with the earth in its degradation: "Come out of the city's human hum / to really hear / the earth screaming."[18]

Marilyn Chin's "We Are Americans Now, We Live in the Tundra" links her own Chinese American background with both African Americans and the environment:

> A blues song; even a Chinese girl gets the blues
> Her reticence is black and blue
>
> Let's talk about the extinct
> Bengal tigers, about giant Pandas—.

If the primary audience for this poem consists of Asian Americans, the poem's imagery and language also enmesh both African Americans and environmentalists, whose spheres the poem connects by likening the minority experience to that of those political representatives of the Chinese environment, Ling Ling and Xing Xing, who are "quoted" in the following lines:

> "Ling Ling loves Xing Xing . . . yet
> We will not mate. We are
>
> Not impotent, we are important.
> We blame the environment, we blame the zoo!"[19]

It is its connective quality that allows current identity poetry to appeal to readers beyond the intended primary audience. Here the experience of Asian Americans relates not only to other human minorities but also to nature itself, caged and displayed like the pandas.

This connection between oppressed human populations and nonhuman nature is at the core of ecofeminist writing. In her formative *Woman and Nature: The Roaring Inside Her,* Susan Griffin makes this connection explicit. The book, which Griffin places "in a realm between essay and poem, between reality and myth," counterpoints the "cool, professional, pretending to objectivity" voice of "cultural authority" with "the chorus of women and nature, an emotional, animal, embodied voice."[20] Griffin is aware of the irony and danger of accepting a characterization developed by others. She begins the prologue of *Woman and Nature* by acknowledging that the connection between woman and nature originates with the patriarchy: "He says that woman speaks with nature" (83). By the end of the prologue, however, it is clear that Griffin intends to use the identification between the two as a source of empowerment and knowledge: "*We are women and nature. And he says he cannot hear us speak. / But we hear*" (83).

Because feminism is fundamentally a liberation movement, ecofeminists have provided environmentalism with a clear sense of the essential and reciprocal relationship between environmental concerns and social justice. In her essay "A Collaborative Intelligence" Griffin argues that "[i]f one would create an egalitarian society, nature must be restored as the common ground of existence. Yet this common ground cannot be reclaimed without the transformation of an unjust social order."[21]

In addition to ecofeminists, other ecopoets are defining a primary audience based on environmental concern. In his environmental poetry, gathered in the collection *Pterodactyl Rose,* William Heyen combines a regional Long Island sensibility he traces to Walt Whitman with the apocalyptic sense he brings to the other major social subject in his work, the Holocaust. Heyen's poems of extinction and despair are especially aimed at placing the individual experience, even when it seems innocent, in the larger sphere of the world economy, where the trivial expands powerfully into nightmare, as in "Fast Food," in which "I sit at McDonald's eating my fragment of forest," and in "The Global Economy," in which a dollar placed in the bank grows into a series of questions culminating with "What happened to all the trees?"[22]

It would not be difficult to identify a substantial canon of contemporary and current ecopoets, whose works are published in *Amicus Journal, Appalachia Journal, Orion,* and in more overtly literary publications like *Petroglyph, Albatross,* and *Green Fuse,* as well as in the mainstream literary journals. If, as I have argued, a reevaluation of the relationship among writer, audience, and subject matter is a key to defining current poetry, it follows that, for ecopoets, who have always been convinced of the significance of subject matter, the transition between the contemporary and the current would be less obvious. For writers such as Gary Snyder and Wendell Berry, subject matter has always been a defining factor in the makeup of their audiences. Although Snyder's prosody has considerable appeal, it is his environmental advocacy and countercultural spirit that has carved him a special niche among readers and kept his books in print. Berry's appeal also involves attachment to his subject matter and a clear sense of duty to his readers.

Given the ecopoet's sense of purposiveness and commitment to both reader and subject matter, it is not surprising that the distinction between contemporary and current poetry is less pronounced among ecopoets than in many other areas of poetry. Nevertheless, the convergence of Rich's tributaries is important to poets of the environment in that it broadens their appeal and sets their work in a new, more expansive, and less-isolated context.

Anthologies, Multiculturalism, and the Ecology of Poets

As is the case with all innovations in literature, critics have engaged in spirited and sometimes acrimonious discussions concerning current identity poetics. The 1996 edition of *The Best American Poetry* evoked pointed criticism from Harold Bloom, who left Rich's edition completely unrepresented in his *Best of the Best* compilation. The third edition of the *Heath Anthology of American Literature,* especially its selection of contemporary poetry, has drawn similar fire. In both cases the critics have claimed that the main criterion for inclusion was the identity group of the author and not the artistry of the work. In the *AWP Chronicle,* published by the Associated Writing Programs, Robert Wallace took the *Heath* to task by claiming that traditional criteria of literary value had been ignored in favor of social and political ones, a choice Wallace sees as a capitulation to political correctness and, worse, as an inappropriate adoption of nonliterary criteria for evaluating literary works.[23] But an anthology's purpose is not necessarily to gather all of the best works of a period. Anthologies also aim to reflect the literary climate of a given place and time. In this light it seems clear that the *Heath Anthology* does provide a legitimate reflection of the literary life of the period following the 1970s, in which hegemonies of class, race, and gender began to give way to a new poetics, pioneered by social poets within contemporary poetry and resulting in the poetry of identity that has flourished since that time. Paul Lauter, editor of the *Heath Anthology,* notes the distinction between pre- and post-1980 literary climates by asserting that "people who don't think writers of color and white women were being widely ignored" should "check out general American literature or poetry anthologies before the 1980s."[24]

Environmental concerns have made their way into the sphere of identity and multicultural literature primarily through the work of Native American poets. The influence of the "Native American Renaissance" of the 1970s is still being felt in multicultural American literature, in which American Indian writing holds a prominent place. A brief survey of *Harper's Anthology of Twentieth Century Native American Poetry* reveals the centrality of environmental themes in the work of Indian poets. In his introduction to this collection, edited by Duane Niatum, Brian Swann, who also serves as poetry editor for the Natural Resources Defense Council's *Amicus Journal,* points out that Indian poets seem "to work from a sense of social responsibility to the group as much as from an intense individuality."[25] Swann goes on to quote contemporary poet Richard Hugo, who considered young Native American poets heirs to the modernist tradition of T. S. Eliot and William Butler Yeats, "who felt we inherited ruined worlds that, before they were ruined, gave man a sense of self-esteem, social unity, spiritual certainty and being at home on the earth" (xxi–xxii). The poems collected by Niatum, himself enrolled in the Klallam tribe, demonstrate that for Native American poets Hugo's "earth" includes physical planet as well as cosmic homeland. The portrayals of nature and the environment in Niatum's collection are varied, but the volume includes many poems embracing central principles of ecopoetics. Some of the poems address ecological destruction. In "Drawings of the Song Animals" Niatum pictures a contemporary Northwest in which "Dams abridge the Columbia Basin,"[26] and Elizabeth Cook-Lynn's "Journey" begins with a landscape in which

> Wet, sickly
> smells of cattle yard silage fill the prairie air
> far beyond the timber; the nightmare only just
> begun, a blackened cloud moves past the sun
> to dim the river's glare, a malady of modern times.[27]

Ecopoets contrast the order found in natural systems with the overbearing but ultimately illusory transformative power of modern technologies. Wendy Rose's "Loo-wit" recalls a Cowlitz personification of Mt. St. Helens, an old woman spitting "her black tobacco," although

> Around her
> machinery growls,
> snarls and ploughs
> great patches
> of her skin.[28]

In Carter Revard's "Driving in Oklahoma" the freedom of the meadowlark is contrasted to the illusion of freedom provided by technology, the open road revealed as a constrained linear progression, the speaker discovering that although he was "feeling / technology is freedom's other name," it is really the lark, not limited to the path of the highway, that "flies so easy, when he sings."[29] Roberta Hill Whiteman's "The White Land" also contrasts twentieth-century technology with natural imagery, the return from the natural and spiritual world of the poem's dream vision disturbed by "the roar of that plane," leaving a troubled anticipation evident in the poem's last two lines: "The dishwater's luminous; a truck / grinds down the street."[30] Images of connection breaking through traditional Western dualities are also apparent throughout the anthology, in poems such as Simon Ortiz's Snyderesque "Bend in the River":

> There are tracks
> at river's edge, raccoon,
> coyote, deer, crow,
> and now my own.[31]

Like Li-young Lee, American Indian writers resist stereotypical characterizations (note, for example, Louise Erdrich's playing with liberal white expectations in "Dear John Wayne" and the unsympathetic portrayal of the white Indian studies professor in Sherman Alexie's novel *Indian Killer*). But current Native American poetry shows that the identification of American Indians with environmental concerns is not simply a matter of white expectations and stereotypes. And American Indian writers have carried these concerns into multicultural anthologies. *An Ear to the Ground,* for example, includes clearly ecopoetic works by such poets as Gogisgi/Carroll Arnett:

> I rise to make
> four prayers of
> thanksgiving for
> this fine clear day,
>
> this good brown
> earth.[32]

And Lance Henson:

> the fog lifts its gray cover to reveal
> the carcasses of two dead deer

two silent places that have fallen upon the earth
at the side of a busy road.[33]

And Paula Gunn Allen:

Great Cities, piling drifting clouds
of chemical poisons that have long since
killed the air? Rivers and lakes long since
dead beneath the burden of filth dumped into
them for years?[34]

In *The Best American Poetry 1996* Native American poets, although less prominent, are represented. Ray A. Young Bear's "Our Bird Aegis" presents an evocative web of connective imagery drawn from nature (the "immature black eagle") and transformed into the mythology of aegis and "Bear-King."[35] The poem's connective web entangles the speaker's personal history in natural and social spheres; the eagle/Bear-King, "subject to physical wounds and human / tragedy," "meditates" on the speaker's "loss / of my younger brother" (239).

Rich's *The Best American Poetry 1996* also contains ecopoetry by Patiann Rogers ("Abundance and Satisfaction") and Heyen, whose "The Steadying" acknowledges environmentalism's debt to Native American cultures by granting Oglala leader Crazy Horse a prominent place in a net of associations linking the Holocaust and the environment ("cattlecars of redwoods voweling toward Gotham in my dream").[36]

A fear evoked by current identity poetics is that it "Balkanizes" American literature by appealing narrowly to one group of readers at the expense of others, adopting an indifferent or even antagonistic stance toward readers not belonging to the primary audience. Rich herself has often been characterized as hostile to readers who are not members of her intended audience, although this criticism, especially in recent years, may say more about the fears of her critics than about her own evolving attitudes. But such criticism neglects current identity poetry's tendency to construct provisional but concentric or overlapping alignments of readers and the resulting encouragement of a profoundly ecological concept of interlocking audiences in which each poet is shown to be connected to many, perhaps all, others.

Claims that poets are included in works like *The Best American Poetry 1996* on the basis of who they are and what group they represent obscure another possible interpretation of the selections. In her introduction Rich rejects any notion of an absolute and static list of best poems or even of American poems.

She does not seek to define aesthetic boundaries, which she sees as analogous to the "official recantation of the *idea* that democracy should be continually expanding, not contracting."[37] Instead Rich sees editing a poetry anthology as a way to create an alternative "space where other human and verbal relationships are possible" (20). This space is home to ever-shifting relationships among writers, readers, and the subject matter of the poem, an ecological interplay of organisms and the environment in which they live.

A number of recent anthologies have been devoted to poetry on ecological themes. Like so many of the developments in current poetry, the "green anthology" originates solidly in contemporary poetry. Robert Bly's *News of the Universe* provides an international selection of past and present poets, although the selection is clearly dominated by Bly's own sense of the centrality of continental European romanticism. It is revealing, though, to contrast Bly's two most recent chronological groupings. Whereas the "Poems of Twofold Consciousness: Early Twentieth Century" chapter consists almost exclusively of well-known male American and European poets, the "1945–1979" section, despite its relatively early closing date, offers a more diverse group of poems, combining selections by "eco-canonical" contemporary figures like Berry, Snyder, Denise Levertov, and Bly himself with works by Ray A. Young Bear, Louis Jenkins, and international poets like Anna Akhmatova and Gabriella Mistral. It is easy to imagine an editor with more inclusive tastes (or a less confining agenda) broadening the selection still further by adding contemporary works not normally identified with ecopoetry, such as Sylvia Plath's "Pheasant," and by incorporating works by Allen, Baca, Antler, Griffin, St. John, and others. The international 1991 anthology *Poetry for the Earth,* edited by Sara Dunn and Alan Scholefield, exemplifies the breadth possible in even a rather slender collection. If multicultural anthologies contextualize environmental concerns in a large field of social issues, environmental poetry collections could also serve to broaden the base of environmentalism by opening up the largely white, upper-middle-class rolls of "card-carrying environmentalists" to other populations who share their concerns but have not always considered themselves welcome in environmentalist circles.

Such combinations are, of course, not always easy, and the more diverse a collection of poets is, the less chance there is that their works will rest easily on the page next to each other. But it is exactly the desire to avoid ideological or aesthetic tension that has resulted in the narrow focus of anthologies such as Bread Loaf's relentlessly mainstream *Poems for a Small Planet* or Bly's *News of the Universe.* A more open collection, including if not uniting a comprehensive spectrum of poets linked by environmental content, would be likely to reveal and foster connections among these poets and among their audiences. Such a collection, instead of serving to reinforce stereotypes of environmental writers and their constituencies, would demonstrate both the underlying common ground shared by such writers and the complicated differences among them. Because ecopoetry has as its subject the world systems that support all life, the web of ecological poets is potentially impressive indeed. Poets as diverse as Susan Griffin and Wendell Berry may never sit comfortably in any sort of critical perspective. But this, perhaps, is the ultimate strength of ecopoetry. The poets remain individual, resisting schools. What links them and their audiences is the concern for the central subject matter. That Griffin and Berry find common ground in sustainable agriculture and in their admiration for the work of Gary Snyder is more surprising, and ultimately more hopeful, than is the often remarked conjunction of Berry and Snyder.

Current Ecopoetry as Environmental Literature

One long-standing criticism of environmental literature in general involves the "whiteness" of both its practitioners and its readers. One need only consult the writings and discussions emanating from the Association for the Study of Literature and the Environment (ASLE) to see how troubling this issue has been to literary environmentalists, and the issue also appears frequently in the mainstream environmental press. The basic contention is that although environmental concern is widespread (that so many toxic waste sites are located in and around minority areas has not escaped the attention of those who live there), environmentalism as such is beholden to the "white hunter romanticism" of Theodore Roosevelt and Ernest Hemingway and to a basically reactionary agrarianism that glosses over the racism of Thomas Jefferson. At the 1999 ASLE convention at Kalamazoo, Michigan, in which the midwestern location seemed to bring out this latter aspect of environmental history, Native American poet Gloria Bird injected some wry, pointed humor by offering to read her poem about Jefferson. In publications like *An Ear to the Ground,* however, environmental concern emerges in the context of a multifaceted populist agenda.

Another criticism of environmental literature is that it is too intellectually confining, that in Joyce Carol Oates's infamous words, it "inspires a painfully limited set of responses in 'nature writers.'"[38] A similar frustration is evident in a recent *Amicus Journal* review of several collections of prose nature writing, in which Lydia Millet claims that the genre often "fails to move beyond the placid inertia of longing."[39] Such comments indicate the degree to which nature and environmental writing have been linked to a particular kind of romanticism, the history of which can be traced in publications like Thomas Lyon's *This Incomperable Lande* and Ann Ronald's *The Sierra Club Trailside Reader.* Responses like Oates's and Millet's may seem insensitive to the nuances of this tradition, but a broader spectrum of environmental concern is available in the work of current poets. Certainly the response to nature in the work of Jimmy Santiago Baca is complex. Baca mixes an understanding of nature as a measure of ultimate reality with the knowledge that less ultimate but overpowering political factors have separated him and his ancestors from their natural context, leaving Hispanic Americans, as he titles one of his books, *Immigrants in Our Own Land.* In "The Sun on Those," the prose poem that opens this collection, the speaker's father is able to cling to the memory of the trees he planted, which "in jail cell after jail cell . . . were his secret." Even in the next generation, "when they captured me," one tree remains, "plunging its roots deeper into the face of progress and land grabbers."[40] In Baca's *Black Mesa Poems* images of nature damaged and degraded are placed in an overtly pastoral context, giving the poems a tension unusual in ecopoetry. In "Day's Blood" the poem's speaker encounters slaughterhouse dogs along the Rio Grande when "walking there myself at night / in the moonlight," and in "A God Loosened" the riparian woods appear like "the upturned claws / of great dead eagles."[41] Socioeconomic barriers, embodied in the "no trespassing signs white flashing past" (62) of "Family Ties," compromise the speaker's access to the natural world. Ultimately, however, the complexity of his relationship with his environment does not alienate Baca from nature. In "Choices" he values a sustaining if difficult agrarianism over the prosperity engendered by the military-industrial economy, a choice the poem's speaker must make when a friend, beset by economic reverses on his farm, takes a job at the Los Alamos Laboratory.[42]

What can the role of poetry be in a time of ecological crisis? At a poetry reading in Arizona in 1994 Richard Shelton, speaking of his own work in defense of the Sonoran Desert, claimed that poetry should not be inconsequential, but at the dawn of the twenty-first century poetry may seem irrelevant and anachronistic. Yet considering the evident popularity of "street poetry" and of poetry in public places such as city buses, and the even more ubiquitous appeal of such popular versions of poetry as the rock or rap song lyric, perhaps it is not unreasonable to think that a poetry conscious of its relationship to subject and audience could have an impact on American culture as a whole. And there are of course the many thousands of readers who are already sampling the offerings of poets from university presses and little magazines. It is also worth considering that, if American nature and environmental writing in prose may still seem to be primarily white and upper class or bourgeois, current ecopoetry is being written by a diverse group of writers in America and around the world. One consequence of current ecopoetry, therefore, is to reveal the environment as a fundamental concern linking university and barrio, wilderness and city, feminist and agrarian. An additional consequence, the assertion that the subject of a poem has value in its own right, reflects a fundamental principle of ecopoetics. In moving from the personal contemporary to the more inclusive assumptions of current poetry, poets reveal that the thing that is said—the content—is the poem's surest connection to both the reader and the earth.

Notes

1. A. Poulin Jr., "Contemporary American Poetry: The Radical Tradition," in *Contemporary American Poetry,* 5th ed., ed. A. Poulin Jr. (Boston: Houghton Mifflin, 1991), 651–670.

2. Marie Harris and Kathleen Aguero, preface to *An Ear to the Ground: An Anthology of Contemporary American Poetry,* ed. Marie Harris and Kathleen Aguero (Athens: University of Georgia Press, 1989), xix–xx.

3. David Lehman, foreword to *The Best American Poetry 1996,* ed. Adrienne Rich (New York: Scribner, 1996), 9.

4. Andrei Codrescu, "Up Late: An Introduction," in *Contemporary Poetry since 1970: Up Late,* ed. Andrei Codrescu (New York: Four Walls Eight Windows, 1987), xxxi, xxxiv.

5. Eliot Weinberger, "A Note on the Selection," *American Poetry since 1950: Innovators and Outsiders,* ed. Eliot Weinberger (New York: Marsilio, 1993), xii.

6. Jimmy Santiago Baca, "Ese Chicano," in Harris and Aguero, 24.

7. Matthew Fluharty, "An Interview with Li-young Lee," *Missouri Review* 23, no. 1 (2000): 89.

8. Adrienne Rich, introduction to *The Best American Poetry 1996,* ed. Adrienne Rich (New York: Scribner, 1996), 17.

9. Lehman, 11.

10. Gary Snyder, *No Nature: New and Selected Poems* (New York: Pantheon, 1992).

11. Harris and Aguero, 322.

12. Lars Nordström, *Theodore Roethke, William Stafford, and Gary Snyder: The Ecological Metaphor as Transformed Realism* (Stockholm: Uppsala, 1989).

13. Timothy Seibles, "The Black Aesthetic," in *A Profile of Twentieth Century Amer-*

ican Poetry, ed. Jack Myers and David Wojahn (Carbondale: Southern Illinois University Press, 1991), 180.

14. Primus St. John, "Listening to the Curandera," *Calapooya Literary Review* 20 (1999): 1.

15. Primus St. John, "Lemon Verbena," *Calapooya Literary Review* 20 (1999): 1.

16. Primus St. John, "*¿Que Pasa?*" *Calapooya Literary Review* 20 (1999): 1.

17. Leonard D. Moore, "From the Field," in *The Garden Thrives: Twentieth Century African-American Poetry,* ed. Clarence Major (New York: HarperCollins, 1996), 400.

18. Esther Iverem, "Earth Screaming," in Major, 410.

19. Marilyn Chin, "We are Americans Now, We Live in the Tundra," in *Unsettling America: An Anthology of Contemporary Multicultural Poetry,* ed. Maria Mazzioti Gillan and Jennifer Gillan (New York: Penguin, 1994): 10.

20. Susan Griffin, *Made from This Earth: An Anthology of Writings* (New York: Harper and Row, 1982), 82.

21. Susan Griffin, *The Eros of Everyday Life: Essays on Ecology, Gender, and Society* (New York: Anchor/Doubleday, 1995), 46.

22. William Heyen, *Pterodactyl Rose: Poems of Ecology* (St. Louis: Time Being Books, 1991), 41, 39.

23. Robert Wallace, "Reconstructing Contemporary American Poetry," *AWP Chronicle,* no. 4 (1994–1995): 14.

24. Paul Lauter, "Overviews and Notes," *Heath Anthology of American Literature,* available from <http://www.georgetown.edu/tamlit/newsletter/13/Lauter.htm> (accessed June 16, 2000).

25. Brian Swann, "Introduction: Only the Beginning," in *Harper's Anthology of Twentieth Century Native American Poetry,* ed. Duane Niatum (New York: Harper and Row, 1988): xix.

26. Niatum, "Drawings of the Song Animals," in Niatum, 116.

27. Elizabeth Cook-Lynn, "Journeys," in Niatum, 41.

28. Wendy Rose, "Loo-wit," in Niatum, 234.

29. Carter Revard, "Driving in Oklahoma," in Niatum, 43.

30. Roberta Hill Whiteman, "The White Land," in Niatum, 219.

31. Simon J. Ortiz, "Bend in the River," in Niatum, 143.

32. Gogisgi/Carol Arnett, "Early Song," in Harris and Aguero, 110.

33. Lance Henson, "sketches near youngstown, ohio," in Harris and Aguero, 120.

34. Paula Gunn Allen, "Molly Brant, Iroquois Matron, Speaks," in Harris and Aguero, 7.

35. Ray A. Young Bear, "Our Bird Aegis," in Rich, 239.

36. Heyen, "The Steadying," in Rich, 100.

37. Rich, 16.

38. Joyce Carol Oates, "Against Nature," in *On Nature: Nature, Landscape, and Natural History*, ed. by Daniel Halpern (San Francisco: North Point Press, 1987), 236.

39. Lydia Millet, reviews of *The Seacoast Reader*, ed John A. Murray; *The River Reader*, ed. Murray; *American Nature Writing 1999*, ed. Murray; *At Home on the Earth*, ed. David Landis Barnhill, all in *Amicus Journal* (summer 2000): 39.

40. Jimmy Santiago Baca, *Immigrants in Our Own Land* (Baton Rouge: Louisiana State University Press, 1979), 1.

41. Jimmy Santiago Baca, *Black Mesa Poems* (New York: New Directions, 1986), 19, 34.

42. Ibid., 60.

Contributors

J. Scott Bryson is assistant professor of English at Mount St. Mary's College in Los Angeles. He is coeditor (with Roger Thompson) of two *Dictionary of Literary Biography* volumes on nature writing. His other publications include work on Joy Harjo, Henry David Thoreau, Thomas Pynchon, and on teaching composition. He is currently completing a second book manuscript, an examination of the ecopoetry of Wendell Berry, Joy Harjo, Mary Oliver, and W. S. Merwin.

Laird Christensen is a ranger, teacher, writer, and native Cascadian, and he has published his poems and essays in a variety of journals, including *Wild Earth, Northwest Review, Renascence, Earth First! Journal,* and *Studies in American Indian Literature.* He is currently assistant professor of English literature at Green Mountain College, an environmental liberal arts college in western Vermont, where he teaches creative writing, American literature, environmental writing, and Native American literatures.

Beverly Curran teaches in the Department of Creativity and Culture (Multicultural Studies) of Aichi Shukutoku University in Nagoya, Japan. She is currently researching the media translation of Canadian poetry into radio plays. Her Japanese translation of Nicole Brossard's *Journal intime* has just been published.

John Elder is Stewart Professor of English and Environmental Studies at Middlebury College, Vermont. He has written widely, including *Imagining the Earth: Poetry and the Vision of Nature, Reading the Mountains of Home,* and *Following the Brush: An American Encounter with Classical Japanese Culture.* He is also the coeditor of *The Norton Book of Nature Writing* (with Robert Finch), *Spirit and Nature: Why the Environment Is a Religious Issue* (with Steven Rockefeller), and *The Family of Earth and Sky: Indigenous Tales of Nature from around the World* (with Hertha Wong), as well as executive editor for *American Nature Writing.*

Deborah Fleming is associate professor of English at Ashland University, where she teaches modern poetry and environmental studies. She is the author of *"A man who does not exist": The Irish Peasant in W. B. Yeats and J. M. Synge* and articles on Yeats, Eamon Grennan, and Robinson Jeffers. Her poetry has appeared in such journals as *Hiram Poetry Review, ISLE, Organization and Environment,* and *Cottonwood.*

Terry Gifford is reader in literature and environment at the University of Leeds and author of *Green Voices: Understanding Contemporary Nature Poetry* (1995) and *Pastoral* (1999). His fifth collection of poetry was *Whale Watching with a Boy and a Goat* (1998), and he has also published a collection of rock-climbing poetry, *The Rope* (1996). Gifford has edited the complete works of John Muir in two volumes: *John Muir: The Eight Wilderness-Discovery Books* (1992) and *John Muir: His Life and Letters and Other Writings* (1996).

David Gilcrest teaches in the English department at Carroll College in Waukesha, Wisconsin. He is the author of *Greening the Lyre: Environmental Poetics and Ethics.*

Maggie Gordon is postdoctoral fellow in English at the University of Mississippi, where she offers literature and gender studies seminars based on her dissertation, "Reconceiving the Sacred: Louise GlŸck and Postmodern Spirituality." She received her Ph.D. from the University of Mississippi in 2000 and has published articles on gender and mythology in twentieth-century American literature and culture in journals including *Literature/Film Quarterly* and *Clues: A Journal of Detection.*

Emily Hegarty received her Ph.D. in American literature from the CUNY Graduate Center and currently teaches at Nassau Community College. She is working on a book-length study of nationalism and ethnicity in American ecopoetry.

Richard Hunt received his Ph.D. from the University of Nevada, Reno, in the Literature and Environment program, in May 2000. He now teaches in both the English and the music departments at Mesabi Range College in Virginia, Minnesota. His primary research interests explore the connections and interactions between science and faith as expressed through American nature writing.

Roy Osamu Kamada is a Ph.D. candidate in the English department at the University of California, Davis. His work has appeared in *The Diasporic Imag-*

ination: Identifying Asian-American Representations in America and will appear in the forthcoming *Asian-American Poets.* He is currently completing work on his dissertation, "Postcolonial Romanticisms: Landscape and the Possibilities of Inheritance."

Mark C. Long is assistant professor of English and American studies at Keene State College, where he teaches courses in American literature and culture, with an emphasis in poetry and poetics, intellectual history and critical theory, literature-and-environment studies, and expository writing. He has published essays on writing program administration, theories of reading in the study of American literature, ecocomposition, the early writing of William Carlos Williams, and the poetics of Denise Levertov.

Bernard Quetchenbach is assistant professor of English at Florida Southern College. He is the author of *Back from the Far Field: American Nature Poetry in the Late Twentieth Century* (2000). He has published articles on American poetry and on literature and the environment in journals such as *New Laurel Review* and *Essays in Arts and Sciences,* and in *Thoreau's Sense of Place: Essays in American Environmental Writing.* His poems have appeared in numerous literary magazines. From 1995–1999 he edited *The River Review/La Revue rivière,* a multidisciplinary international annual.

Leonard M. Scigaj is professor of English at Virginia Tech, where he has taught twentieth-century literature courses since 1978. He has authored two critical studies and edited a collection of essays on Ted Hughes. He has also published numerous articles on such poets as Sylvia Plath, A. R. Ammons, and Gary Snyder; on science fiction authors such as Frank Herbert and Ray Bradbury; and on environmental poetry theory. His most recent book, *Sustainable Poetry: Four American Ecopoets* [Ammons, Berry, Merwin, and Snyder], was published in 1999.

Roger Thompson is assistant professor of English at Virginia Military Institute, where he teaches courses in American literature, rhetoric, and environmental literature. He is coeditor (with Scott Bryson) of two *Dictionary of Literary Biography* volumes on nature writing. His research is primarily in nineteenth-century American literature and rhetorical theory, and he has published articles in *Rhetoric Review* and in a collection of essays on kairos edited by Philip Sipiora and James Baumlin. His current work includes an investigation of nineteenth-century American literacy reform and its intersection with gender roles, an exploration of transatlantic rhetorical theory, and an examination of the rhetoric of John McPhee.

Jeffrey Thomson's collection of poetry, *The Halo Brace,* was published in 2000. He has also published poetry and nonfiction in *Quarterly West, Puerto del Sol, Gulf Coast,* and *Willow Springs.* He directs the creative writing program in environmental nonfiction at Chatham College in Pittsburgh.

Gyorgyi Voros, a poet, essayist, and scholar, teaches English at Virginia Tech. She is the author of *Notations of the Wild: Ecology in the Poetry of Wallace Stevens* (1997). Her current book project explores how metaphors for the human-nature relationship in contemporary literature and the visual arts have been altered by land transformation, ecological consciousness, and the environmental movement. She lives in Blacksburg, Virginia.

Zhou Xiaojing teaches Asian American literature and Asian American studies at the Sate University of New York, Buffalo. She is the author of *Elizabeth Bishop: Rebel "in Shades and Shadows"* (1999). Her publications include numerous articles on Asian American poets. Currently she is coediting a critical anthology on Asian American literature and is working on a book-length study on Asian American poetry.

Index

Abbey, Edward, 6
Adams, Carol J., 222, 225
Aguero, Kathleen, 246
Albatross, 252
Alford, Jean, 137
Alighieri, Dante, 117–8, 123; *Divine Comedy*, 117–18
Allan, Gilbert, 39
Allen, Paula Gunn, 171, 172n2, 248, 256
Almon, Bert, 79
Altieri, Charles, 39
Amicus Journal, 252, 254, 258
Ammons, A. R., x–xi, 88–100; *Glare*, 92–93, 96–97; *Garbage*, 97
Anderson, Maggie, 250
anti-pastoral poetry, 77–78
Appalachia Journal, 252
Arnold, Matthew, 81
Atwood, Margaret, x, 232–44; *Morning in the Burning House*, 232, 241; *Surfacing*, 232; *The Circle Game*, 233; *The Animals in That Country*, 234; *The Journals of Susanna Moodie*, 235; *Procedures for Underground*, 236; *Power Politics*, 237; *You Are Happy*, 238; *Two-Headed Poems*, 239; *True Stories*, 240; *Interlunar*, 241
Augustine, 25, 37n2, 117

Baca, Jimmy Santiago, 247, 259; *Black Mesa Poems*, 259
Baldwin, James, 68
Barnes, Jim, 163
Barrell, John, 217n4
Basho, x, 24
Bass, Rick: *Fiber*, 78
Bate, Jonathan: *The Song of the Earth*, 2; *Romantic Ecology: Wordsworth and the Environmental Tradition*, 12n1, 70n3, 79
Berleant, Arnold, 188
Berry, Patricia, 97
Berry, Wendell, x, 35, 117–34, 207, 250, 252–53, 258; *A Timbered Choir*, 117–34; *The Gift of Good Land*, 118; *Sabbaths*, 119; *Sabbaths: 1987–1990*, 119; *Openings*, 122
Bible, 117–34
Bird, Gloria, 258
Bishop, Elizabeth, ix, 153–54
Black Arts Movement, 248
Black Elk, 6
Blake, William, 78, 81, 84
Bloom, Harold, 253
Blue Cloud, Peter, 6
Bly, Robert, 2, 245–46, 247; *News of the Universe: Poems of a Twofold Consciousness*, 12n2, 70n3, 257
Bonds, Diane, 140
Bowering, George, 195
Bradstreet, Anne, 3
Brooks, Charles Timothy, 32
Brooks, Gwendolyn, 246
Brown, George Mackay: *Fishermen with Ploughs*, 77
Bryson, J. Scott, 12n3
Buber, Martin, 139–40, 227
Buell, Lawrence, 5, 77, 78
Burris, Sidney, 155
Butler, Judith: *Gender Trouble*, 219n13
Byers, Thomas B., 107, 111–12
Byron, Lord (George Gordon): *Don Juan*, 77

Callicot, J. Baird, 136
Campbell, SueEllen, 150n1
Capra, Fritjof, 189
Carr, Brenda, 196
Carson, Anne, 88, 90, 96
Carson, Rachel, 3
Cheng, Anne, 211
Chin, Marilyn, 251
Christiansen, Laird, 12n3, 27n6, 70n3
Churchill, Ward, 173n15
Clare, John, 217
Codrescu, Andrei, 246–47
Coetzee, J. M., 208
Coleridge, Samuel Taylor, 40
Collier, Mary: *The Woman's Labour*, 77
Cook-Lynn, Elizabeth, 254
Crabbe, George: *The Village*, 77
Creeley, Robert, 195
Cummings, E. E., 68
current environmental identity poetry, 245–62

Daniel, John: *Wild Song: Poems of the Natural World*, 12n2, 70n3
Davey, Frank, 195
Davis, Cheri, 110
Davison, Peter, 111
d'Eaubonne, Françoise, 222
de Chardin, Teilhard, 117
Diggory, Terence, 45, 46
Dillard, Annie, 207, 233
Dove, Rita, 246
Duck, Stephen: *The Thresher's Labour*, 77
Dun, Tan, 193n27
Dunn, Sara: *Beneath the Wide Wide Heaven: Poetry of the Environment from Antiquity to the Present* (with Alan Scholefield), 12n2, 70n3, 257

Eckhart, Meister, 118, 123, *Meditations*, 118
ecocriticism, 1, 59–60, 208; and avoidance of "black concerns," 208
ecofeminism, 78, 222–31, 252; history and characteristics of, 222
ecology, ix, 89, 135–36, 149–50, 167, 180–8, 199–200, 222
ecopoetry, x, 18–9, 79, 101, 109–10, 162, 167, 180, 184, 222. 232–33, 245, 248, 256–58; definition and history of, 2–7, 18–20; and rhetoric, 29–38; and language, 58–74; and the "ecological Indian," 169; and physical sciences, 179–94; and postcolonial criticism, 207–20
Elder, John, 59, 66, 146; *Imagining the Earth: Poetry and the Vision of Nature*, 1, 59, 70n3, 70n4
elegy, contemporary, 153–61
Eliot, T. S., 64, 254
Elton, Charles, 135
Emerson, Ralph Waldo, ix, 6, 30–32, 155
Endrezze, Anita, 168
England, Charles R., 173n2
Erdrich, Louise, 255
Evernden, Neil, 27n6

Fiumara, Gemma Corradi: *The Other Side of Language*, 199–200
Foster, John Wilson, 233
Fox, Matthew, 117, 118, 120, 124; *The Coming of the Cosmic Christ*, 117, 118
Fox, Warwick, 242
Frazier, Jane, 104
Freud, Sigmund, 211
Frost, Robert, ix, 2, 36, 89

Gale, Vi, 250
Gelpi, Albert, 6
genocide, Native American, 162–75
Georgian Poetry, 77
Gifford, Terry: *Green Voices: Understanding Contemporary Nature Poetry*, 1, 5, 70n3, 70n4

Gilbert, Roger, 89
Gilcrest, David, 12n3, 70n3
Gilman, Charlotte Perkins, 230n7
Ginsberg, Allen, 245–46
Glück, Louise, x, 221–31; *Firstborn*, 222, 223, 228; *The House on Marshland*, 223; *Descending Figure*, 223; *The Triumph of Achilles*, 223; *The Wild Iris*, 223, 226, 228; *Vita Nova*, 223, 226; *Ararat*, 226; *Meadowlands*, 226, 228
Gogisgi/Carol Arnett, 255
Grabes, Herbert, 91
Green Fuse, 252
Griffin, Susan, 258; *Woman and Nature: The Roaring Inside Her*, 251–52
Grontkowski, Christine B., 99

Hale, Dorothy, 213
Han-shan, 20–21
Harjo, Joy, 6, 167, 169
Harper's Anthology of Twentieth Century Native American Poetry, 254
Harries-Jones, Peter, 188
Harris, Marie, 246
Hass, Robert, 221–22, 229; *Field Guide*, 222; *Sun under Wood*, 222
Hatt, Michael, 168
Hawking, Stephen, 192n2
Head, Dominic, 208
Heath Anthology of American Literature, 253
Hemingway, Ernest, 258
Hensen, Lance, 255
Heyen, William: *Pterodactyl Rose*, 252, 256
Hildegard of Bingen: *Illuminations*, 117, 123
Hogan, Linda, 162–75; *Mean Spirit*, 164; *Power*, 169
Hopkins, Gerard Manley, 80
Howard, Ben, 139
Howard, Richard, 111
Howells, Coral Ann, 233
Huggan, Graham, 218–19n11
Hughes, Ted, 77, 79, 81; *Moortown Diary*, 77
Hugo, Richard, 254

Iverem, Esther, 251

Jeffers, Robinson, ix, 2, 6, 39–57, 89
Jefferson, Thomas, 258
Jonas, Hans, 99
Jost, Walter, 36–37

Kaufman, Bob: *Solitudes Crowded with Loneliness*, 250
Kavanagh, Patrick: *The Great Hunger*, 77
Keller, Evelyn Fox, 99
Kenyon, Jane, 155–57, 160
King, Ynestra, 222–23, 224
Kinnell, Galway, 11, 246
Klee, Paul: *Notebooks*, 132
Kolodny, Annette: *The Lay of the Land: Fantasy and Experience of the American Frontiers, 1630–1860*, 151n29
Kumar, Sehdev, 117

LaDuke, Winona, 173n15
Langbaum, Robert, 2
l=a=n=g=u=a=g=e poets, 247
Lazer, Hank, 34
Lee, Li–young, 249, 255
Lehman, David, 246
Leopold, Aldo, x, 72, 241–42
Levertov, Denise, 3, 67
Lickbarrow, Isabella: *Poetical Effusions*, 77
literary criticism, 208, 210; as an ecosystem, x–xi
Lopez, Barry: *Arctic Dreams*, 207
Lowell, Robert, 245
Lyon, Thomas: *This Incomperable Lande*, 259

Maclean, Sorley, 82
Macy, Joanna, 136
Major, Clarence: *The Garden Thrives*, 250–51
Makdisi, Saree: *Romantic Imperialism: Universal Empire and the Culture of Modernity*, 219n11
Marlatt, Daphne, x, 195–206; *Vancouver Poems*, 195–6; *Stevetson*, 196–206; *Ana Historic*, 197; *Touch to My Tongue*, 201; *Salvage*, 202
Marx, Leo, 77
Matthews, Freya, 27n6
McCombs, Judith, 233
McNew, Janet, 142, 144
Mechtild of Magdeburg, 118, 124; *Meditations*, 118
Merchant, Carolyn, 88
Merleau-Ponty, Maurice: *The Prose of the World*, 121, 128–9; *The Visible and the Invisible*, 122, 125
Merrill, Christopher: *The Forgotten Language: Contemporary Poets and Nature*, 12n2
Merwin, W. S., x, 3–5, 29, 34–36, 101–16, 247, 250; *Drunk in the Furnace*, 102; *Rain in the Trees*, 102; *The River Sound*, 102–3, 108; *The Vixen*, 108; *Writings to an Unfinished Accompaniment*, 111; *The Moving Target*, 111, 112
Millet, Lydia, 258
Milosz, Czeslaw, 229
Milton, John, 153
Minden, Robert, 197–98
Missouri Review, The, 249
Mitchell, W. J. T., 43–44
Moore, Lawrence D., 250–51
Moore, Marianne, ix, 2, 3
Muir, John, 78
Murphy, Patrick, 78

Naess, Arne, 188–89
Native American Renaissance, 253–54
Niatum, Duane, 254
Nielsen, Dorothy, 167
Nordström, Lars, 250

Oates, Joyce Carol, 258
Oliver, Mary, x, 135–52, 157–61, 169, 250; *Twelve Moons*, 137, 143; *House of Light*, 138, 141, 144, 147; *Winter Hours*, 139; *New and Selected Poems*, 145; *American Primitive*, 147, 157
Olson, Charles, 60, 195; *Maximus Poems*, 196
Ong, Walter J.: *Interfaces of the Word: Studies in the Evolution of Consciousness and Culture*, 99
Orion, 252
Ortiz, Simon, 168, 255

Pack, Robert: *Poems for a Small Planet: Contemporary American Nature Poetry* (with Jay Parini), 12n2, 70n3
panentheism, 120
Parini, Jay: *Poems for a Small Planet: Contemporary American Nature Poetry* (with Robert Pack), 12n2, 70n3
pastoral poetry, 77–78, 187, 250
Pelikan, Jaroslav, 117
Pennybacker, Mindy, 173n15
Perloff, Marjorie, 89
Petroglyph, 252
Phillips, Dana, 60
Plath, Sylvia, 257
Plato, 20–25, 37n2
Poems for a Small Planet, 257
Pope, Alexander: *Windsor Forest*, 77
post-pastoral poetry, 77–87; defined, 79
Poulin, A., Jr.: *Contemporary American Poetry*, 245

Quetchenbach, Bernard W.: *Back from the Far Field: American Nature Poets in the Late Twentieth Century*, 2, 70n3

Raglon, Rebecca, 241
Ramazani, Jahan: *The Poetry of Mourning*, 154
Revard, Carter, 254–55
Rich, Adrienne, 67–68, 165, 246, 248, 249, 256
Roethke, Theodore, 11
Rogers, Pattiann, 11, 256
Ronald, Ann: *The Sierra Club Trailside Reader*, 259
Roosevelt, Theodore, 258
Rorty, Richard: *Philosophy and the Mirror of Nature*, 91
Rose, Wendy, 254
Ross, Gary, 233
Rotella, Guy: *Reading & Writing Nature: The Poetry of Robert Frost, Wallace Stevens, Marianne Moore, and Elizabeth Bishop*, 12n1, 70n3
Rueckert, William, 36

Sacks, Peter: *The English Elegy*, 153
Scholefield, Alan: *Beneath the Wide Wide Heaven: Poetry of the Environment from Antiquity to the Present* (with Sara Dunn), 12n2, 70n3, 257
Schwartz, Judith, 187
Scigaj, Leonard M., 5, 66, 78, 95, 113, 116n37; *Sustainable Poetry: Four Ecopoets*, 2, 18–9, 59, 180, 189
Scott, Winfield Townley, 45
Seibles, Timothy, 250
Sessions, George, 27n6
Shelley, Percy Bysshe, 88–89
Shelton, Richard, 250, 259
Silko, Leslie Marmon, 11, 167
Slaymaker, William, 208
Snyder, Gary, x, 3, 7, 79–87, 137, 167, 174n31, 249, 250, 252–53, 258; *Turtle Island*, 36, 174n31; *Myths and Texts*, 78; *No Nature*, 83, 250
Spretnak, Charlene, 225, 226–27
Ssu-K'ung T'u, 21–22
St. Francis of Assisi, 117, 123
St. John, Primus, 250
Stafford, William, 171, 250
Stevens, Wallace, ix, 2, 3, 40, 89
Suzuki, D. T., 19
Swann, Brian, 254
Sydney, Sir Phillip: *Arcadia*, 77
Sze, Arthur, x, 179–94; *The Redshifting Web*, 179; *Archipelago*, 180–85; *Dazzled* 186

Theocritus: *Idylls*, 77
Thieme, John: *Derek Walcott*, 218
Thoreau, Henry David, 77, 89
Todd, Judith, 173n15
transcendentalists, 30–34, 88
Tuan, Yi-Fu, 104–5; *Space and Place: The Perspective of Experience*, 101–2
Turner, Jack, 27n6

von Halberg, Robert, 69
Voros, Gyorgyi, 99; *Notations of the Wild: Ecology in the Poetry of Wallace Stevens*, 1, 70n3, 70n4

Walcott, Derek, x, 207–20; *The Schooner Flight*, 209; *Omeros*, 218n8; *The Odyssey*, 218n8
Walker, David, 60
Wallace, Robert, 253
Weinberger, Eliot, 247
Weir, Lorraine, 201
White, Lynn, Jr., 118, 175

White, Nicholas P., 27n11
Whiteman, Roberta Hill, 255
Whitman, Walt, 3–5, 30, 147, 153, 168, 252
Williams, Raymond: *The Country and the City*, 43
Williams, Terry Tempest, 207
Williams, William Carlos, ix, 2, 40, 58–74, 195; *In the American Grain*, 61–62; *Paterson*, 62–65, 196
Wordsworth, William, ix, 82, 148, 208, 217n4
Wright, Charles, x, 17
Wright, James, 246

Yeats, W. B., ix, 39–57, 254
Young, Robert, 209–10
Young Bear, Ray A., 256
Yuasa, Nobuyuki, 24

Zaller, Robert, 39